New Inside Out

Sue Kay, Vaughan Jones,

Helena Gomm, David Seymour,

Caroline Brown & Chris Dawson

Beginner

Teacher's Book

MACMILLAN

Macmillan Education
Between Towns Road, Oxford OX4 3PP
A division of Macmillan Publishers Limited
Companies and representatives throughout the world

ISBN 978-1-4050-7062-1

Text © Sue Kay and Vaughan Jones 2007
Text by Helena Gomm
Design and illustration © Macmillan Publishers Limited 2007

First published 2007

Designed by 320 Design
Page layout by Carolyn Gibson
Illustrated by Chris Davidson, Phil Garner, Peter Harper, Ben Hasler and Ed McLachlan
Cover design by Andrew Oliver

The authors and publishers would like to thank the following for permission to
reproduce their material: Quotation from *Language and Problems of Knowledge* by Noam
Chomsky copyright © Noam Chomsky 1988 Massachusetts Institute of Technology,
reprinted by permission of The MIT Press, Cambridge, Massachusetts. Quotation from
Understanding Second Language Acquisition by Rod Ellis copyright © Rod Ellis 1985,
reproduced by permission of Oxford University Press. *Friday I'm in Love* Words by Robert
Smith, Music by Robert Smith, Simon Gallup, Porl Thompson, Boris Williams and Perry
Bamonte copyright © Fictions Songs Limited 1992, reprinted by permission of Music
Sales Ltd. All Rights Reserved. International Copyright Secured.
What a Wonderful World Words and Music by George David Weiss and Bob Thiele
copyright © Range Road Music, Inc., Quartet Music Inc. and Abilene Music Inc., USA
1967, copyright renewed, reprinted by permission of Carlin Music Corporation, London,
NW1 8BD and Memory Lane Music Ltd. All rights Reserved.

Dave Seymour would like to thank Xanthe Sturt-Taylor and Des O'Sullivan for their
input and support.

The authors and publishers would like to thank the following for permission to
reproduce their photographic material: Corbis/Ian Hodgson/Reuters, Corbis/Fotoreport
Berry/dpa, Corbis/Matteo Bazzi/epa, Corbis/Hulton-Deutsch Collection, Corbis/Fred
Prouser/Reuters, Corbis/Ethan Miller/Reuters, Corbis/Pablo Corral Vega,
Corbis/Bettmann, Corbis/Reuters.

Whilst every effort has been made to locate the owners of copyright material in this book,
there may have been some cases when the publishers have been unable to contact the
owners. We should be grateful to hear from anyone who recognises copyright material
and who is unacknowledged. We shall be pleased to make the necessary amendments in
future editions of the book.

Printed in Thailand

2014 2013 2012 2011
11 10 9 8 7 6 5

Contents

TEACHER'S NOTES

RESOURCE MATERIALS

Student's Book contents map

WB = **Workbook**. Each unit of the Workbook contains a one-page section which develops practical writing skills.

Introduction

Welcome to New Inside Out!

New Inside Out is the fruit of many years teaching, writing and developing material. Everything we write is informed by the reactions we get from our students. Our aim is simply to produce a set of materials that will help you create optimum conditions in your classroom for learning to take place.

Engaging content

The American linguist and philosopher Noam Chomsky once said:

'The truth of the matter is that about 99% of teaching is making the students feel interested in the material. Then the other 1% has to do with your methods.'

While we might want to quibble with the percentages, we would nevertheless agree whole-heartedly with the central message in Professor Chomsky's assertion: namely, students learn best when they're interested in the material. It's as simple as that. A text might contain six beautifully-crafted examples of the past simple, a good spread of high frequency lexical items and exemplify some useful functional language, but if it doesn't engage the students, if they can't relate to it, if it feels alien to them, then the most important ingredient for successful learning is missing.

In *New Inside Out*, we've drawn on our own classroom experience, and that of our colleagues around the world, to select topics, texts and tasks that engage students both emotionally and intellectually. Students are our richest resource. They come to class with their own knowledge of the world, their own tastes, feelings and opinions. It's up to us to exploit this rich resource by organising learning around topics that they can relate to – topics that are part of their life experience.

Structured support

We all know that learning a language is a messy, non-linear business. We're dismayed when there seems to be little correlation between what is taught and what is learned! However, there is plenty of evidence to suggest that 'instructed' learners (those who attend classes or follow a course of study) learn faster, and ultimately attain a higher level of proficiency than 'non-instructed' learners.

In *New Inside Out*, new language input is carefully controlled: we aim to maximise exposure to high frequency language appropriate to this level. Students are encouraged to notice new grammar and new vocabulary in contexts where the meaning is clear. They are then given opportunities to manipulate the new language and try it out in different situations. They discover why using one particular form rather than another one actually matters: not just because it's right or wrong, but because it does or doesn't communicate a meaning successfully. The emphasis is always on what students can do with the language rather than what they know about the language. The new language is systematically reviewed and recycled until finally the students feel confident enough to use it to make their own meanings. It becomes part of their available repertoire. It has been 'learned'.

Real world tasks

We're strong believers in the old adage: 'practice makes perfect'. *New Inside Out* emphasises output, particularly speaking, and there are a huge number of tasks that are designed to develop fluency. Students practise functional language in sections entitled *Useful phrases*. But for the most part, the speaking tasks simply encourage the students to talk about things that actually matter to them, rather than playing roles or exchanging invented information. One of our main objectives is to ensure that the language our students spend time rehearsing in the classroom is transferable to the real world. By orchestrating tasks that require the students to use grammar and vocabulary to make meaningful utterances, this objective becomes obtainable. As the linguist and academic Rod Ellis reminds us:

'It is the need to get meanings across and the pleasure experienced when this is achieved that motivates second language acquisition.'

www.insideout.net
'the art of communication'

Components of the course

Student's materials

- Student's Book *see page viii–x*
- CD-ROM *see page xi*
- Workbook and Audio CD
  see page xi

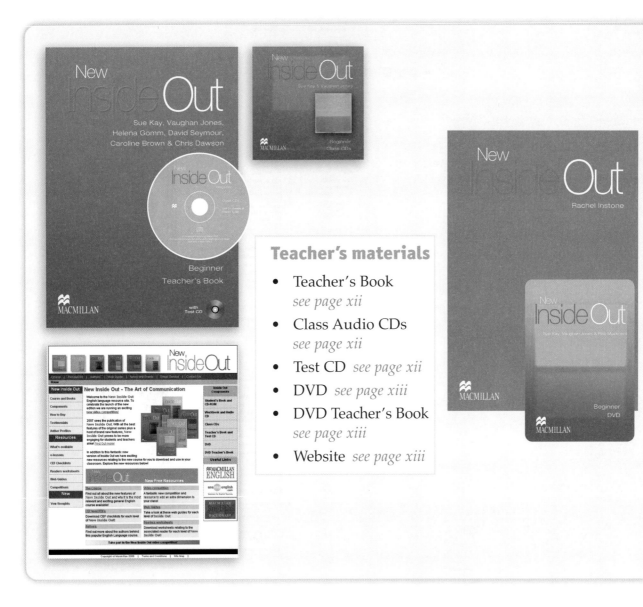

Teacher's materials

- Teacher's Book
  see page xii
- Class Audio CDs
  see page xii
- Test CD *see page xii*
- DVD *see page xiii*
- DVD Teacher's Book
  see page xiii
- Website *see page xiii*

Student's materials A typical Student's Book unit (Unit 4)

Headings throughout the units provide clear explanations of what students are studying and why.

New vocabulary is presented in a meaningful context and supported by clear pictures.

Students listen and repeat before they manipulate the form.

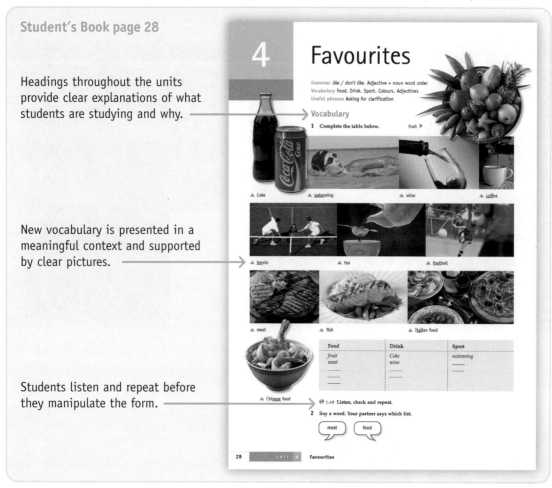

New Inside Out Beginner includes an average of two Grammar sections in every unit. Typically, these follow a five-stage approach.

1 New grammar is presented in a realistic context, usually a dialogue or a short text.

2 Students focus on the way the new language works.

3 Students listen to the sentences and do choral repetition of the new language.

4 The practice stage is designed to be realistic and meaningful.

5 Students use the target sentences for controlled, personalised practice.

Additional support is provided in the margin.

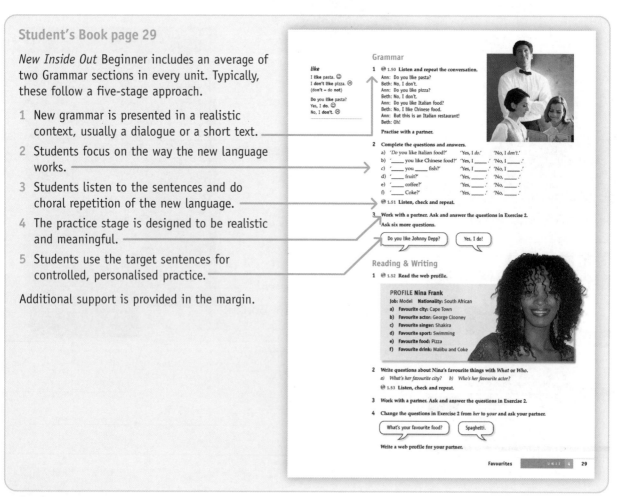

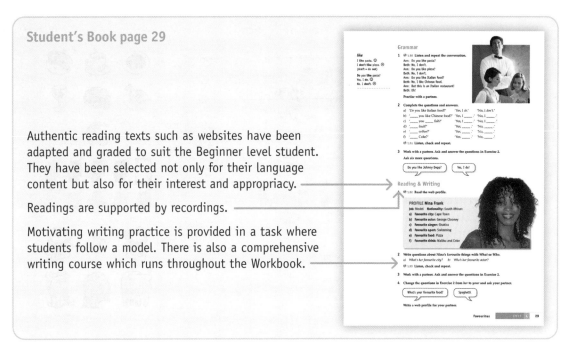

Authentic reading texts such as websites have been adapted and graded to suit the Beginner level student. They have been selected not only for their language content but also for their interest and appropriacy.

Readings are supported by recordings.

Motivating writing practice is provided in a task where students follow a model. There is also a comprehensive writing course which runs throughout the Workbook.

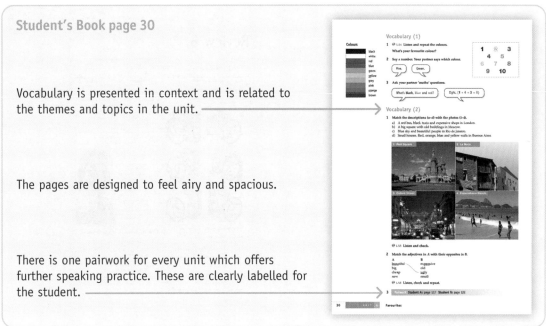

Vocabulary is presented in context and is related to the themes and topics in the unit.

The pages are designed to feel airy and spacious.

There is one pairwork for every unit which offers further speaking practice. These are clearly labelled for the student.

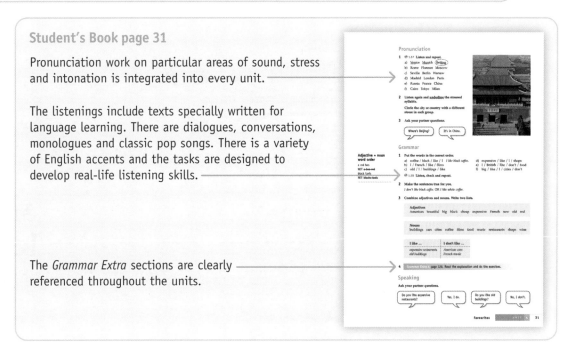

Pronunciation work on particular areas of sound, stress and intonation is integrated into every unit.

The listenings include texts specially written for language learning. There are dialogues, conversations, monologues and classic pop songs. There is a variety of English accents and the tasks are designed to develop real-life listening skills.

The *Grammar Extra* sections are clearly referenced throughout the units.

Student's Book page 32

Useful phrases gives students a portable toolkit of functional language. These sections are designed to be fun and engaging and the phrases are recorded on the Audio CD.

Student's Book page 33

The *Vocabulary Extra* pages at the end of every unit recycle the key vocabulary items taught in the unit. This provides students with an activated wordlist and a useful bank of vocabulary.

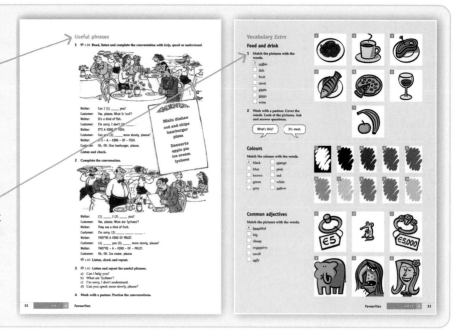

Student's Book page 46

There are five Review units in *New Inside Out* Beginner Student's Book. Each Review unit revises the new structures taught in the previous three teaching units.

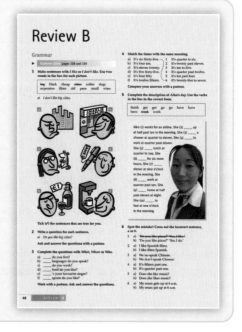

Student's Book pages 128 and 129

The *Grammar Extra* pages at the back of the Student's Book provide a summary of the new grammatical structures as well as extra practice.

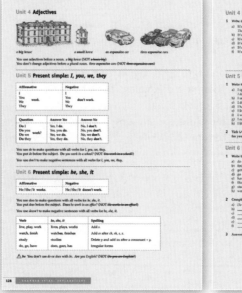
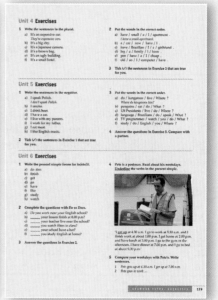

CD-ROM

The CD-ROM in the back of every Student's Book provides a wealth of interactive practice activities along with integrated listening material.

Workbook pages 16 and 19

The Workbook provides revision of all the main points in the Student's Book, plus extra listening practice, pronunciation work and a complete self-contained writing course. There are with and without key versions, and a story is included in the back of the Workbook.

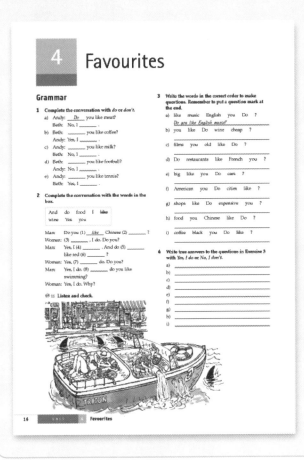

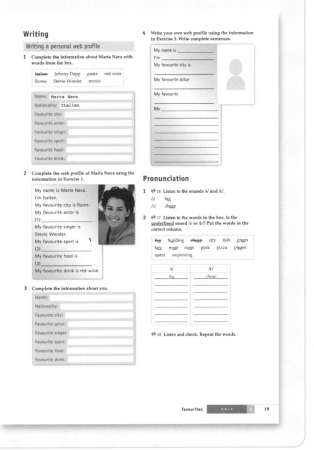

Teacher's materials

Teacher's Book

The 6-in-1 Teacher's Book contains:

- an Introduction
- Practical methodology
- Council of Europe (CEF) checklists
- complete teaching notes with answer keys
- a bank of extra photocopiable grammar, vocabulary and communicative activities
- a Test CD with word files that you can edit

4 Grammar

Do you like it?

German		tea	
French		food	
English		books	
Brazilian		football	
Italian		coffee	
American		music	
Spanish		wine	
Japanese		cars	

Class CD set

The Class CDs contain:

- the dialogues and listening activities from the Student's Book
- recordings of the songs
- recordings of the reading texts
- listening activities for the tests

DVD and DVD Teacher's Book

The DVD contains programmes which complement the topics in the Student's Book. There is a wide variety of formats including interviews, profiles, documentaries and video diaries. The DVD Teacher's Book contains related teaching notes and photocopiable worksheets.

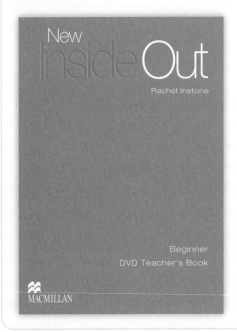

Website

www.insideout.net

Visit www.insideout.net to find out more details about the course and its authors. The new magazine-style website provides downloadable resources and more information about *New Inside Out*.

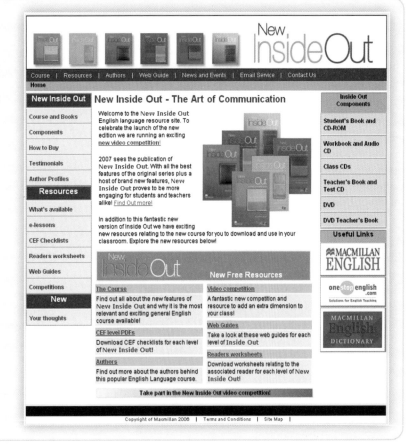

Practical methodology

Teaching beginners

In this age of the internet, international travel and world-dominance of English-language pop music, 'real' or 'absolute' beginners are relatively rare. Most students have at least some prior knowledge of the language, even if it's only a set phrase like *Don't worry, be happy*. In *New Inside Out* Beginner, drawing on our own experience of teaching beginners, and having talked to many English teachers teaching beginners in a wide variety of contexts, we decided that it was best to assume no prior knowledge of the language. We opted for a building-block approach – low and slow – where the content of each unit builds on the previous one, and where the grammar and vocabulary is frequently and systematically reviewed and recycled.

Right from the start

Every teacher has their own way of setting up their classroom, interacting with their students and conducting their lessons. Here are a few things we've found useful to bear in mind in our beginner classrooms.

The right atmosphere

It's important to do everything you can to create a supportive learning environment. Start by memorising every student's name and learn as much information as you can about them.

Beginners are often shy about speaking in English. As anyone who has learnt a foreign language will know, in the very early stages it takes a great deal of courage to open your mouth and say something. Yet we know that the sooner you start, the more practice you get, the more confident you feel and the easier it becomes.

In *New Inside Out* Beginner we've used a number of strategies to help build up the students' confidence. Students aren't required to use new language before they've had a chance to listen and repeat words and phrases chorally. 'Drilling' is the technique most teachers use to help their students get their tongues around new language. However, when you're focusing on form, it doesn't follow that you have to abandon meaning. In *New Inside Out* language practice, however controlled, is always meaningful.

- Instructions are simple and the same ones are repeated throughout the course.

- Activity-types are repeated, especially in the grammar sections, so that the students get used to what is expected of them.

- Students are encouraged to work in pairs and groups, so that they can rehearse the language 'in private' rather than be immediately required to speak in the more intimidating arena of the class.

Beginners need much more time to think. It's perfectly normal to have moments of silence while students absorb and process new information, write down new vocabulary from the board, or think about their answers. Don't be afraid of the 'pregnant pause'!

The right environment

Your classroom might be the only exposure to English that students get. Make that exposure as rich as you can by decorating the walls with maps and posters. Here are some further ideas.

- Stick up useful formulaic phrases. For example, phrases from Unit 1 *Useful phrases*: *Can you spell that please?, Can you repeat that please?*, or Unit 4 *Useful phrases*: *What's ....?, I don't understand.*, etc.

- Keep a 'wordbox' on your table, where words or phrases that come up in the lesson are recorded on strips of paper and put in the box. Alternatively, you could institute the 'class scribe' idea. One student in the class is given the role of recording any new language that comes up during the lesson that isn't necessarily the target language of that lesson. This record is then photocopied for everyone in the class, including the teacher who can use the data for revision activities. The role of class scribe is rotated.

- Introduce your students to simplified graded readers. Many of them now come as 'talking books' with CDs. This is invaluable input. Get your students hooked on books!

- Use English in the classroom. It's very tempting to slip into the students' language – particularly if you're teaching beginners in a monolingual situation. Try to use the L1 only for an occasional quick translation or brief explanation.

The right learning skills

If this is their first experience of learning a second language, or if they haven't been very successful in their previous attempts, beginners need some help with learning strategies. Here are some thoughts.

- Spend time encouraging students to experiment with how they record words and phrases from the lesson. Get them to draw the word rather than translate it. They're then associating the word with the concept rather than with another word. Make sure they note the part of speech – verb, noun, adjective, etc. Tell them to find a way of noting the pronunciation of the word, either using phonemic script (in the back of the Student's Book), or by developing their own system. Ask them to write complete personalised sentences putting the new word or phrase in a real context and thereby making it more memorable.

- A dictionary is a very important language learning tool and most students will buy one. Beginners prefer a bilingual dictionary as this provides them with a quick translation of the word they need. Although at beginner level most of the vocabulary they need is straightforward, it's important to begin teaching them good dictionary skills.

The right amount of practice

In our experience of teaching beginners, the most successful lessons consist of a manageable amount of new input, and then a lot of meaningful practice. For this reason, we've tried to provide maximum practice activities in *New Inside Out*, both in the Student's Book and in the other supporting components.

The TOP 10 activities for beginners

These tried and trusted activities can be used as lead-ins, warmers, fillers, pair-forming activities, or for revision and recycling. Most of them require very little or no preparation and can be adapted to cover a wide variety of different language points. You may be familiar with some of the ideas and others may be new. In any event, we hope they provide a useful extension to your teaching repertoire. They certainly get used and re-used in our own classrooms!

It is always useful to have a stock of small white cards and access to a stock of pictures. Magazine pictures are ideal, and can be filed in alphabetical order according to topics.

Alternatively, use the pictures in the *Vocabulary Extra* section at the end of each unit in *New Inside Out* Beginner Student's Book.

1 Standing in line

a) Alphabetical order

Aim

This is a great way to review *What's your first name / surname?* after Unit 1.

Preparation

None.

Procedure

- Write three names of students in your class on the board. Underline the first letter of each name, and re-write the names in alphabetical order. Then ask all the students to stand up and put themselves in alphabetical order according to the first letter of their first name.

- Show the class where the line should begin. Encourage them to ask one another *What's your first name?* so that they can put themselves in order. Once they've lined up, check that they're in the correct order by asking them to take it in turns down the line to say *My name's …*

- Repeat the same procedure using their middle names, their surnames, their mother's or father's first name, etc.

b) Numerical order

Aim

To recycle numbers.

Preparation

You'll need one card for each student in the class. On each card, write a number that you want to practise.

Procedure

- Ask the students to stand up and take a card each. On the card is a number. Tell them not to show it to anyone. Ask them to repeat their number aloud until they can organise themselves numerically. Show the class where the line should begin with the lowest number. Then, when they're in line, ask them to hold up their card and say their number to check they're in the correct order.

- Here are some more ideas for line-ups:
  1. To practise dates and months: line up in order of the date and month of birth.
  2. To practise saying times: hand out a clock face with a different time on it to each student in the class. Ask them to line up in chronological order by saying the time on their clock.
  3. To recycle vocabulary: hand out one picture card to each student. Ask them to line up according to the first letter of the word it represents by saying their word aloud.
  4. To recycle vocabulary: divide the class into groups, mix up the letters of a word and give one letter to each student in the group. Call out the complete word and ask them to get into the correct order to spell the word.
  5. To revise word order: mix up the words of a sentence and give one word to each student in the group. Ask them to arrange themselves in the correct order to make a sentence by saying their word aloud.

Follow-up

Once the students have completed a line-up activity, you can divide them into pairs or small groups before they sit down by asking them to work with the student(s) they're standing next to. This works well in a class where students always tend to sit in the same place.

2 Battleships

Aim

To practise the alphabet and revise vocabulary.

Preparation

Each student will need a grid of roughly ten to twelve squares across and down (see below). Graph paper is ideal for this activity.

Procedure

- Demonstrate the activity by drawing a blank grid on the board. Think of a word or words you want to revise and write them onto a different grid on a piece of paper, but don't tell the students what they are yet. You should write the words horizontally, one letter per square, as shown below.

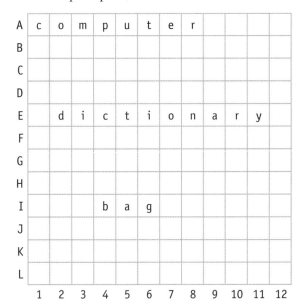

- Now tell the students that there are some words hidden in the grid. Explain that they need to find the squares with letters in them. Tell them to guess squares by giving letter and number references. For example, C–2, F–12, J–4, etc. When a student guesses a square with a letter in, write it in the square. Continue like this until they've found all the words.

- Now ask the students to work in pairs. First, they should draw two grids. One of them should remain blank, and on the other they need to write words, but without showing their partner. Either you can let the students choose their own words, or else you can give them a topic. For example, write three countries / nationalities / jobs / classroom objects / names.

- When they've written their words, tell the students to take it in turns to name a square on their partner's grid. If there's a letter in the square, their partner should say what the letter is and they should write it in the blank grid.

- As soon as they think they know their partner's word, they can guess. If it's wrong, they miss a turn.

3 Hangman

Aim

This game reviews vocabulary and practises the alphabet, so it's a perfect game for beginners.

Preparation

None.

Procedure

- The game can be played as a whole group activity, but also in pairs or small groups when the students know the game. The students can use any vocabulary they know, or you can limit it by telling them to choose from a category. For example, food or a famous person, a verb or a place.

- Demonstrate on the board. Choose a word for the students to find. For example, *computer*. Write up on the board:

  _ _ _ _ _ _ _ _

- Ask the students to guess a letter. If necessary, suggest a letter yourself, for example the letter *E* and then write it above the appropriate line:

  _ _ _ _ _ _ *E* _

- Ask the students for another letter. If they suggest a letter which is in the word, write it in the appropriate place. If they suggest a letter which isn't in the word, begin to draw the hangman with a vertical line. For the second incorrect guess, draw the horizontal support. For the third, the rope, the fourth is a circle for the head, then a line for  the body, one arm, then the second arm, then a leg and finally the second leg.

- If they find the word before the hangman is complete, they win. However, if the hangman is complete, then they lose.

4 Category dictation

Aim

This activity can be adapted to review almost any vocabulary. It can also be used to review certain pronunciation and grammar points.

Preparation

Choose the language you want to review and devise a way of categorising it into two or more categories.

Procedure

- Write the category headings on the board and ask the students to copy them onto a piece of paper. Two simple categories is usually best. More than three can get complicated. Then dictate the words (ten–twelve maximum) slowly and clearly, and ask the students to write them down in the correct category.

  For example, you want to revise jobs from Unit 5. Your categories might be jobs you do inside and jobs you do outside. So, write the following on the board and ask the students to copy it down.

Inside	Outside

- Then dictate the words: e.g. *a farmer, a teacher, a doctor, a taxi driver*, etc. The students write down the words in the correct category. When you've dictated ten or twelve words, ask the students to compare their lists. When they've done this, ask them to call out their answers and write them on the board in the correct category, so that they can check the spelling. Alternatively, you could ask the students to take it in turns to write the answers on the board.

- Here are some more ideas for categories:
  1 Revise common objects. (Unit 1)
    Suggested categories: *Singular* and *Plural; In the classroom* and *Not in the classroom; In my pocket/bag* and *Not in my pocket/bag*, etc.
  2 Revise numbers. (Unit 2)
    Suggested categories: *1 to 20* and *20 to 100; Even numbers* and *Odd numbers*.
  3 Revise furniture. (Unit 8)
    Suggested categories: *Usually in a living room* and *Not usually in a living room; Cost under $100* and *Cost over $100*.
  4 Revise sports. (Unit 12)
    Suggested categories: *Sports with a ball* and *Sports without a ball; Sports you play in teams* and *Sports you play individually*.
  5 Revise parts of the body. (Unit 14)
    Suggested categories: *Above the waist* and *Below the waist*, or *You have one of these* and *You have two of these*.

5 Chain memorisation

Aim

This memory activity can be used to review vocabulary or a grammatical structure. It's also very useful for beginners, because it gives them an opportunity to get their tongues around longer utterances.

Preparation

Some simple prompt cards can be helpful, but they aren't essential.

Procedure

- If you have a very large group, it's better to split the group into two or three smaller groups, so that everyone has the opportunity to speak before the sentences get too long!

- First, demonstrate how the game will work before you split the group. For example, to practise *There's / There are* and the vocabulary from Unit 7, prepare prompt cards based on the vocabulary of the lesson, in this case, features of a city. Model the phrase *In my city, there's a …*, turn over a card and add the relevant word, for example, *a statue*. Ask the first student to repeat *In my city, there's a statue*.

- As they finish, add the words *and there …*, and turn over another card indicating that you want the next student to add this to the sentence. For example, *In my city there's a statue and there's a museum*. Repeat this procedure with several students. Encourage them to memorise the sentence as it grows. If they falter, you can show them the card as a prompt.

- When they've understood how the activity works, split the class into groups and if necessary, give a set of prompt cards to each group. Alternatively, the students can choose the words to add sentence themselves.

- Alternative chain sentences at this level include:
  In my house there's a … + furniture. (Unit 8)
  I went to market and I bought … + food. (Unit 9)
  Last weekend, I played/went … + sport. (Unit 12)

6 Mill drills

Aim

To provide controlled practice of new language in a drill-like way, and to give students the opportunity to repeat the same language with several different partners.

Preparation

Organise your classroom so that the students can move around and speak to one another. Prepare one prompt card for each student in the class. The prompts will depend on the language you want to practise. See Procedure point 2 below for examples of cue cards.

Procedure

- Tell the students that they're going to spend ten to fifteen minutes practising the new language, and that you're going to show them how to do this.

- Give one card to each student in the class, and keep one for yourself. Write a sample dialogue on the board. Point to the part of the dialogue to be supplied by the picture or word prompts on the card. For example:

side 1	side 2	Sample dialogue on board
![bag]	It's a bag.	A: *What's this?* B: *It's a bag.*

side 1	side 2	Sample dialogue on board
![taxi]	Mike	A: *What does Mike do?* B: *He's a taxi driver.*

side 1	side 2	Sample dialogue on board
![bananas]	?	A: *Do you like bananas?* B: *Yes, I do.*

- Explain that the language will change according to the prompt on the card. Show the students how to hold their cards. This is important because cards must be held in such a way that when the students are talking to a partner, they're both able to see each other's cards.

- Choose a confident student to demonstrate the activity with you. Then ask two or three pairs of students to demonstrate the dialogue.

- Ask all the students to stand up and to go round the class or group, repeating the dialogue with as many different partners as possible, and using their cards as prompts.

- Stop the activity after a few moments, and ask the students to either exchange cards with another student or turn their card around so that the students get the opportunity to make new responses.

- A mill drill is a controlled practice activity and it's important that the students use the language accurately. Therefore, while the students are doing the drill, go round the class and correct any mistakes in grammar and pronunciation.

7 Crosswords

Aim

This activity is good for revising lexical sets and can help with spelling.

Preparation

Choose a lexical set you want to revise. For example, *countries* or *nationalities* (Unit 2), *colours* (Unit 4), *jobs* (Unit 5), *clothes* (Unit 10), etc.

Procedure

- Students work in pairs. They'll need a piece of paper, preferably graph paper with squares on.

- Choose a topic, for example, *nationalities*.

- Student A writes 'Across' words, and Student B writes 'Down' words.

- It's a good idea to provide the first word across, and make sure that it's a long one. Student B then adds another nationality down the paper from top to bottom. This word must intersect with the nationality word written across the page.

- Student A then writes another nationality across that intersects with the nationality Student B has written down. Students continue taking it in turns to write in their words.

- The students build up a crossword until they can't think of any more nationalities. (You could make it into a game by saying that the last person to write a nationality is a winner.) Note that the students must leave one square empty between each word – this is why it's better and clearer to use squared paper.

8 TPR (Total Physical Response)

Aim

To give students the opportunity to show that they understand language without having to respond orally.

Preparation

Provide cue cards or realia as required.

Procedure

- Minimal pairs for pronunciation practice: for each student, prepare a set of cue cards for pairs of words that students often confuse, for example *hat* and *hot*, *here* and *hair*, *know* and *now*, etc. Hand out a set to each student. Read out a word and ask the students to hold up the word they hear. This also works well with numbers *13/30*, *14/40*, etc.

- *Stand up / Sit down* to show comprehension: in a listening activity, ask different students to listen out for different words. Ask them to stand up when they hear their word, and sit down when they hear it again. Useful for pop song activities.

- Follow instructions: to practise prepositions of place, and recycle fruit and vegetable vocabulary, bring a bag of fruit and vegetables to the class. Ask the students to arrange the fruit according to your instructions. For example, put the banana next to the apple, etc.

9 Odd one out

Aim

This activity can be used to revise almost any language.

Preparation

Think of the vocabulary, pronunciation or grammar point you want to revise.

Procedure

- Write five words on the board and ask the students which one is the odd one out. The students then explain why. Either in the L1 or in the L2. This usually relates to the meaning of the word.

| blue | dog | pink | red | yellow |

  dog is the odd one out because it's an animal. The other words are colours.

- Note that it doesn't matter if the students can't explain in perfect English why *dog* is the odd one out. They important thing is that they're looking at and thinking about the words you want to revise.

- You can use this format to practise and revise all sorts of things. Here are some examples.

  1 For meaning:
  sister / grandfather / daughter / wife / mother
  grandfather is the odd one out because he's a man. The other words describe women.

  2 For spelling:
  pen / book / bag / phone / diary
  diary is the odd one out because you spell the plural *ies*. The other words you just add *s*.

  3 For pronunciation: sounds
  A / I / H / J / K
  I is the odd one out because the vowel sound is different.

  4 For pronunciation: stress
  hospital / banana / potato / Italian / computer
  hospital is the odd one out because the stress is on the first syllable. The other words have the stress on the second syllable.

  5 For collocation:
  boat / bus / foot / train / car
  foot is the odd one out because you say *on foot*. For the other words you use *by*.

  6 For grammar:
  work / go / see / take / swim
  work is the odd one out because it's regular. The other verbs are irregular.

- You should tell the students what the criteria is, for example 'think about meaning' or 'think about the sounds'. To make the activity a little more challenging, instead of writing the words on the board you can dictate them. As a follow-up, ask the students to write their own odd ones out.

10 Board bingo

Aim

This activity is good for revising any type of vocabulary.

Preparation

Write down twelve to fifteen words you want to revise on the board.

Procedure

- Ask the students to choose five of the words and write them down. When they've done that, tell the students that you're going to read out words in random order and that they should cross out one of their words if they hear it. When they've crossed out all five words, they shout *Bingo!* Make sure you keep a record of the words you call out so that you can check the students' answers.

- You can make this more challenging by reading out dictionary definitions of the words rather than the words themselves. (Or if you teach a monolingual class then you could read out a translation of each word). Alternatively, you can turn it into a listening exercise and choose words that are phonetically similar, i.e. *work* /wɜːk/, *walk* /wɑːk/ and *woke* /wəʊk/, etc.

- At the beginning of the course, you could simplify the activity by writing up single letters (especially the vowels) or numbers (or a mixture of cardinal and ordinal numbers).

Key concepts in *New Inside Out*

The following excerpts are from *An A–Z of ELT* by Scott Thornbury (Macmillan Books for Teachers, 2006). They give clear authoritive definitions and explanations of some of the most important concepts in *New Inside Out*.

Contents

Note: SLA = Second Language Acquisition

classroom interaction METHODOLOGY

Classroom interaction is the general term for what goes on between the people in the classroom, particularly when it involves language. In traditional classrooms, most interaction is initiated by the teacher, and learners either respond individually, or in unison. Teacher-centred interaction of this kind is associated with *transmissive* teaching, such as a lecture or presentation, where the teacher *transmits* the content of the lesson to the learners. In order to increase the amount of student involvement and interaction, teacher–learner interaction is often combined with **pairwork** and **groupwork**, where learners interact among themselves in pairs or small groups. Other kinds of interaction include *mingling* or *milling*. Pairwork and groupwork are associated with a more **learner-centred** approach. Rather than passively receiving the lesson content, the learners are actively engaged in using language and discovering things for themselves. The value of pairwork and groupwork has been reinforced by the belief that **interaction** facilitates language learning. Some would go as far as to say that it is *all* that is required.

The potential for classroom interaction is obviously constrained by such factors as the number of students, the size of the room, the furniture, and the purpose or type of activity. Not all activities lend themselves to pairwork or groupwork. Some activities, such as reading, are best done as *individual work*. On the other hand, listening activities (such as listening to an audio recording, or to the teacher) favour a *whole class* format, as do grammar presentations. The whole class is also an appropriate form of organization when reviewing the results of an activity, as, for example, when spokespersons from each group are reporting on the results of a discussion or survey.

The success of any classroom interaction will also depend on the extent to which the learners know what they are meant to be doing and why, which in turn depends on how clearly and efficiently the interaction has been set up. Pair- and groupwork can be a complete waste of time if learners are neither properly prepared for it, nor sure of its purpose or outcome.

Finally, the success of pair- and groupwork will depend on the kind of group **dynamics** that have been established. Do the students know one another? Are they happy working together? Do they mind working without constant teacher supervision? Establishing a productive classroom dynamic may involve making decisions as to who works with whom. It may also mean deliberately staging the introduction of different kinds of interactions, starting off with the more controlled, teacher-led interactions before, over time, allowing learners to work in pairs and finally in groups.

collocation VOCABULARY

If two words *collocate*, they frequently occur together. The relation between the words may be grammatical, as when certain verbs collocate with particular prepositions, such as *depend on, account for, abstain from*, or when a verb, like *make, take*, or *do*, collocates with a noun, as in *make an arrangement, take advantage, do the shopping*. The collocation may also be lexical, as when two **content words** regularly co-occur, as in *a broad hint, a narrow escape* (but not **a wide hint* or **a tight escape*). The strength of the collocation can vary: *a broad street* or *a narrow path* are weak collocations, since both elements can co-occur with lots of other words: *a broad river, a busy street*, etc. *Broad hint* and *narrow escape* are stronger. Stronger still are combinations where one element rarely occurs without the other, as in *moot point, slim pickings* and *scot free*. Strongest of all are those where both elements never or rarely occur without the other, such as *dire straits* and *spick and span*. These have acquired the frozen status of *fixed expressions*.

Unsurprisingly, learners lack intuitions as to which words go with which, and this accounts for many errors, such as *You can completely enjoy it* (instead of *thoroughly*), *On Saturday we made shopping* (instead of *went*), and *We went the incorrect way* (for *wrong*). Using texts to highlight particular collocations, and teaching new words in association with their most frequent collocations are two ways of approaching the problem. Nowadays learners' dictionaries also include useful collocational information.

communicative activity METHODOLOGY

A communicative activity is one in which real communication occurs. Communicative activities belong to that generation of classroom **activities** that emerged in response to the need for a more **communicative approach** in the teaching of second languages. (In their more evolved form as **tasks**, communicative activities are central to **task-based learning**). They attempt to import into a practice activity the key features of 'real-life' communication. These are

- *purposefulness*: speakers are motivated by a communicative goal (such as getting information, making a request, giving instructions) and not simply by the need to display the correct use of language for its own sake
- *reciprocity*: to achieve a purpose, speakers need to interact, and there is as much need to listen as to speak

- *negotiation*: following from the above, they may need to check and **repair** the communication in order to be understood by each other
- *unpredictability*: neither the process, nor the outcome, nor the language used in the exchange, is entirely predictable
- *heterogeneity*: participants can use any communicative means at their disposal; in other words, they are not restricted to the use of a pre-specified grammar item.

And, in the case of spoken language in particular:

- *synchronicity*: the exchange takes place in real time

The best known communicative activity is the *information gap* activity. Here, the information necessary to complete the task is either in the possession of just one of the participants, or distributed among them. In order to achieve the goal of the task, therefore, the learners have to share the information that they have. For example, in a *describe-and-draw* activity, one student has a picture which is hidden from his or her partner. The task is for that student to describe the picture so that the partner can accurately draw it. In a *spot-the-difference* task, both students of a pair have pictures (or texts) that are the same apart from some minor details. The goal is to identify these differences. In a *jigsaw activity*, each member of a group has different information. One might have a bus timetable, another a map, and another a list of hotels. They have to share this information in order to plan a weekend break together.

Information gap activities have been criticized on the grounds that they lack **authenticity**. Nor are information gap activities always as productive as might be wished: unsupervised, learners may resort to **communication strategies** in order to simplify the task. A more exploitable information gap, arguably, is the one that exists between the learners themselves, ie, what they don't know – but might like to know – about one another (→ **personalization**).

context LINGUISTICS

The context of a language item is its adjacent language items. In the absence of context, it is often impossible to assign exact meaning to an item. A sentence like *Ben takes the bus to work*, for example, could have past, present, or future reference, depending on the context:

> I know this chap called Ben. One day *Ben takes the bus to work*, and just as …
> Most days *Ben takes the bus to work*, but sometimes he rides his bike …
> If *Ben takes the bus to work* tomorrow, he'll be late, because there's a strike …

Likewise, a sentence like *You use it like this* is meaningless in the absence of a context. By the same token, a word or sentence in one context can have a very different meaning in another. The sign *NO BICYCLES* in a public park means something different to *NO BICYCLES* outside a bicycle rental shop. It is sometimes necessary to distinguish between different kinds of context. On the one hand, there is the context of the accompanying **text**, sometimes called the *co-text*. The co-text of this sentence, for example, includes the sentences that precede and follow it, as well as the paragraph of which it forms a part. It is the co-text that offers clues as to the meaning of unfamiliar vocabulary in a text. The *situational* context (also *context of situation, context of use*), on the other hand, is the physical and temporal setting in which an instance of language use occurs. The typical context for the spoken question *Are you being served?* is in a shop, for example. Both co-text and context influence the production and interpretation of language. **Discourse analysis** studies the relationship between language and co-text, including the way that sentences or utterances are connected. **Pragmatics** studies the relationship between language and its contexts of use, including the way meaning can be inferred by reference to context factors.

Various theories have been proposed in order to account for the ways that language choices are determined by contextual factors. One of the best known of these is Michael Halliday's **systemic functional linguistics**. Halliday distinguishes three variables in any context that systematically impact on language choices and which, together, determine a text's **register**:

- the *field*: what the language is being used to talk about, and for what purposes
- the *tenor*: the participants in the language event, and their relationship
- the *mode*: how language is being used in the exchange, eg is it written or spoken?

For example, this short text shows the influence of all three factors:

> Do u fancy film either 2nite or 2moro? Call me.

The field is 'making arrangements about leisure activities', hence the use of words like *film, 2nite* (*tonight*), *2moro* (*tomorrow*). The tenor is one of familiarity and equality (accounting for the informal *fancy* and the imperative: *call me*); and the mode is that of a written text message, which explains its brevity, its use of abbreviated forms (*u, 2nite*) and the absence of salutations. A change in any of these contextual factors is likely to have a significant effect on the text.

Language learners, it is argued, need to know how these contextual factors correlate with language choices in order to produce language that is appropriate to the context. One way of doing this is to ask them to make changes to a text (such as the text message above) that take into account adjustments to the field, tenor, or mode.

drill METHODOLOGY

A drill is repetitive oral practice of a language item, whether a sound, a word, a phrase or a sentence structure. Drills that are targeted at sentence structures are sometimes called *pattern practice drills*.

Drills follow a prompt–response sequence, where the prompt usually comes from the teacher, and the students respond, either in chorus (a *choral drill*) or individually. An *imitation drill* simply involves repeating the prompt, as in:

| Teacher | They have been watching TV. |
| Student | They have been watching TV. |

A *substitution drill* requires the students to substitute one element of the pattern with the prompt, making any necessary adjustments:

Teacher	They have been watching TV.
Student	They have been watching TV.
Teacher	She
Student	She has been watching TV.
Teacher	I
Student	I have been watching TV.

etc.

A *variable substitution drill* is the same, but the prompts are not restricted to one element of the pattern:

Teacher	They have been watching TV.
Student	They have been watching TV.
Teacher	She
Student	She has been watching TV.
Teacher	radio
Student	She has been listening to the radio.
Teacher	We
Student	We have been listening to the radio.

etc.

Drills were a defining feature of the **audiolingual** method, and were designed to reinforce good language 'habits'. The invention of language laboratories allowed sustained drilling without the need for a teacher to supply the prompts. With the demise of audiolingualism, drilling fell from favour. However, many teachers – even those who subscribe to a **communicative approach** – feel the need for some form of repetition practice of the kind that drills provide. This may be for the purpose of developing **accuracy**, or as a form of **fluency** training, ie, in order to develop **automaticity**. Hence, communicative drills were developed. A communicative drill is still essentially repetitive, and focuses on a particular structure or pattern, but it has an *information gap* element built in. Learners can perform the drill in pairs, or as a *milling activity* (→ **classroom interaction**) and they are required to attend to what they hear as much as what they say. The milling activity popularly known as *Find someone who …* is one such activity. Students are set the task of finding other students in the class who, for example, can ride a horse, can speak French, can play the guitar, etc. They mill around, asking questions of the type *Can you …?* until they have asked all the other students their questions, and then they report their findings.

dynamics: group, classroom METHODOLOGY

Dynamics are the actions and interactions, both conscious and unconscious, that take place between members of a group, whether the whole class or subgroups. Group dynamics are instrumental in forging a productive and motivating classroom environment. They are determined by such factors as: the composition of the group (including the age, sex, and relative status of the members, as well as their different attitudes, beliefs, learning styles and abilities); the patterns of relationships between members of the group, including how well they know each other, and the roles they each assume, such as group leader, spokesperson, etc; physical factors such as the size of the group and the way it is seated; and the tasks that the group are set, eg: Does the task require everyone to contribute? Does it encourage co-operation or competition? Are the goals of the task clear to the group members?

Ways that the teacher can promote a positive group (and class) dynamic include:

- ensuring all class or group members can see and hear one another, and that they know (and use) each other's names
- keeping groups from getting too big – three to six members is optimal
- setting – or negotiating – clear rules for groupwork, such as using only the target language, giving everyone a turn to speak, allowing individuals to 'pass' if they don't want to say anything too personal
- using 'ice-breaking' activities to encourage interaction, laughter, and relaxation
- ensuring that group tasks are purposeful, interactive, and collaborative
- personalizing tasks, ie, setting tasks that involve the sharing of personal experiences and opinions
- defining the roles and responsibilities within the group, and varying these regularly, eg by appointing a different spokesperson each time
- monitoring groupwork in progress, and being alert to any possible conflicts or tensions between members, and reconstituting groups, if necessary
- discussing the importance of groupwork with learners, and getting feedback on group processes

fluency SLA

If someone is said to be fluent in a language, or to speak a language fluently, it is generally understood that they are able to speak the language idiomatically and accurately, without undue pausing, without an intrusive accent, and in a manner appropriate to the context. In fact, research into listeners' perceptions of fluency suggests that fluency is primarily the ability to produce and maintain speech in *real time*. To do this, fluent speakers are capable of:

- appropriate pausing, ie:
  - their pauses may be long but are not frequent
  - their pauses are usually filled, eg with **pause fillers** like *erm, you know, sort of*
  - their pauses occur at meaningful transition points, eg at the intersections of clauses or phrases, rather than midway in a phrase
- long runs, ie, there are many syllables and words between pauses

All of the above factors depend on the speaker having a well-developed grammar, an extensive vocabulary, and, crucially, a store of memorized *chunks*. Being able to draw on this store of chunks means not having to depend on grammar to construct each utterance from scratch. This allows the speaker to devote **attention** to other aspects of the interaction, such as planning ahead. Speakers also use a number of 'tricks' or *production strategies* to convey the illusion of fluency. One such strategy is disguising pauses by filling them, or by repeating a word or phrase.

Some proponents of the **communicative approach** re-defined fluency so as to distinguish it from **accuracy**. Fluency came to mean 'communicative effectiveness', regardless of formal accuracy or speed of delivery. Activities that are communicative, such as information-gap activities, are said to be *fluency-focused*. This is the case even for activities that produce short, halting utterances. Separating accuracy and fluency, and defining the latter as *communicative* language use, is misleading, though. There are many speech events whose communicativeness depends on their accuracy. Air traffic control talk is just one. Moreover, many learners aspire to being more than merely communicative.

Classroom activities that target fluency need to prepare the learner for real-time speech production. Learning and memorizing lexical chunks, including useful conversational gambits, is one approach. **Drills** may help here, as will some types of **communicative activity** that involve repetition. Research has also shown that fluency improves the more times a **task** is repeated. Fluency may also benefit from activities that manage to distract learners' attention away from formal accuracy so that they are not tempted to slow down. (This has been called 'parking their attention'). Some interactive and competitive language **games** have this effect. **Drama** activities, such as roleplays, recreate conditions of real-time language use, and are therefore good for developing fluency. Finally, learners can achieve greater fluency from learning a repertoire of **communication strategies**, ie, techniques for getting around potential problems caused by a lack of the relevant words or structures.

focus on form SLA

When learners focus on form, they direct conscious attention to some formal feature of the language **input**. The feature may be the fact that the past of *has* is *had*, or that *enjoy* is followed by verb forms ending in *-ing*, or that adjectives do not have plural forms in English. The learners' attention may be self-directed, or it may be directed by the teacher or by another learner. Either way, it has been argued that a focus on **form** is a necessary condition for language learning. Simply focusing on the **meaning** of the input is not enough. Focusing on form is, of course, not a new idea: most teaching methods devote a great deal of time to the forms of the language, eg when new grammar items are presented. But the term *focus on form* captures the fact that this focus can, theoretically, occur at any stage in classroom instruction. Thus, **correction**, especially in the form of negative **feedback**, is a kind of focus on form. In fact, some researchers argue that the most effective form focus is that which arises incidentally, in the context of communication, as when the teacher quickly elicits a correction during a classroom discussion. This incidental approach contrasts with the more traditional and deliberate approach, where teaching is based on a **syllabus** of graded structures (or *forms*), and these are pre-taught in advance of activities designed to practise them. This traditional approach is called – by some researchers – a *focus on formS*.

function LINGUISTICS

The function of a language item is its communicative purpose. Language is more than simply **forms** and their associated meanings (ie, **usage**). It is also the communicative **uses** to which these forms and meanings are put. These two sentences, for example, share the same forms, but function quite differently:

[in an email] *Thank you for sending me the disk.*
[a notice in a taxi] *Thank you for not smoking.*

The function of the first is *expressing thanks*, while the second is more like a *prohibition*. Likewise, the same function can be expressed by different forms:

[a notice in a taxi] *Thank you for not smoking.*
[a sign in a classroom] *No smoking.*

Thus, there is no one-to-one match between form and function. Assigning a function to a text or an utterance usually requires knowledge of the **context** in which the text is used. The study of how context and function are interrelated is called **pragmatics**.

Communicative functions can be categorized very broadly and also at increasing levels of detail. The 'big' functions, or macrofunctions, describe the way language is used in very general terms. These include the use of language for *expressive* purposes (eg poetry), for *regulatory* purposes (eg for getting people to do things), for *interpersonal* purposes (eg for socializing), and for *representational* purposes (eg to inform). More useful, from the point of view of designing language syllabuses, are microfunctions. These are usually expressed as **speech acts**, such as *agreeing and disagreeing, reporting, warning, apologizing, thanking, greeting,* etc. Such categories form the basis of **functional syllabuses**, a development associated with the **communicative approach**. They often appear as one strand of a coursebook **syllabus**. Functions differ from notions in that the latter describe areas of meaning – such as *ability, duration, quantity, frequency,* etc – rather than the uses to which these meanings are put.

One way to teach functions is to adopt a 'phrasebook' approach, and teach useful ways of expressing common functions (what are called *functional exponents*), such as *Would you like ...?* (*inviting*) and *Could you ..., please?* (*requesting*). More memorable, though, is to teach these expressions in

the contexts of **dialogues**, so that the functional exponents are associated not only with common situations in which they are used, but with related functions (such as *accepting* and *refusing*). The term *function*, in contrast to **form**, is also used in linguistics, specifically with regard to the functions of the different elements of a **clause** (such as subject and object).

grammar teaching METHODOLOGY

Like the word **grammar** itself, the topic of grammar teaching is a controversial one, and teachers often take opposing views. Historically, language teaching methods have positioned themselves along a scale from 'zero grammar' to 'total grammar', according to their approach to grammar teaching. Proponents of *natural methods*, who model their approach to teaching second languages on the way that first languages are acquired, reject any explicit teaching of grammar at all. (They may, however, teach according to a grammar **syllabus**, even if no mention of grammar as such is made in the classroom). This implicit approach is common both to the **direct method** and to **audiolingualism**. Through exposure to demonstrations, situations or examples, learners are expected to pick up the rules of grammar by **inductive learning**. At the other end of the spectrum, there are approaches, such as **grammar-translation**, that adopt an explicit and **deductive learning** approach. From the outset, learners are presented with rules which they study and then practise. Occupying a midway point between zero grammar and total grammar is the approach called **consciousness-raising**. Instead of being given rules, learners are presented with language data which challenge them to re-think (and *restructure*) their existing mental grammar. This data might take the form of **input** that has been manipulated in some way. For example, pairs of sentences, such as the following, have to be matched to pictures, forcing learners to discriminate between them, and, in theory, **notice** the difference (→ **noticing**):

The Queen drove to the airport.
The Queen was driven to the airport.

(This is sometimes called a *grammar interpretation task*, or *structured input*.) In order to do the task, learners have to process not just the individual words, but also their grammatical form. That is why this approach to teaching grammar is sometimes called *processing instruction*. There are other researchers who argue that it is by means of manipulating the learner's output, eg through productive practice, that mental restructuring is best effected.

The **communicative approach** accommodates different approaches to grammar teaching. Proponents of **task-based learning**, for example, argue that, if the learner is engaged in solving problems using language, then the mental grammar will develop of its own accord. However, advocates of the weaker version of the communicative approach (and the version that is most widespread) justify a role for the pre-teaching of grammar in advance of production. This view finds support in **cognitive learning theory**, which suggests that conscious attention to grammatical form (called **focus on form**) speeds up language learning, and is a necessary corrective against premature **fossilization**. There is some debate, though, as to whether this form focus should be planned or incidental. Incidental grammar teaching occurs when the teacher deals with grammar issues as and when they come up, eg in the form of **correction**, or task **feedback**. In this way (it is argued) grammar teaching follows the learners' own 'syllabus'. Such an approach attempts to address one of the dilemmas of grammar teaching: the fact that the learner's mental grammar, and the way it develops, bears only an accidental relation to a formal grammar syllabus.

Nevertheless, the research into these different choices is still inconclusive. It may be the case that some items of grammar respond better to explicit teaching, while others are more easily picked up through exposure. There are also different learner types: some prefer learning and applying rules, while others are happier with a more 'deep-end' approach (→ **learning style**). Most current teaching materials hedge their bets on these issues. They offer both deductive and inductive grammar presentations, and opportunities for incidental as well as for planned learning.

learner-centred instruction, learner-centredness
METHODOLOGY

Learner-centred instruction aims to give learners more say in areas that are traditionally considered the domain of the teacher or of the institution. Learner-centred instruction is true to the spirit of progressive education, including the movement towards providing learners with greater **autonomy**. For example, a learner-centred **curriculum** would involve learners in negotiating decisions relating to the choice of syllabus content, of materials, of activity-types, and of assessment procedures. Learner-centredness also describes ways of organizing **classroom interaction** so that the focus is directed away from the teacher, and on to the learners, who perform tasks in pairs or small groups. This contrasts with traditional, teacher-centred, classroom interaction. Some writers believe that the dichotomy between learner-centred (= good) and teacher-centred (= bad) is a false one. It might be more useful to talk about *learning-centred instruction*, ie, instruction which prioritizes sound learning principles. In a learning-centred approach there would be room for both learner-centred *and* teacher-centred interactions.

learning style PSYCHOLOGY

Your learning style is your preferred way of learning. This style may be influenced by biographical factors (such as how you were taught as a child) or by innately endowed factors (such as whether you have a 'good ear' for different sounds). Types of learning style are often presented in the form of polarities (some of which may overlap), such as:

- analytic versus global (or holistic) thinkers, ie, learners who tend to focus on the details, versus learners who tend to see 'the big picture'
- rule-users versus data-gatherers, ie, learners who learn and apply rules, versus those who prefer exposure to lots of examples
- reflective versus impulsive learners
- group-oriented versus solitary learners
- extrovert versus introverted learners
- verbal versus visual learners
- passive versus active learners

Attempts have been made to group these polarities and relate them to brain lateralization. So, a bias towards left-brain processing correlates with analytic, rule-forming and verbal learners, while a bias towards right-brain processing correlates with their opposite. A less binary view of learning style is that proposed by the psychologist Howard Gardner. He identified at least seven distinct intelligences that all individuals possess but to different degrees. These include the *logical/mathematical*, the *verbal/linguistic*, and the *visual/spatial*. Similarly, proponents of **neuro-linguistic programming** distinguish between different sensory orientations, including the *visual, aural* and *kinesthetic* (ie, related to movement, touch). So far, though, there is no convincing evidence that any of these dispositions correlates with specific learning behaviours. Nor has it been shown that a preference in one area predicts success in language learning. In fact, it is very difficult to separate learning style from other potentially influential factors, such as personality, intelligence, and previous learning experience. Nor is it clear to what extent learning style can be manipulated, eg through **learner training**. The best that can be said is that, if the learner's preferred learning style is out of synch with the type of instruction on offer, then success is much less likely than if the two are well matched. This supports the case for an **eclectic** approach, on the one hand, and the individualization of learning, on the other.

listening METHODOLOGY

Listening is the skill of understanding spoken language. It is also the name given to classroom activities that are designed to develop this skill – what are also called *listening comprehension* activities – as in 'today we're going to do a listening'. Listening is one of the four language **skills**, and, along with **reading**, was once thought of as being a 'passive' skill. In fact, although receptive, listening is anything but passive. It is a goal-oriented activity, involving not only processing of the incoming speech signals (called *bottom-up processing*) but also the use of prior knowledge, contextual clues, and expectations (*top-down processing*) in order to create meaning. Among the sub-skills of listening are:

- perceiving and discriminating individual sounds
- segmenting the stream of speech into recognizable units such as words and phrases

- using **stress** and **intonation** cues to distinguish given information from new information
- attending to **discourse markers** and using these to predict changes in the direction of the talk
- guessing the meaning of unfamiliar words
- using clues in the text (such as vocabulary) and context clues to predict what is coming
- making inferences about what is not stated
- selecting key information relevant to the purpose for listening
- integrating incoming information into the mental 'picture' (or **schema**) of the speech event so far

Also, since listening is normally interactive, listeners need to be capable of:

- recognizing when speakers have finished their turns, or when it is appropriate to interrupt
- providing ongoing signals of understanding, interest, etc. (*backchannelling*)
- asking for clarification, asking someone to repeat what they have just said, and repairing misunderstandings

These sub-skills exist across languages, so, in theory, learners should be able to transfer them from their first language into their second. In fact, there are a number of reasons why this does not always happen. One is that speakers of different languages process speech signals differently, depending on the phonetic characteristics of the language they are used to. This means that speakers of some languages will find it harder than others to match the spoken word to the way that the word is represented in their mind. They simply do not recognize the word. Another problem is lack of sufficient L2 knowledge, such as vocabulary or grammar. A third problem is that learners may lack the means (and the confidence) to negotiate breakdowns in understanding. Finally, many learners simply lack exposure to spoken language, and therefore have not had sufficient opportunities to experience listening. These problems can be compounded in classrooms because:

- Listening to audio recordings deprives the learners of useful visual information, and allows the learners no opportunity to interact and repair misunderstandings.
- Classroom acoustics are seldom ideal.
- If learners do not know what they are listening for (in the absence, for example, of some pre-set listening task) they may try to process as much information as possible, rather than being selective in their listening. This can lead to listening overload, which in turn can cause inhibiting anxiety.
- Listening texts that have been specially written for classroom use are often simplified. But if this simplification means eliminating a lot of redundant language, such as speaker repetitions, pause fillers and vague language, the density of information that results may make it harder – not easier – to process.

For this reason, the use of audio recordings to develop listening skills needs to be balanced against the advantages of using other media, such as video, and face-to-face interaction with the teacher or another speaker.

Nevertheless, the use of audio recordings is an established part of classroom practice, so it is important to know how to use them to best advantage. The following approach is one that is often recommended:

- Provide some minimum contextual information, eg who is talking to whom about what, and why. This helps to compensate for lack of visual information, and allows learners to activate the relevant mental **schema**, which in turn helps top-down processing, including the sub-skill of prediction.
- Pre-teach key vocabulary: this helps with bottom-up processing, although too much help may mean that learners don't get sufficient practice in guessing from context.
- Set some 'while-listening' questions. Initially, these should focus on the overall *gist* of the text. For example: true/false questions, selecting, ordering or matching pictures, ticking items on a list, following a map
- Play a small section of the recording first, to give learners an opportunity to familiarize themselves with the different voices, and to trigger accurate expectations as to what they will hear.
- Play the recording right through, and then allow learners to consult on the answers to the pre-set task. Check these answers. If necessary, re-play the recording until satisfied that learners have 'got the gist'.
- Set a more demanding task, requiring more intensive listening, such as listening for detail, or inferring speakers' attitudes, intentions, etc. If the recording is a long one, it may pay to stage the intensive listening in sections. Again, allow learners to consult in pairs, before checking the task in open class.
- On the basis of the learners' success with these tasks, identify problem sections of the recording and return to these, playing and re-playing them, and perhaps eliciting a word-by-word transcription and writing this on the board.
- Distribute copies of the transcript of the recording (if available) and re-play the recording while learners read the transcript. This allows the learners to clear up any remaining problems, and also to match what they hear to what they see.

The above approach can be adapted to suit different kinds of recorded texts and different classroom needs. For higher level learners, for example, it may be counter-productive to make listening *too* easy. The approach can also be adapted to the use of video, and even to *live listenings*, such as listening to the teacher or a guest.

motivation PSYCHOLOGY

Motivation is what drives learners to achieve a goal, and is a key factor determining success or failure in language learning. The learner's goal may be a short-term one, such as successfully performing a classroom task, or a long-term one, such as achieving native-like proficiency in the language. With regard to long-term goals, a distinction is often made between *instrumental motivation* and *integrative motivation*. Instrumental motivation is when the learner has a functional objective, such as passing an exam or getting a job. Integrative motivation, on the other hand, is when the learner wants to be identified with the target language community. Intersecting with these two motivational *orientations* are two different *sources* of motivation: *intrinsic* (eg the pleasure of doing a task for its own sake) and *extrinsic* (eg the 'carrot and stick' approach). Another motivational source that has been identified is success: experience of succeeding can result in increased motivation (called *resultative motivation*), which raises the question as to whether motivation is as much a result as a cause of learning.

Various theories of motivation have been proposed. Most of these identify a variety of factors that, in combination, contribute to overall motivation, such as:

- *attitudes*, eg to the target language and to speakers of the language
- *goals*, both long-term and short-term, and the learners' *orientation* to these goals
- how much *value* the learner attaches to achieving the goals, especially as weighed against *expectancy of success*; expectancy of success may come from the learner's assessment of their own abilities, and how they account for previous successes or failures
- *self-esteem*, and the need to achieve and maintain it
- *intrinsic interest*, *pleasure*, *relevance* or *challenge* of the task
- *group dynamic*: is it competitive, collaborative, or individualistic?
- *teacher's attitudes*, eg what expectations does the teacher project about the learners' likelihood of success?

As the last point suggests, teachers can play a key role in motivating learners, not just in terms of choosing activities that are intrinsically motivating, but in the attitudes they project. Two researchers on motivation offer the following advice for teachers:

> Ten commandments for motivating language learners
>
> 1. Set a personal example with your own behaviour
> 2. Create a pleasant, relaxed atmosphere in the classroom.
> 3. Present the tasks properly.
> 4. Develop a good relationship with the learners.
> 5. Increase the learner's linguistic self-confidence.
> 6. Make the language classes interesting.
> 7. Promote learner autonomy.
> 8. Personalise the learning process.
> 9. Increase the learners' goal-orientedness.
> 10. Familiarise learners with the target language culture.

noticing SLA

If you notice a feature of the language that you are exposed to, it attracts your attention and you make a mental note of it. For example, a learner might notice (without necessarily understanding) the sign *Mind the gap*, repeated several times on a railway station platform. That same day, the learner hears the teacher say *would you mind* in the context of making a request in class. A day or two later, the same learner hears someone else say *I don't mind*. Each successive 'noticing' both primes the learner to notice new occurrences of *mind*, and at the same time contributes to a growing understanding of the use and meaning of *mind*. Proponents of **cognitive learning theory** believe that noticing is a prerequisite for learning: without it input would remain as mere 'noise'. The *noticing hypothesis*, then, claims that noticing is a necessary condition for acquisition, although not the only one. Some kind of mental processing of what has been noticed is also necessary before the **input** becomes *intake*, ie before it is moved into long-term **memory**.

Teachers obviously play an important role in helping learners to notice features of the language. They do this when they repeat words or structures, write them on the board, or even drill them. One way of increasing the chance of learners' noticing an item is to include it lots of times in a text, a technique called *input flood*. For example, learners read a text with the word *mind* included several times. They then categorize these examples according to their meaning. A set of **concordance** lines for a particular word can be used in the same way.

There is another type of noticing, called *noticing the gap*. This is when learners are made aware of a gap in their language knowledge. This might happen when they do a **dictation**, for example. When they compare their version with the correct version, they may notice certain differences, such as the lack of past tense endings, that represent a gap in their **interlanguage**. It has been argued that noticing the gap can trigger the **restructuring** of interlanguage. That is, 'minding the gap' leads learners to 'fill the gap'.

personalization METHODOLOGY

When you personalize language you use it to talk about your knowledge, experience and feelings. Personalization of the type *Now write five true sentences about yourself using 'used to'* is often motivated by the need to provide further practice of pre-taught grammar structures. But it is also good preparation for the kinds of situations of genuine language use that learners might encounter outside the classroom. These advantages are lost, though, if the teacher's response is to treat the exercise as *only* an exercise, and correct the learners' errors without responding to the content. The influence of **humanistic approaches** has given a fresh impetus to personalization, both in terms of providing a more coherent rationale and suggesting a broader range of activity types. For a start (it is argued), personalization creates better classroom **dynamics**. This is because groups are more likely to form and bond if the individuals in them know more about one another. And the mental and emotional effort that is involved in finding personal associations with a language item is likely to make that item more memorable. This quality is called cognitive and affective *depth*. Finally, lessons are likely to be more interesting, and hence more motivating, if at least some of the content concerns the people in the room, rather than the characters in coursebooks. On these grounds, some writers have suggested that personalization should not be considered simply as an 'add-on', but should be the principle on which most, if not all, classroom content should be based. One teaching approach that is committed to this view is **community language learning**. In this approach, all the content of the lesson comes from the learners themselves. Personalization is not without risks, though. Teachers need to be sensitive to learner resistance: learners should have the right to 'pass' on questions that they consider too intrusive. And teachers should be authentic in the way that they respond to learners' personalizations. This means that they should respond to *what* their learners are saying, not just how they say it.

practice METHODOLOGY

If you practise a skill, you experience doing it a number of times in order to gain control of it. The idea that 'practice makes perfect' is fundamental to **cognitive learning theory**. It is through practice that the skill becomes automatic. **Sociocultural learning theory** finds room for practice too. Performing a skill with the assistance of someone who is good at it can help in the **appropriation** of the skill. At issue, then, is not so much whether practice is beneficial, but what form it should take, when, and how much of it is necessary. In addressing these questions, it is customary to distinguish between different kinds of practice, such as *controlled practice* vs *free practice*, *mechanical practice* vs *meaningful/communicative practice*, and *receptive practice* vs *productive practice*.

Controlled practice is associated with the second P of the **PPP** instructional model. Practice can be controlled in at least two senses: *language control* and *interactional control*. In the first, the language that is being practised is restricted to what has just been presented (hence it is also called *restricted practice*). For example, if the first **conditional** has been presented, learners practise this, and only this, structure, and in a repetitive way, eg through a sequence of **drills**. Practice is also said to be controlled if the learners' participation is overtly managed and monitored by the teacher, such as in open-class work, as opposed to closed **pairwork** or **groupwork**. One reason for this degree of control is

that it maintains a focus on accuracy, and pre-empts or corrects errors. *Free practice*, on the other hand, allows learners a measure of creativity, and the opportunity to integrate the new item into their existing language 'pool'. It is also less controlled in terms of the interactions, with pairwork and groupwork being favoured. Typical free practice activities might be **games**, **discussions** or **drama**-based activities.

Mechanical practice is a form of controlled practice, where the focus is less on the meaning of an item than on manipulating its component parts. Mechanical practice can be either oral or written: many traditional **exercises** are mechanical in this sense, such as when learners transform sentences from active into passive, or from direct speech into reported speech. The arguments in favour of controlled and mechanical practice have lost their force since the decline of **behaviourism** and its belief that learning is simply habit-formation.

Meaningful practice requires learners to display some understanding of what the item that they are practising actually means. One way of doing this is through **personalization**. *Communicative practice* involves the learners interacting in order to complete some kind of task, such as in an *information gap* activity (→ **communicative activity**). Proponents of a communicative approach argue that it is only this kind of practice that is truly effective. This is because learners are not simply practising language, but are practising the behaviours associated with the language, and this is a pre-condition for long-term behavioural change.

Finally, some practice activities are purely *receptive*. They involve the learners in identifying, selecting, or discriminating between language items, but not actually producing them. Many **consciousness-raising** activities are receptive, on the grounds that learners first need to understand a new structure before they can properly internalize it. Receptive practice is also associated with comprehension-based approaches to teaching. *Productive practice*, on the other hand, requires learners to produce the targeted items (either orally or in writing), and is associated with output-based models of learning.

There is fairly general agreement nowadays that the most effective practice activity combines at least some of the following features:

- It is meaningful, which may mean that is personalized.
- It is communicative, thus it will require learners to interact.
- It involves a degree of repetition – not of the mindless type associated with imitation drills, but of the type associated with many games.
- It is language-rich, ie, learners have to interpret or produce a lot of language.
- Learners can be creative and take risks, but support is at hand if they need it.
- Learners are pushed, at least some of the time, to the limits of their competence
- Learners get **feedback**.

pronunciation teaching PHONOLOGY

Pronunciation is the general term for that part of language classes and courses that deals with aspects of the **phonology** of English. This includes the individual sounds (**phonemes**) of English, sounds in **connected speech**, word and sentence **stress**, **rhythm** and **intonation**. These components are customarily divided into two groups: the *segmental* features of pronunciation, ie, the individual sounds and the way they combine, and the *suprasegmental* features, ie, stress, rhythm and intonation. **Paralinguistic** features of speech production such as voice quality, tempo and loudness, are also classed as suprasegmental.

Effective pronunciation teaching needs to consider what goals, course design and methodology are most appropriate for the learners in question. The goal of acquiring a native-like **accent** is generally thought to be unachievable for most learners (and perhaps even undesirable). Instead, the goal of **intelligibility** is nowadays considered more realistic, if less easily measurable. It is often claimed that suprasegmental features play a greater role in intelligibility than do segmental ones. Unfortunately, however, some of these suprasegmental features, such as intonation, are considered by many teachers to be unteachable. Moreover, learners intending to interact with native speakers may need to set different goals from those learners whose purpose is to learn **English as an international language (EIL)**. For this latter group, the so-called **phonological core** is a checklist of those pronunciation features considered critical for intelligibility in EIL.

In terms of the design of course content, a basic choice is whether the pronunciation focus is *integrated* or *segregated*. In an integrated approach, pronunciation is dealt with as part of the teaching of grammar and vocabulary, or of speaking and listening. In a segregated approach it is treated in isolation. A classical segregated exercise is the **minimal pairs** task, in which learners are taught to discriminate and produce two contrasted phonemes (as in *hit* and *heat*). There are doubts as to whether this item-by-item approach to pronunciation reflects the way that the features of pronunciation are interconnected. Nor does it reflect the way that they jointly emerge over time ('as a photo emerges in the darkroom'). A related issue is whether pronunciation teaching should be *pre-emptive* or *reactive*. That is to say, should pronunciation teaching be planned around a syllabus of pre-selected items, or should the focus on pronunciation emerge *out of* practice activities, in the form, for example, of **correction**? There is evidence that the latter approach is more effective than the former.

In 1964 the writer (and former language teacher) Anthony Burgess wrote, 'Nothing is more important than to acquire a set of foreign phonemes that shall be entirely acceptable to your hosts'. However, there is generally less emphasis given to pronunciation teaching nowadays. Indeed, some teachers are sceptical as to the value of teaching pronunciation at all. This view is reinforced by research that suggests that the best predictors of intelligible pronunciation are 'having a good ear' and prolonged residence in an English-speaking country. On the other hand, faulty pronunciation is one of the most common causes of misunderstandings. This is an argument for demanding higher standards than the learners can realistically achieve, in the hope that they will meet you 'halfway'.

reading METHODOLOGY

Reading is a receptive **skill**. But the fact that it is receptive does not mean that it is passive: reading is an active, even interactive, process. Readers bring their own questions to the text, which are based on their background knowledge, and they use these to interrogate the text, modifying their questions and coming up with new ones according to the answers they get. In order to do this, they draw on a range of knowledge bases. They need to be able to decode the letters, words and grammatical structures of the individual sentences – what is called *bottom-up processing*. But they also enlist *top-down processes*, such as drawing on **discourse** and schematic knowledge, as well as on immediate contextual information. Discourse knowledge is knowing how different text-types – such as news reports, recipes or academic papers – are organized. Schematic knowledge is the reader's existing knowledge of the topic. Reading involves an interaction between these different 'levels' of knowledge, where knowledge at one 'level' can compensate for lack of knowledge at another.

Readers also bring their own *purposes* to texts, and these in turn determine the way they go about reading a text. The two main purposes for reading are for *information* (such as when consulting a directory), and for *pleasure* (such as when reading a novel), although these purposes may overlap. Different ways of reading include:

- *skimming* (*skim-reading, reading for gist*): rapidly reading a text in order to get the *gist*, or the main ideas or sense of a text. For example, a reader might skim a film review in order to see if the reviewer liked the film or not.
- *scanning*: reading a text in search of specific information, and ignoring everything else, such as when consulting a bus timetable for a particular time and destination.
- *detailed reading*: reading a text in order to extract the maximum detail from it, such as when following the instructions for installing a household appliance.
- *reading aloud*: such as when reading a prepared speech or lecture, or reading a story aloud, or an extract from the newspaper.

A reader's purpose usually matches the writer's intentions for the text. Readers seldom read telephone books from cover to cover, for example. Nor do they normally skim through a novel looking for names beginning with *Vron* .... In classrooms, however, texts are frequently used for purposes other than those for which they were originally intended. They are often used not so much as vehicles of information or of pleasure, but as 'linguistic objects', that is, as contexts for the study of features of the language. A distinction needs to be made, therefore, between two types of classroom reading: reading as *skills development*, and reading as *language study*. There is no reason why the same text cannot be used for both purposes.

Another distinction that is often made is between *intensive reading* and *extensive reading*. The former applies to the way short texts are subject to close and detailed classroom study. Extensive reading, on the other hand, means the more leisurely reading of longer texts, primarily for pleasure, or in order to accumulate vocabulary, or simply to develop sound habits of reading. This is typically done outside class, using graded **readers**, authentic texts, or literary texts.

A third important distinction is between testing reading and teaching reading. Traditional reading tasks usually involve reading a text and then answering **comprehension questions** about it. This is the testing approach. A teaching approach, on the other hand, aims to help learners to become more effective readers by training them in the *sub-skills* of reading, and by teaching them *reading strategies*. Some of the sub-skills of reading are:

- understanding words and identifying their grammatical function
- recognizing grammar features, such as word endings, and 'unpacking' (or **parsing**) the syntax of sentences
- identifying the topic of the text, and recognizing topic changes
- identifying text-type, text purpose, and text organization, and identifying and understanding **discourse markers** and other cohesive devices
- distinguishing key information from less important information
- identifying and understanding the gist
- inferring the writer's attitude
- following the development of an argument
- following the sequence of a narrative
- paraphrasing the text

Activities designed to develop these sub-skills include: underlining topic-related words; contrasting different text-types; comparing different examples of the same text type and identifying *generic* features; circling and categorizing discourse markers; identifying what the pronouns refer to; predicting the direction the text will take at each discourse marker; choosing the best summary of a text; putting a set of pictures in order; extracting key information on to a grid, writing a summary of the text, etc. *Strategy training* involves training learners in ways of overcoming problems when they are reading. Some useful strategies include:

- using contextual and extra-linguistic information (such as pictures, layout, headlines) to make predictions regarding what the text is about

- brainstorming background (or schematic) knowledge in advance of reading
- skimming a text in advance of a more detailed reading
- keeping the purpose of the text in mind
- guessing the meaning of words from context
- **dictionary** use

There is some argument, however, as to the value of a 'skills and strategies' approach to teaching reading. Most adult learners of English come to English texts with already well-developed reading skills in their own language. They already know how to skim, scan, use context clues, enlist background knowledge, and so on. Theoretically, at least, these skills are transferable. What makes reading difficult is not so much lack of reading skills as lack of *language knowledge*. That is, learners lack sufficient vocabulary and grammar to unpack sentences, and they cannot easily identify the ways that sentences are connected. This can result in 'tunnel vision', with readers becoming distracted by unfamiliar words, at the expense of working out meaning from context. On the other hand, it can also result in an over-reliance on guesswork, and on superficial 'text attack' strategies such as skimming. This suggests that texts needs to be chosen that do not over-stretch learners' ability to read them fluently. At the same time, texts should not be so easy that learners can process them simply by skimming. It also means that tasks need to be chosen that both match the original purpose of the text, and that encourage learners to transfer their first language reading skills. Such tasks are likely to be those that motivate learners to *want* to read the text. This might mean activating interest in the topic of the text, through, for example, a pre-reading quiz. At the same time, classroom reading texts should be exploited, not just for their potential in developing reading skills, but as sources of language input. This will involve, at some point, detailed study of the text's formal features, such as its linking devices, its collocations or its grammar.

speaking METHODOLOGY

Speaking is generally thought to be the most important of the four **skills**. The ability to speak a second language is often equated with proficiency in the language, as in *She speaks excellent French*. Indeed, one frustration commonly voiced by learners is that they have spent years studying English, but still can't speak it. One of the main difficulties, of course, is that speaking usually takes place spontaneously and in real time, which means that planning and production overlap. If too much **attention** is paid to planning, production suffers, and the effect is a loss of **fluency**. On the other hand, if the speaker's attention is directed solely on production, it is likely that **accuracy** will suffer, which could prejudice **intelligibility**. In order to free up attention, therefore, the speaker needs to have achieved a degree of **automaticity** in both planning and production. One way of doing this is to use memorized routines, such as **formulaic language**. Another is to use *production strategies*, such as the use of **pause fillers**, in order to 'buy' planning time. The situation is complicated by the fact that most speaking is interactive. Speakers are jointly having to manage the flow of talk. The management of interaction involves *turn-taking skills*, such as knowing how and when to take, keep, and relinquish speaker turns, and also knowing how to repair misunderstandings.

For language learners these processing demands are magnified through lack of basic knowledge of grammar and vocabulary. For the purposes of most day-to-day talk, however, the grammar that is required is not as complex nor need be as accurate as the grammar that is required for writing. Nor do speakers need an enormous vocabulary, especially if they have developed some **communication strategies** for getting round gaps in their knowledge. A core vocabulary of 1000–1500 high-frequency words and expressions will provide most learners with a solid basis for speaking.

Activating this knowledge, though, requires **practice**. This in turn suggests that the more speaking practice opportunities that learners are given, and the sooner, the easier speaking will become. Speaking practice means more than simply answering the teacher's questions, or repeating sentences, as in grammar practice activities. It means interacting with other speakers, sustaining long turns of talk, speaking spontaneously, and speaking about topics of the learners' choice.

Approaches to teaching speaking vary. Traditionally, speaking was considered to be a by-product of teaching grammar and vocabulary, reinforced with work on **pronunciation**. This view has been replaced by approaches that treat speaking as a skill in its own right. One such approach is to break down the speaking skill into a number of discrete sub-skills, such as *opening and closing conversations, turn-taking, repairing, paraphrasing, interrupting,* etc. Another approach is to focus on the different *purposes* of speaking and their associated **genres**, such as *narrating, obtaining service, giving a presentation, making small talk,* etc. This approach is particularly well suited to learners who have a specific purpose for learning English. A third is to adopt a topic-based approach, where learners are encouraged to speak freely on a range of topics, at least some of which they have chosen themselves. This is the format used in many conversation classes. Typical activity types for the teaching of speaking include: **dialogues, drama** activities (including *roleplays* and *simulations*), many **games, discussions** and debates, as well as informal classroom chat.

task METHODOLOGY

A task is a classroom activity whose focus is on communicating meaning. The objective of a task may be to reach some consensus on an issue, to solve a problem, to draft a plan, to design something, or to persuade someone to do something. In contrast, practising a pre-selected item of language (such as the present perfect) for its own sake would not be a valid task objective. In the performance of the task, learners are expected to make use of their own language resources. In theory, tasks may be receptive or productive, and may be done individually or in pairs or small groups. However, in practice, most activities that are labelled 'tasks' in coursebooks involve production (either speaking or writing, or both) and require learners to interact with one another.

Tasks are the organizing principle in **task-based learning**. In order to devise a syllabus of tasks it is necessary both to classify tasks, and to identify the factors that make one task more difficult than another. Different criteria for classifying tasks have been suggested. For example, tasks can be *open-ended* or *closed*. An open-ended task is one in which learners know there is no predetermined solution. It might be planning an excursion, or debating a topical issue. A closed task, on the other hand, requires learners to discover the solution to a problem, such as identifying the differences in a *spot-the-difference* task (→ **communicative activity**). Tasks can also be classified according to the kinds of operations they involve, such as *ranking, selecting, sorting, comparing, surveying* and *problem-solving*.

Factors which influence the degree of difficulty of the task, and hence which affect the grading of tasks, include:

- *linguistic factors*: How complex is the language that learners will need to draw on, in order to do the task? How much help, either before, or during the task, will they get with their language needs?
- *cognitive factors*: Does the task require the processing of complex data? Is the task type familiar to learners?
- *performance factors*: Do the learners have to interact in real time in order to do the task? Do they have time to rehearse? Do they have to 'go public'?

The term *task* is now widely accepted as a useful way of labelling certain types of classroom activity, including many which have a thinly disguised grammar agenda. But the concept of task is not without its critics. Some writers feel that the associations of task with 'work' undervalues the more playful – and possibly less authentic or communicative – types of classroom activity, such as games, songs and drama.

vocabulary teaching METHODOLOGY

Vocabulary describes that area of language learning that is concerned with word knowledge. Vocabulary learning is a major goal in most teaching programmes. It hasn't always been so. In methods such as **audiolingualism**, vocabulary was subordinated to the teaching of grammar structures. Words were simply there to fill the slots in the sentence patterns. The move towards *semantic* (ie, meaning-based) **syllabuses** in the 1970s, along with the use of **authentic** materials, saw a revival of interest in vocabulary teaching. Subsequently, developments in **corpus** linguistics and **discourse analysis** started to blur the distinction between vocabulary and grammar. In the 1990s the **lexical**

approach ushered in a major re-think regarding the role of vocabulary. This concerned both the *selection* of items (**frequency** being a deciding factor) and the *type* of items: **formulaic language** (or lexical chunks) were recognized as being essential for both **fluency** and **idiomaticity**. These developments have influenced the design of teaching materials. Most contemporary coursebooks incorporate a lexical syllabus alongside the grammar one. Recent developments in lexicography have complemented this trend. There is now a wide range of **dictionaries** available for learners, many of which come with sophisticated software for accessing databases of examples and collocations.

It is now generally agreed that, in terms of goals, learners need a receptive vocabulary of around 3000 high-frequency words (or, better, **word families**) in order to achieve independent user status. This will give them around ninety per cent coverage of normal text. For a productive vocabulary, especially for speaking, they may only need half this number.

Classroom approaches to achieving these goals include dedicated vocabulary lessons. Typically these take the form of teaching *lexical sets* of words (ie, groups of thematically linked words) using a variety of means, including visual **aids**, demonstration, situations, texts and dictionary work. As well as the **meaning** of the items, the **form**, both spoken (ie, **pronunciation**) and written (ie, **spelling**), needs to be dealt with, especially if the words are being taught for productive use. Other aspects of word knowledge that may need to be highlighted include **connotation** and **style**, **collocation**, derived forms, and grammatical features, such as the word's **word class**. Vocabulary is also taught as preparation for listening or reading (*pre-teaching vocabulary*) or as a by-product of these skills.

It would be impossible, in class, to teach all the words that learners need. Learners therefore need opportunities for *incidental* learning, eg through *extensive reading*. They may also benefit from training in how to make the most of these opportunities, eg by means of dictionary use, note-keeping, etc. Some strategies for deducing the meaning of unfamiliar words will also help.

Amassing a fully-functioning vocabulary is essentially a **memory** task, and techniques to help in the memorizing of words can be usefully taught, too. It also helps to provide learners with repeated encounters with new words, eg through the re-reading of texts, or by reading several texts about the same topic. Constant recycling of newly learned words is essential. One simple way of doing this is to have a *word box* (or word bag) in the classroom. New words are written on to small cards and added to the word box. At the beginning of the next lesson, these words can be used as the basis for a review activity. For example, the teacher can take words out of the box and ask learners to define them, provide a translation or put them into a sentence. The words can also form the basis for peer-testing activities, in which learners take a number of word cards and test each other in pairs or small groups.

writing METHODOLOGY

Like speaking, writing is a productive **skill**, and, like other skills, writing involves a hierarchy of *sub-skills*. These range from the most mechanical (such as handwriting or typing legibly) through to the ability to organize the written text and lay it out according to the conventions of the particular text type. Along the way, writers also need to be able to:

- produce grammatically accurate sentences
- connect and punctuate these sentences
- select and maintain an appropriate style
- signal the direction that the message is taking
- anticipate the reader's likely questions so as to be able to structure the message accordingly

In order to enable these skills, writers need an extensive knowledge base, not only at the level of vocabulary and grammar, but at the level of connected discourse. This includes familiarity with a range of different text types, such as *informal letters*, *instructions*, *product descriptions*, etc. It follows that if classroom writing is mainly spelling- or grammar-focused, many of the sub-skills of writing will be neglected.

Nevertheless, the teaching of writing has tended to focus on the 'lower-level' features of the skill, such as being able to write sentences that are both accurate and complex, that demonstrate internal cohesion, and that are connected to the sentences next to them. This language-based approach is justified on the grounds that stricter standards of accuracy are usually required in writing than in speaking. Also, writing demands a greater degree of explicitness than speaking, since writers and their readers are separated in time and space. They therefore can't rely on immediate feedback in order to clear up mis-understandings.

By contrast, a text-based approach to teaching writing takes a more 'top-down' view. This approach finds support in **discourse analysis**, which shows that a **text** is more than a series of sentences, however neatly linked. Instead, texts are organized according to larger *macrostructures*, such as problem-solution, or definition-examples. Hence, learners need explicit guidance in how texts are structured. This typically involves analysing and imitating models of particular text types. For example, a business letter might be analysed in terms of its overall layout, the purpose of each of its paragraphs, the grammatical and lexical choices within each paragraph, and the punctuation. Each of these features is then practised in isolation. They are then recombined in tasks aimed first at reproducing the original text and then at producing similar texts incorporating different content.

This approach is called a *product approach* to the teaching of writing, since the focus is exclusively on producing a text (the product) that reproduces the model. By contrast, a *process approach* argues that writers do not in fact start with a clear idea of the finished product. Rather, the text emerges out of a creative process. This process includes: *planning* (*generating ideas, goal setting* and *organizing*), *drafting* and *re-drafting; reviewing*, including *editing* and *proofreading*, and, finally, 'publishing'. Advocates of a process approach argue for a more organic sequence of classroom activities, beginning with the brainstorming of ideas, writing preliminary drafts, comparing drafts, re-drafting, and *conferencing*, that is, talking through their draft with the teacher, in order to fine-tune their ideas.

The process approach to writing has a lot in common with the **communicative approach** to language teaching, and each has drawn support from the other. The communicative approach views writing as an act of communication in which the writer interacts with a reader or readers for a particular purpose. The purpose might be to ask for information about a language course, to relay personal news, to complain about being overcharged at a hotel, or simply to entertain and amuse. Thus, advocates of a communicative approach argue that classroom writing tasks should be motivated by a clear purpose and that writers should have their reader(s) in mind at all stages of the writing process. Such principles are now reflected in the design of writing tasks in public examinations, such as this one, from the Cambridge ESOL First Certificate in English (FCE) paper:

> The school where you learn English has decided to buy some videos in English. You have been asked to write a report to the Principal, suggesting what kinds of videos the school should buy. In your report you should also explain why students at the school will like these videos.
>
> Write your report.

The social purposes of writing are also foregrounded by proponents of a *genre-based approach*. **Genre** analysis attempts to show how the structure of particular text-types are shaped by the purposes they serve in specific social and cultural contexts. Put simply, a business letter is the way it is because of what it does. Advocates of genre-based teaching reject a process approach to teaching writing. They argue that to emphasize self-expression at the expense of teaching the generic structures of texts may in fact disempower learners. Many learners, especially those who are learning English as a *second* language, need a command of those genres – such as writing a CV, or requesting a bank loan – that permit access to the host community. A genre approach to teaching writing is not unlike a product approach, therefore. It starts with model texts that are subjected to analysis and replication. The difference is that these models are closely associated with their contexts of use, and they are analysed in functional terms as much as in linguistic ones. The genre approach has been particularly influential in the teaching of academic writing.

In reality, none of these approaches is entirely incompatible with any other. Resourceful teachers tend to blend elements of each. For example, they may encourage learners to 'discover' what they want to write, using a process approach. They may then give them a model text, both as a source of useful language items, and as a template for the final product. They may also provide exercises in specific sub-skills, such as linking sentences, or using a formal style.

The Common European Framework and *New Inside Out*

The Common European Framework for language learning

Introduction

The Common European Framework (CEF) is a widely used standard created by the Council of Europe. In the classroom, familiarity with the CEF can be of great help to any teacher in identifying students' actual progress and helping them to set their learning priorities.

Students can use the descriptors (description of competences) at any point to get a detailed, articulated, and personal picture of their own individual progress. This is important, as no two language learners progress in the same way, and consequently it's always rather artificial to apply a 'framework level' to a class as a whole, or to a course or coursebook.

The European Language Portfolio is another Council of Europe project, designed to give every learner a structure for keeping a record of their language learning experiences and their progress as described in the CEF. Up-to-date information about developments with the CEF and Portfolio can be found on www.coe.int/portfolio.

The Swiss-based Eurocentres Foundation played a major role in the development of the levels and the descriptors for the CEF and the prototype Portfolio[1]. The CEF descriptors, developed in a Swiss National Research Foundation project, were presented in clearer, simpler, self-assessment form in the prototype (Swiss) Portfolio. There are now dozens of different national versions of the Portfolio for different educational sectors, but the only version for adults is that developed from the Swiss version by EAQUALS (European Association for Quality Language Services) in collaboration with ALTE[2]. The descriptors used in this guide are taken from the EAQUALS/ALTE Portfolio. An electronic version that can be completed on-line can be downloaded in English or French from www.eelp.org. The EAQUALS/ALTE portfolio descriptors have been used in this guide, as they're more concrete and practical than the original CEFR descriptors.

New Inside Out CEF checklists

New Inside Out Beginner is appropriate for students who have had no previous contact with the language, or whose knowledge of the language is very sketchy. By the end of *New Inside Out* Beginner, if the students have had access to English outside the classroom, and have had the opportunity to practise, they should be able to do most of the things described at the A1 level. They'll probably also be able to perform a number of the A2 descriptors: every student will be different.

In order to help the teacher and student assess their progress, we've provided a list of the A1 descriptors for each unit of *New Inside Out* Beginner. So, for example, in Unit 1 nearly all of the descriptors listed are things that the students certainly won't feel confident about doing yet. However, with a lot of help and support from the teacher, many of the students should be feeling that they can try to do a range of things in English by the end of the unit. Once they've studied more units, they should begin to feel more confident about certain aspects of the language. The descriptors in these charts allow the teacher to see a typical pattern of language acquisition.

At beginner level, students will need the help of the teacher if they're to use the self-assessment at all, since they won't be able to understand the descriptors. The descriptors may be of use to the teacher; not in formally assessing the students, but in gauging their progress through the course across the whole range of language abilities. This will help clarify for the teacher which students are making quicker or slower progress in the different areas, and will assist them in planning the focus of future lessons.

New Inside Out offers a wide range of teaching materials in its various components, which together give teachers the opportunity to develop all aspects of their students' language ability. The CEF can be used to follow their progress. By checking whether the students' confidence is at an appropriate level across the whole range of language skills at any point in the course, the teacher can decide if there is an area that requires more practice. Suggested targets for the checklist are provided on the website www.insideout.net and on the Test CD at the back of the Teacher's Book.

1 Schneider, Günther, & North, Brian (2000): "Fremdsprachen können – was heisst das?" Zürich, Rüegger
North, Brian (2000): "The Development of a Common Framework Scale of Language Proficiency", New York, Peter Lang

2 EAQUALS is a pan-European language school accreditation body with over 100 full members. ALTE is an association dedicated to raising standards in language testing and encompasses the major European examination providers. Eurocentres provides high quality language teaching in countries where the language concerned is spoken. EAQUALS, ALTE and Eurocentres are the three NGOS advisers for language learning to the Council of Europe and all three implement the CEFR.

CEF Student checklists

Unit 1

Complete the checklist.

1 = I can do this with a lot of help from my teacher
2 = I can do this with a little help
3 = I can do this fairly well
4 = I can do this really well
5 = I can do this almost perfectly

Competences	Page	Your score				
I can very simply ask somebody to repeat what they said.	10	1	2	3	4	5
I can understand a questionnaire (entry permit form, hotel registration form) well enough to give the most important information about myself (name, surname, date of birth, nationality).	7, 10	1	2	3	4	5
I can understand when someone speaks very slowly to me and articulates carefully, with long pauses for me to assimilate meaning.	9, 10	1	2	3	4	5
I can understand numbers, prices and times.	7, 11	1	2	3	4	5
I can introduce somebody and use basic greeting and leave-taking expressions.	6	1	2	3	4	5

Unit 2

Complete the checklist.

1 = I can do this with a lot of help from my teacher
2 = I can do this with a little help
3 = I can do this fairly well
4 = I can do this really well
5 = I can do this almost perfectly

Competences	Page	Your score				
I can understand numbers, prices and times.	14, 15, 16, 17	1	2	3	4	5
I can handle numbers, quantities, cost and time.	14, 15, 16	1	2	3	4	5
I can understand information about people (place of residence, age, etc.) in newspapers.	14	1	2	3	4	5
I can make simple purchases where pointing or other gestures can support what I say.	15, 16	1	2	3	4	5
I can ask people questions about where they live, people they know, things they have, etc. and answer such questions addressed to me provided they are articulated slowly and clearly.	12, 13	1	2	3	4	5

Unit 3

Complete the checklist.

1 = I can do this with a lot of help from my teacher
2 = I can do this with a little help
3 = I can do this fairly well
4 = I can do this really well
5 = I can do this almost perfectly

Competences	Page	Your score				
I can introduce somebody and use basic greeting and leave-taking expressions.	18, 22	1	2	3	4	5
I can understand when someone speaks very slowly to me and articulates carefully, with long pauses for me to assimilate meaning.	18, 19	1	2	3	4	5
I can give personal information (address, telephone number, nationality, age, family and hobbies).	18, 19, 23	1	2	3	4	5
I can make myself understood in a simple way but I am dependent on my partner being prepared to repeat more slowly and rephrase what I say and to help me to say what I want.	20, 21	1	2	3	4	5
I can write sentences and simple phrases about myself, for example where I live and what I do.	19, 21	1	2	3	4	5

Review A

Complete the checklist.

1 = I can do this with a lot of help from my teacher
2 = I can do this with a little help
3 = I can do this fairly well
4 = I can do this really well
5 = I can do this almost perfectly

Competences	Page	Your score				
I can understand numbers, prices and times.	25, 26	1	2	3	4	5
I can fill in a questionnaire with my personal details (job, age, address, hobbies).	27	1	2	3	4	5

 New Inside Out Beginner Teacher's Book © Macmillan Publishers Limited 2007

Unit 4

Complete the checklist.

1 = I can do this with a lot of help from my teacher
2 = I can do this with a little help
3 = I can do this fairly well
4 = I can do this really well
5 = I can do this almost perfectly

Competences	Page	Your score				
I can very simply ask somebody to repeat what they said.	32	1	2	3	4	5
I can say when I don't understand.	32	1	2	3	4	5
I can understand words and phrases on signs encountered in everyday life (for instance *station, car park, no parking, no smoking, keep left*).	28, 33	1	2	3	4	5
I can make simple purchases where pointing or other gestures can support what I say.	28, 33	1	2	3	4	5
I can understand short simple messages on postcards, for example holiday greetings.	30	1	2	3	4	5

Unit 5

Complete the checklist.

1 = I can do this with a lot of help from my teacher
2 = I can do this with a little help
3 = I can do this fairly well
4 = I can do this really well
5 = I can do this almost perfectly

Competences	Page	Your score				
I can introduce somebody and use basic greeting and leave-taking expressions.	36, 39	1	2	3	4	5
I can understand questions and instructions addressed carefully and slowly to me and follow, short, simple directions.	37	1	2	3	4	5
I can ask and answer simple questions, initiate and respond to simple statements in areas of immediate need or on very familiar topics.	35, 36, 37	1	2	3	4	5
I can ask people questions about where they live, people they know, things they have, etc. and answer such questions addressed to me provided they are articulated slowly and clearly.	35, 36, 37	1	2	3	4	5
I can write sentences and simple phrases about myself, for example where I live and what I do.	35, 39	1	2	3	4	5

Unit 6

Complete the checklist.

1 = I can do this with a lot of help from my teacher
2 = I can do this with a little help
3 = I can do this fairly well
4 = I can do this really well
5 = I can do this almost perfectly

Competences	Page	Your score				
I can understand numbers, prices and times.	40, 41, 45	1	2	3	4	5
I can describe where I live.	42	1	2	3	4	5
I can locate a concert or film on calendars of public events or posters and identify where it takes place and at what time it starts.	41, 45	1	2	3	4	5
In everyday situations I can understand simple messages written by friends or colleagues, for example *back at four o'clock*.	41	1	2	3	4	5
I can indicate time by such phrases as *next week, last Friday, in November, three o'clock*.	41	1	2	3	4	5

Review B

Complete the checklist.

1 = I can do this with a lot of help from my teacher
2 = I can do this with a little help
3 = I can do this fairly well
4 = I can do this really well
5 = I can do this almost perfectly

Competences	Page	Your score				
I can understand information about people (place of residence, age, etc.) in newspapers.	48	1	2	3	4	5
I can make myself understood in a simple way but I am dependent on my partner being prepared to repeat more slowly and rephrase what I say and to help me to say what I want.	46, 47	1	2	3	4	5

 New Inside Out **Beginner Teacher's Book**

Unit 7

Complete the checklist.

1 = I can do this with a lot of help from my teacher
2 = I can do this with a little help
3 = I can do this fairly well
4 = I can do this really well
5 = I can do this almost perfectly

Competences	Page	Your score				
I can write a note to tell somebody where I am or where we are to meet.	52	1	2	3	4	5
I can understand simple directions about how to get from X to Y, on foot or by public transport.	50, 54, 55	1	2	3	4	5
I can understand questions and instructions addressed carefully and slowly to me and follow, short, simple directions.	54, 55	1	2	3	4	5
I can locate a concert or film on calendars of public events or posters and identify where it takes place and at what time it starts.	51, 52, 55	1	2	3	4	5
I can describe where I live.	50, 51, 52, 53 ,55	1	2	3	4	5

Unit 8

Complete the checklist.

1 = I can do this with a lot of help from my teacher
2 = I can do this with a little help
3 = I can do this fairly well
4 = I can do this really well
5 = I can do this almost perfectly

Competences	Page	Your score				
I can introduce somebody and use basic greeting and leave-taking expressions.	60	1	2	3	4	5
I can describe where I live.	57, 61	1	2	3	4	5
I can understand when someone speaks very slowly to me and articulates carefully, with long pauses for me to assimilate meaning.	57	1	2	3	4	5
I can ask and answer simple questions, initiate and respond to simple statements in areas of immediate need or on very familiar topics.	58, 59, 60	1	2	3	4	5
I can ask people questions about where they live, people they know, things they have, etc. and answer such questions addressed to me provided they are articulated slowly and clearly.	57, 58, 59	1	2	3	4	5

Unit 9

Complete the checklist.

1 = I can do this with a lot of help from my teacher
2 = I can do this with a little help
3 = I can do this fairly well
4 = I can do this really well
5 = I can do this almost perfectly

Competences	Page	Your score				
I can understand numbers, prices and times.	66	1	2	3	4	5
I can handle numbers, quantities, cost and time.	63, 66	1	2	3	4	5
I can understand information about people (place of residence, age, etc.) in newspapers.	64	1	2	3	4	5
I can make simple purchases where pointing or other gestures can support what I say.	63, 66, 67	1	2	3	4	5
I can ask people for things and give people things.	66, 67	1	2	3	4	5

Review C

Complete the checklist.

1 = I can do this with a lot of help from my teacher
2 = I can do this with a little help
3 = I can do this fairly well
4 = I can do this really well
5 = I can do this almost perfectly

Competences	Page	Your score				
I can understand a questionnaire (entry permit form, hotel registration form) well enough to give the most important information about myself (name, surname, date of birth, nationality).	70	1	2	3	4	5
I can write sentences and simple phrases about myself, for example where I live and what I do.	71	1	2	3	4	5

 New Inside Out Beginner Teacher's Book

Unit 10

Complete the checklist.

1 = I can do this with a lot of help from my teacher
2 = I can do this with a little help
3 = I can do this fairly well
4 = I can do this really well
5 = I can do this almost perfectly

Competences	Page	Your score				
I can describe where I live.	72	1	2	3	4	5
I can understand when someone speaks very slowly to me and articulates carefully, with long pauses for me to assimilate meaning.	74	1	2	3	4	5
I can ask and answer simple questions, initiate and respond to simple statements in areas of immediate need or on very familiar topics.	74, 77	1	2	3	4	5
I can make simple purchases where pointing or other gestures can support what I say.	72, 76, 77	1	2	3	4	5
I can make myself understood in a simple way but I am dependent on my partner being prepared to repeat more slowly and rephrase what I say and to help me to say what I want.	73, 74, 75	1	2	3	4	5

Unit 11

Complete the checklist.

1 = I can do this with a lot of help from my teacher
2 = I can do this with a little help
3 = I can do this fairly well
4 = I can do this really well
5 = I can do this almost perfectly

Competences	Page	Your score				
I can understand questions and instructions addressed carefully and slowly to me and follow, short, simple directions.	82	1	2	3	4	5
I can understand information about people (place of residence, age, etc.) in newspapers.	78, 80	1	2	3	4	5
I can locate a concert or film on calendars of public events or posters and identify where it takes place and at what time it starts.	78, 82	1	2	3	4	5
I can understand words and phrases on signs encountered in everyday life (for instance *station, car park, no parking, no smoking, keep left*).	78, 82	1	2	3	4	5
I can indicate time by such phrases as *next week, last Friday, in November, three o'clock*.	78, 81	1	2	3	4	5

Unit 12

Complete the checklist.

1 = I can do this with a lot of help from my teacher
2 = I can do this with a little help
3 = I can do this fairly well
4 = I can do this really well
5 = I can do this almost perfectly

Competences	Page	Your score				
I can understand when someone speaks very slowly to me and articulates carefully, with long pauses for me to assimilate meaning.	84, 87	1	2	3	4	5
I can understand a questionnaire (entry permit form, hotel registration form) well enough to give the most important information about myself (name, surname, date of birth, nationality).	85	1	2	3	4	5
I can write a greeting card, for instance a birthday card.	88	1	2	3	4	5
I can ask people questions about where they live, people they know, things they have, etc. and answer such questions addressed to me provided they are articulated slowly and clearly.	85	1	2	3	4	5
I can indicate time by such phrases as *next week, last Friday, in November, three o'clock*.	85	1	2	3	4	5

Review D

Complete the checklist.

1 = I can do this with a lot of help from my teacher
2 = I can do this with a little help
3 = I can do this fairly well
4 = I can do this really well
5 = I can do this almost perfectly

Competences	Page	Your score				
I can write sentences and simple phrases about myself, for example where I live and what I do.	93	1	2	3	4	5
I can make myself understood in a simple way but I am dependent on my partner being prepared to repeat more slowly and rephrase what I say and to help me to say what I want.	90, 91	1	2	3	4	5

 New Inside Out Beginner Teacher's Book

Unit 13

Complete the checklist.

1 = I can do this with a lot of help from my teacher
2 = I can do this with a little help
3 = I can do this fairly well
4 = I can do this really well
5 = I can do this almost perfectly

Competences	Page	Your score				
I can understand simple directions about how to get from X to Y, on foot or by public transport.	94	1	2	3	4	5
I can handle numbers, quantities, cost and time.	98	1	2	3	4	5
I can ask people for things and give people things.	98	1	2	3	4	5
I can give personal information (address, telephone number, nationality, age, family and hobbies).	95	1	2	3	4	5
I can ask people questions about where they live, people they know, things they have, etc. and answer such questions addressed to me provided they are articulated slowly and clearly.	97	1	2	3	4	5

Unit 14

Complete the checklist.

1 = I can do this with a lot of help from my teacher
2 = I can do this with a little help
3 = I can do this fairly well
4 = I can do this really well
5 = I can do this almost perfectly

Competences	Page	Your score				
I can ask and answer simple questions, initiate and respond to simple statements in areas of immediate need or on very familiar topics.	101, 102, 103, 104, 105	1	2	3	4	5
I can fill in a questionnaire with my personal details (job, age, address, hobbies).	102	1	2	3	4	5
I can understand information about people (place of residence, age, etc.) in newspapers.	94	1	2	3	4	5
I can make myself understood in a simple way but I am dependent on my partner being prepared to repeat more slowly and rephrase what I say and to help me to say what I want.	101, 105	1	2	3	4	5
I can indicate time by such phrases as *next week, last Friday, in November, three o'clock*.	100	1	2	3	4	5

Unit 15

Complete the checklist.

1 = I can do this with a lot of help from my teacher
2 = I can do this with a little help
3 = I can do this fairly well
4 = I can do this really well
5 = I can do this almost perfectly

Competences	Page	Your score				
I can locate a concert or film on calendars of public events or posters and identify where it takes place and at what time it starts.	108	1	2	3	4	5
I can understand short simple messages on postcards, for example holiday greetings.	110	1	2	3	4	5
In everyday situations I can understand simple messages written by friends or colleagues, for example *back at four o'clock*.	110	1	2	3	4	5
I can make simple purchases where pointing or other gestures can support what I say.	106, 107	1	2	3	4	5
I can indicate time by such phrases as *next week, last Friday, in November, three o'clock*.	107, 108	1	2	3	4	5

Review E

Complete the checklist.

1 = I can do this with a lot of help from my teacher
2 = I can do this with a little help
3 = I can do this fairly well
4 = I can do this really well
5 = I can do this almost perfectly

Competences	Page	Your score				
I can write a simple postcard (for example with holiday greetings).	115	1	2	3	4	5
I can ask people questions about where they live, people they know, things they have, etc. and answer such questions addressed to me provided they are articulated slowly and clearly.	115	1	2	3	4	5

   New Inside Out Beginner Teacher's Book

0 Instructions *Teacher's notes*

This introductory unit equips students with some basic language for following spoken and written classroom instructions. The exercises are simple, asking the students just to listen and repeat or follow a simple instruction.

1 🌐 **1.01**

Focus the students' attention on the photo and give them a minute or two to look at it. Students are going to listen to the words printed on the photo and repeat them after the speaker. Play the recording. When the students have repeated the words as a class, you could ask for individual repetition of the words.

> ### Extra activity
>
> You could give further practice by saying the words and getting the students to mime the actions. i.e. *Point* – students point. *Listen* – students exaggerate listening by cupping their hand over their ear. You could then get the students to do this in pairs.

2 🌐 **1.02**

This is another listen and repeat exercise, but this time all the instructions are full sentences rather than individual words. Focus the students' attention on the photos and read the captions with the class. Make sure everyone understands all the instructions by getting students to mime the actions. Then play the recording and ask the students to repeat each sentence after the speaker. Do this chorally at first and then get individual students to say the instructions. Again, you could get students to mime the actions.

3 🌐 **1.03**

This exercise introduces some more basic instructions. Illustrate the meaning of each of the words by doing the action on the board, i.e. you write *Hello. My name's _____* on the board and then you pause and say *Complete* before completing the sentence with your name. Then play the recording and ask them to listen to the instructions.

4

- Now students get the chance to put the rubric instructions they have learnt into practice. Begin this with the whole class. Focus the students' attention on item 1 and point out that this corresponds to item a) in Exercise 3. Ask the students to complete the sentence using their own names. Do the same with item 2, pointing out that

this corresponds to item b) in Exercise 3. Point out the other correspondences.

- Then ask students to work individually to complete the exercise. Go round checking that everyone knows what to do and has fully understood all the instructions. You may need to explain the male and female symbols in item 4.

Now that your students have studied some basic classroom language in English, try to use it as much as possible in subsequent lessons. If the students look uncertain when you give an instruction in English, take them back to this unit and remind them of the meaning.

> ### Before the next lesson
>
> Bring in the following objects for Grammar, Exercise 2, on page 8 of the student's book: a bag; two or three books; some pens; some keys and a mobile phone.

1 ID *Overview*

Section	Aims	What the students are doing
Grammar **SB page 6**	*Grammar*: possessive determiners – *my* and *your* *be* contractions	• Listening and completing short sentences with possessive determiners – *my* and *your*. • Practising the use of *be* contractions in introductions.
Speaking **SB page 6**	*Conversation skills*: introductions	• Substituting students' own names in a simple introduction conversation.
Grammar **SB page 7**	*Grammar*: possessive determiners – *his* and *her*	• Listening and completing introductions with *his* and *her*. • Asking questions about the names of other students in the class.
Vocabulary **SB page 7**	*Vocabulary*: numbers *0* to *10*	• Listening and repeating numbers. • Listening to and writing down phone numbers
Speaking **SB page 7**	*Vocabulary*: names and personal information *Conversation skills*: asking for personal information	• Asking questions and completing a page from an address book with names and phone numbers of other students.
Vocabulary **SB page 8**	*Vocabulary*: common objects, plurals	• Listening to and repeating words for common objects. • Identifying common objects.
Grammar **SB page 8**	*Grammar*: *this* and *these*	• Asking questions and identifying objects. • Asking questions with *this* and *these*.
Listening **SB page 9**	*Listening skills*: listening for specific details	• Listening to a conversation and ticking the things the speakers have.
Pronunciation **SB page 9**	*Pronunciation*: the alphabet	• Listening to and repeating the letters of the alphabet. • Listening to and identifying abbreviations.
Useful phrases **SB page 10**	*Vocabulary*: useful phrases for communicating personal information	• Listening to and completing conversations. • Listening to and repeating useful phrases. • Writing and practising new conversations.
Vocabulary *Extra* **SB page 11**	*Vocabulary*: revision of words from the unit: everyday objects; numbers	• Matching pictures with words.
Writing **WB page 7**	Using capital letters	

ID *Teacher's notes*

Warm-up

Introduce yourself to the class with a simple friendly greeting such as *Hello, I'm (name)*. Go round each of the students and greet them individually, encouraging them to respond with *Hello, I'm (Julio)*.

Language note

Vocabulary: *ID*

ID is a shortened form of 'identity' and is now widely used. For example, *Can I see some ID, please?* You pronounce the two letters separately /aɪˈdiː/.

Grammar (SB page 6)

Possessive determiners

1 🌐 **1.04**

- Focus the students' attention on the photo taken from the James Bond film *Die Another Day* (see *Cultural notes* on this page). Then focus attention on the gapped conversation and remind students of the instruction *complete* from the introductory unit. Ask students to listen to the recording and complete the conversation with the correct word.

- Focus the students' attention on the use of *your* and *my*. Make sure they know the difference between them. You could then ask several pairs of students to roleplay the conversation.

- Point out the information about contractions of the verb *be* in the margin. Ask students to find the contractions in the conversation they have just practised (*What's* and *name's*).

> My name's Bond ... James Bond.

Language notes

Grammar: possessive determiners

The possessive determiners *my, your, his, her, its, our, their* are sometimes know as 'possessive adjectives' in older grammars and coursebooks. In this unit, only *my, your, his* and *her* are presented. There is more work on possessive determiners in Unit 3.

Grammar: contractions

Throughout the book encourage the use of contractions because it sounds more natural. While it's grammatically correct not to use contractions, native speakers will generally do so when speaking.

Vocabulary: name

The phrase *My name's Bond ... James Bond* has been repeated in all the James Bond films and has achieved a kind of iconic status as the way James Bond always introduces himself. Some of your students may recognise this from having seen some of the films. In fact, the most appropriate answer to the question *What's your name?* is usually to give your first name only. In more formal situations, students should probably give both their first name and their surname.

Cultural notes

James Bond

- James Bond is a fictional British spy, code named 007. The first Bond novel *Casino Royale* was written by Ian Fleming in 1953. The first Bond film *Dr No* was shown in 1962. Bond has been played by six actors including Sean Connery, Roger Moore, Pierce Brosnan and Daniel Craig.

- The photo shows James Bond meeting Jinx in the film *Die Another Day* (2000). In this film, James Bond stops the plans of a British billionaire that would lead to global war.

2 🌐 **1.05**

- Again, focus the students' attention on the photo. Students listen to the recording and complete the conversation with *my* and *your*.

- Note the useful phrase *Nice to meet you* which completes the introduction. Ask the students to work in pairs and roleplay the meeting between James Bond and Jinx. Then focus their attention on the contraction *I'm* in the conversation.

> What's your name?
> My name's Bond ... James Bond.

Speaking (SB page 6)

- Read out the conversation in the speech bubbles to the class. Then choose a confident student and demonstrate the conversation using your own names.
- Put the students in pairs and ask them to practise the conversation using their own names. When they have finished, they can mingle around the class introducing themselves to other students. Monitor and help where necessary.
- If you like, ask the students to practise the conversation 'Bond-style': *My name's Ramirez … Ana Ramirez.*

Grammar (SB page 7)

Possessive determiners

1 🌐 1.06

- Focus the students' attention on the possessive determiners *his* and *her* in the margin. Point out that *his* is used for men and *her* for women. With speakers of some languages you may need to explain that the choice of adjective is governed by the sex of the owner of the object, not the object itself.
- Ask the students to look at the photo of Pierce Brosnan as James Bond, and Teri Hatcher as Paris Carver in the film *Tomorrow Never Dies*.
- Play the recording and ask the students to complete a) and b).

> a) What's his name?
>   His name's Pierce Brosnan.
> b) What's her name?
>   Her name's Teri Hatcher.

Cultural note

Tomorrow Never Dies (1997)

In this film, James Bond (Pierce Brosnan), with the help of Paris (Teri Hatcher), stop Britain and China from going to war with each other.

2

- Read the speech bubbles with the class, and demonstrate the activity by asking questions about the names of some male and female students with one or two confident students.
- Then ask the students to mingle and ask each other about the names of the other students in the class. Monitor and help, making sure they're using *his* to ask about male students and *her* to ask about female students.

Vocabulary (SB page 7)

Numbers

1 🌐 1.07

- Point out the list of numbers in the margin. Ask why they think the first parts of *zero* and *seven* are underlined (these are words with more than one syllable and the underlining indicates the main stress), and get them to practise saying these two words correctly. Ask them what *007* at the bottom of the list is (James Bond's secret agent number).
- Play the recording and ask the students to repeat the numbers after the speaker. When they have done this chorally, ask individual students to repeat numbers after you. Encourage students to get the intonation right when saying *zero* and *seven*.

Language notes

Vocabulary: numbers

- *Oh* is often pronounced like the letter 'O' when saying numbers one figure at a time – for example, in a reference number or telephone number. Note that *Oh* can also be pronounced *zero*.
- When a figure is repeated, we can say *double three* or *three three*. However, James Bond (*007*) is always known as *double Oh seven*.

2 🌐 1.08

- Do the first one as an example with the class and then ask them to work in pairs to complete the rest.
- When they have finished, play the recording for them to check their answers. Then ask them to repeat the numbers after the speakers.

> a) three, four, five   c) six, eight, ten
> b) three, two, one   d) seven, nine

Extra activity

- To give further practice of the numbers, do a finger dictation. Demonstrate to the students by calling out a number and holding up the corresponding number of fingers. Repeat until all the students are holding up the correct number of fingers. Then call out another number and check they are holding up the correct number of fingers again. Repeat until everyone has the correct number.
- Ask a stronger or more confident student to take over your role and then give everyone a turn around the class.

3 🌐 1.09

- Make sure they know the difference between a home phone number and a mobile phone number. Demonstrate mobile phone number by holding up your mobile phone and saying *My mobile phone number is …* and give the first four numbers.Then play the recording and ask the students to complete the numbers they hear.

> a) 020-7413-6995   b) 07007-856-321

- Check answers with the class, then go round asking a few students for their own home and mobile phone numbers.

Language note
Vocabulary: *mobile number*

A 'mobile phone' in British English is called a 'cell phone' in American English. A 'mobile number' in British English is called a 'cell number' in American English.

Speaking (SB page 7)
Names

- Focus the students' attention on the information in the margin and make sure they know the difference between a *first name* and a *surname* (sometimes also called a *family name*). Demonstrate with your own first name and surname. Practise the conversation from the speech bubbles with a confident student. Get the student to ask the questions and respond with your own first name and surname.

- Focus the students' attention on the address book. With the class, make a list on the board of the questions they need to find out the missing information. Then ask the students to mingle and find two students to question. They should write the information they gather in the address book.

Vocabulary (SB page 8)
1 🌐 1.10

- This exercise introduces the students to some more vocabulary: common objects. Focus attention on the photo, then play the recording. Tell them to point to the objects in the photo as they hear them, and ask them to repeat the words after the speakers. Encourage them to get the stress in the right place in *computer, camera, mobile phone* and *passport*. Remind the students that the underlining will help them get the main stress on the correct part of the word.

- Note that the words *pens, keys* and *books* are plural: there are four pens, several keys and three books in the photo. Tell them that the single objects (*bag, computer, camera,* etc.) could be made plural by the addition of an *s* at the end. Explain also that the plural words don't have the indefinite article *a* in front of them.

2

- Demonstrate this simple game with a confident student. Cover the list of words in your books and then say a number and get the student to identify the object in the photo that has that number. Then change roles with the student calling out a number and you identifying the correct object.

- Put the students in pairs and encourage them to play the game. Make sure they have covered the list of words.

Grammar (SB page 8)
Nouns; *this/these*

1 🌐 1.11

- Focus the students' attention on the information in the margin about the use of *this* and *these*. Get them to practise saying the two words, making sure they differentiate between the short /ɪ/ sound of *this* and the longer /iː/ sound of *these*. Make sure they know that you use *this* with singular words and *these* with plurals. Also check that they can pronounce *they're* /ðeə/ correctly, and that they understand that *are* is the plural form of *is*.

- Look at first item with the whole class. Make sure they know that in the photo there's only one bag, so the question is: *What's this?* and the answer: *It's a bag.* Then ask them to go through the other items and underline the correct answers.

- Play the recording for the students to check their answers. Then play it again and ask them to repeat after the speakers.

1 It's a bag.	5 They're keys.
2 It's a computer.	6 It's a mobile phone.
3 They're books.	7 It's a passport.
4 They're pens.	8 It's a camera.

Extra activity

- Take some of the items in Exercise 1 from your own bag or pocket. Ask students to identify them

- Put the things in a box at the front of the class and allow students to come up, put their hand in the box and pull out an item to ask the rest of the class about.

Language notes
Vocabulary: objects from pocket

- Avoid 'money' which is an uncountable noun and cannot be used with this structure.

- Here are some possible objects that the students might find in their pockets: a bus ticket, a wallet, a purse, a photo, a packet of chewing gum, ID card, coins.

2 *Grammar Extra* 1

Ask the students to turn to *Grammar Extra* 1 on page 126 of the Student's Book. Here they'll find an explanation of the grammar they've been studying and further exercises to practise it.

1	2
a) It's a pen.	a) They're pens.
b) It's a book.	b) They're books.
c) It's a computer.	c) They're computers.
d) It's a bus.	d) They're buses.
e) It's a passport.	e) They're passports.
f) It's a dictionary.	f) They're dictionaries.

3
a) What's this? It's a bag.
b) What are these? They're photos.
c) What's this? It's a camera.
d) What's this? It's a mobile phone.
e) What are these? They're keys.

Language note

Vocabulary: plurals

Be careful of plural forms of some objects which students might find in their pocket or bag. For example, *watch/watches, brush/brushes, diary/diaries*.

If your students need further practice, you could use Photocopiable Worksheet *1 Grammar* here.

Listening (SB page 9)

1 🌐 **1.12**

- Focus the students' attention on the photo and give them time to think about the situation.

- Ask the students to look at the chart. Point out that there's a column for them to tick the things that are in the woman's bag, and a column for them to tick the things that are in the man's bag. There's already a tick in the woman's column to show that she has a computer. Note that they'll find out what is in each bag by listening to the conversation.

- Play the recording for the students to listen and tick the correct objects. You may need to play it more than once.

- Check answers with the class.

> Her bag: a computer, a camera, books,
> a mobile phone, a passport.
> His bag: a mobile phone.

> 🌐 **1.12** (G = Greg; T = Tina)
> G: Hi, Tina.
> T: Oh, hi, Greg.
> G: What's in your bag?
> T: *A computer, a camera, three books, a mobile phone*, er … *my passport* … What's in your bag?
> G: *A mobile phone*.
> T: Oh. Where's your computer?
> G: In my mobile phone.
> T: Where's your camera?
> G: In my mobile phone.
> T: Where's your passport?
> G: Passport? Oh no!

2

Ask the students what isn't in his bag.

> A passport.

Pronunciation (SB page 9)

The alphabet

1 🌐 **1.13**

- Note how the letters of the alphabet are divided up in the table in the margin. They form a kind of poem as the students will hear when they listen to the recording.

- Play the recording and ask the students to repeat the letters in the margin line by line.

- Note that in British English the letter z is pronounced /zed/ and so the rhyme doesn't work. It works in American English where z is pronounced /ziː/.

Language note

Pronunciation: the alphabet

Some students confuse the pronunciation of A /eɪ/, E /iː/ and I /aɪ/, so it's worth giving these sounds extra practice. Other letters that can cause problems are: J /jeɪ/ and G /jiː/, and B /biː/ and V /vː/. It's a good idea to give extra attention to the pronunciation of the letters that cause your students most difficulties.

2 🌐 **1.14**

- Read out the first line of letters (*B, C, D*, etc.) and tell the students that they all have the same vowel sound /iː/. Point out the phonetic symbols at the beginning of the line and explain that these symbols are used in dictionaries to show how a word should be pronounced.

- Explain that the letters of the alphabet can be grouped according to their vowel sound. The letter *E* goes in this first group because it has the same sound as *B, C, D*, etc.

- Play the recording and ask the students to complete the groups with the missing letters from the box.
- Play the recording again for them to repeat the letters.

> 1 E   3 A   4 U   5 I   6 O

3 🌐 **1.15**

- Explain that abbreviations, or more properly acronyms, are words made up of the initial letters of a group of words, often forming the name of a country or organisation. For example, *USA* stands for *United States of America*.
- Play the recording and ask the students to number the abbreviations as they hear them.
- Check answers with the class and then ask them to repeat the abbreviations.
- Note that the odd one out in this list is *OK* whose letters don't actually stand for any words beginning with *O* and *K*. *OK* simply means *all right*. The others are: *CIA* = Central Intelligence Agency, *VIP* = very important person, *NYC* = New York City, *UK* = United Kingdom, *USA* = United States of America.
- Ask the students to suggest any more abbreviations that they know. Write any ideas on the board and get the students to practise saying them aloud. Suggestions they might come up with include *BBC* (British Broadcasting Corporation), *CNN* (Central News Network), *DJ* (disk jockey).

> 1 USA   2 UK   3 VIP   4 OK
> 5 NYC   6 CIA

Extra activity

- To give further practice of the alphabet, do an alphabet dictation, spelling out words that the students have already seen in the unit. For example, *nice, meet, Jinx, my, five, number, first*.
- As you dictate, get the students to write down the letters. They should then call out the word. Finally, ask them to find examples of this word in the book.

Language note

Pronunciation: additional abbreviations

Note that some acronyms are pronounced as words, for example, NATO /ˈneɪ təʊ/, FIFA /ˈfiːfə/, UNICEF /ˈjuːnisef/.

If your students need further practice, you could use Photocopiable Worksheet 1 Vocabulary here.

Useful phrases (SB page 10)

1 🌐 **1.16**

- Focus the students' attention on the illustration which shows a male receptionist and a female student in a language school. He's taking down the student's details. Give students time to look at the illustration and think about what's happening.
- Play the recording for the students to listen and complete the conversation. You may need to play it more than once.
- Check answers with the class.

> 1 R–O–O–N–R–A–K–V–I–T
> 2 R– O–O–N–R–A–K–V–I–T
> 3 Roonrakvit

Language note

Grammar: *can*

Can you …? in this context is a polite request. For *can* for ability, see Unit 14.

2 🌐 **1.17**

Play the recording. The students repeat the phrases after the speaker. Encourage them to match the speaker's intonation. In a) the speaker stresses the word *spell*, in b) *repeat* and in c) *Nut*.

3

- Pairwork. Students choose one of the people from the illustrations and work together to write a new conversation, using Exercise 1 as a model. Go round monitoring and giving help.
- When the students have finished, ask pairs to perform their conversations for the rest of the class. Encourage them, where possible, to make eye contact with each other when they say their lines, rather than simply reading them out.

If your students need further practice, you could use Photocopiable Worksheet 1 Communication here.

4 Pairwork

- The pairwork exercise for this unit is on pages 116 and 121 of the Student's Book. Put the students in pairs and tell them who will be Student A, and who will be Student B.
- While they're doing the exercise, go round monitoring and giving help. Take note of any errors which may need focusing on later, and also any examples of good language use which you can praise. Check answers with the class.

> 1 Denzel Washington   4 Scarlet Johansson
> 2 Christina Aguilera   5 Johnny Depp
> 3 Nicole Kidman   6 Orlando Bloom

Cultural notes

Denzel Washington (born 1954)
Denzel Washington has been in television and films in the US since the 1980s. He appeared in the popular television series *St Elsewhere*, and the films *Cry Freedom*, *Philadelphia*, and *Inside Man*. He's also started to direct his own films.

Christina Aguilera (born 1980)
Christina Aguilera is an American pop singer and songwriter. Her first big hit song was *Genie in a Bottle*. Since then she's had many other successful hits including *Beautiful*. She's won four Grammy awards.

Nicole Kidman (born 1967)
Australian actress Nicole Kidman has made countless films, such as *The Others* and *Moulin Rouge*, and has won an Oscar for the film *The Hours* (2002). She was married to the film star Tom Cruise for eleven years.

Scarlett Johansson (born 1984)
Scarlett Johansson was born in New York. She made her name as an actress in the film *The Horse Whisperer* (1998). She starred in the film *Lost in Translation* (2003) opposite Bill Murray.

Johnny Depp (born 1963)
Johnny Depp's film debut was in *Nightmare On Elm Street* (1984). He then acted in the popular TV series *21 Jump Street*, before starring in the film *Edward Scissorhands* (1990), directed by Tim Burton. His most popular films to date are probably acting as Jack Sparrow in the *Pirates of the Caribbean* trilogy.

Orlando Bloom (born 1977)
Orlando Bloom made his film debut in *Wilde* (1997). He became internationally famous in the role of Legolas in the *Lord of the Rings* trilogy (2001–2003). He also stars in the *Pirates of the Caribbean* films.

Vocabulary *Extra* (SB page 11)

Everyday objects

1

- Focus the students' attention on the list of words and point out that they're all to do with everyday objects. Point out that the underlining indicates the syllable of the word that has the strongest stress. Check that the students can pronounce all of the words correctly.

- Ask the students to look at the pictures and match each one with one of the words. Point out that the first one has been done for them.

6 a bag	5 a key
8 a book	7 a mobile phone
2 a camera	9 a passport
1 a computer	4 a pen
3 a dictionary	

2

- Pairwork. Demonstrate the activity with a confident student. Begin by asking the question in the example and eliciting the answer. Then get the student to ask you a question about one of the other objects in Exercise 1.

- The students then continue the activity in pairs. Go round, giving help and encouragement and check that they're pronouncing the words correctly.

Numbers

1

Ask the students to work individually to match the figures with the words. Allow them to compare answers in pairs.

1 one	6 six
2 two	7 seven
3 three	8 eight
4 four	9 nine
5 five	10 ten

2

Demonstrate the activity with a confident student, tell them that they should write the words for the numbers rather than the figures. Then put the students into pairs to continue the activity. Go round, giving help and encouragement. Make sure each student takes a turn at dictating the numbers.

Writing

Workbook page 7
Using capital letters

Photocopiable resource materials

Grammar: *It's her pen.* (Teacher's notes page 121. Worksheet page 144.)

Vocabulary: *What's his name?* (Teacher's notes page 121. Worksheet page 145.)

Communication: *What's your number?* (Teacher's notes page 122. Worksheet page 146.)

Test CD

See *Test Unit 1* on the CD.

💿 CD-ROM

For more activities go to Unit 1: *ID*.

For the best activities for beginner students, see pages xvi–xxi

For practical methodology, from *Classroom interaction* to *Writing*, see pages xxii–xxxv

What can your students do now? See self-evaluation checklists on pages xxxvi–xlvi

2 International *Overview*

Section	Aims	What the students are doing
🌐 Vocabulary **SB page 12**	*Vocabulary*: names of countries	• Listening to introductions of game show contestants and identifying their countries.
🌐 Grammar **SB page 12**	*Grammar*: *be* (present simple)	• Asking and answering questions about where people are from.
🌐 Grammar **SB page 13**	*Grammar*: prepositions – *in* and *near*	• Listening and underlining the correct answers. • Completing a sentence about where they are from.
Speaking **SB page 13**	*Conversation skills*: fluency practice	• Asking people where they are from. • Asking about where other students in the class are from.
🌐 Vocabulary (1) **SB page 14**	*Vocabulary*: nationalities	• Matching nationalities with photos.
🌐 Vocabulary (2) **SB page 14**	*Vocabulary*: numbers *11* to *19*, and *20* to *199*	• Practising numbers from *11* to *19*, and numbers *20* to *199*.
🌐 Pronunciation **SB page 15**	*Pronunciation*: units of currency	• Listening and matching signs to units of currency. • Listening and circling prices.
🌐 Listening **SB page 15**	*Listening skills*: prices	• Listening and completing a table with prices.
🌐 Grammar **SB page 15**	*Grammar*: *How much ...?*	• Reordering jumbled sentences. • Asking questions using *How much ...?*
🌐 Useful phrases **SB page 16**	*Vocabulary*: useful phrases with *How much ...?* (for shopping)	• Listening and completing conversations. • Listening and repeating useful phrases. • Practising conversations.
Vocabulary *Extra* **SB page 17**	*Vocabulary*: revision of words from the unit: countries and nationalities; numbers	• Matching photos with words.
Writing **WB page 11**	Punctuation (question mark/full stop) Writing short questions and answers	

Warm-up

- Play hangman with the students. Choose a famous person – one they've seen in the pairwork exercise in Unit 1, e.g. Johnny Depp, or another famous person they'll know. Write a dash for each letter of the person's name on the board and tell them that it's the name of a famous person.

- Invite the students to guess a letter. If necessary, suggest a letter yourself, for example the letter *E*, and then write it above the appropriate line:

_ _ _ _ _ _ _E_ _ _

- Ask the students for another letter. If they suggest a letter which is in the name, write it in the appropriate place. Encourage the students to pronounce the letters correctly so if they say /iː/, write E even if they mean I. If they suggest a letter which isn't in the name, begin to draw the hangman with a vertical line. For the second incorrect guess, draw the horizontal support. For the third, the rope, the fourth is a circle for the head, then a line for the body, one arm, then the second arm, then a leg and finally the second leg. If they find the word before the hangman is complete, they win. However, if the hangman is complete, then they lose.

Vocabulary (SB page 12)

1 🌐 **1.18**

- Focus the students' attention on the photos and the flags beside them. Note that the people shown are contestants in a TV show; they have to sing in order to win the title *International Pop Star*.

- Write *Italy* on the board and read it out, emphasising the first syllable. Ask the students to repeat it after you. Make sure that they're all pronouncing it correctly. Then focus their attention on the table and the stress boxes at the top. Repeat the word *Italy*, explaining that the three stress boxes show it's a three-syllable word, and that the larger box at the beginning shows that this is the syllable that receives most stress.

- Focus the students' attention on the stress boxes at the top of the other columns in the table. Demonstrate how these words should be stressed. You could use a nonsense syllable like *da* to illustrate. So, the second column would be DAda, the third daDA, the fourth DA. Ask students to repeat after you.

- Ask the students to listen to the recording and pay attention to the way the names of the countries in the box are pronounced. Give them a few minutes to write them in the correct columns of the table before playing the recording again for them to check their answers.

1 Italy	2 Germany	3 Poland	4 Japan
5 Brazil	6 Spain		

🌐 **1.18**

And now on International Pop Star, please welcome …
Number 1 from Italy!
Number 2 from Germany!
Number 3 from Poland!
Number 4 from Japan!
Number 5 from Brazil!
Number 6 from Spain!

Language notes

Pronunciation: stress

- You can check the stress of any word by looking in your dictionary. Dictionaries usually mark the stress of a word as well as giving the phonetic script, i.e. Brazil /brəˈzɪl/. In *New Inside Out* the stressed <u>syl</u>lable is <u>al</u>ways under<u>lined</u>.

- Note that geographical names and nationalities are normally listed at the back of dictionaries rather than appearing alphabetically in the body of the book.

- Some online dictionaries also provide an audio sample of each word.

2 🌐 **1.19**

- Ask the students to listen and repeat all the country words. Begin with choral repetition, then ask individual students to say the words. Check that their intonation is correct each time.

- Finally, ask what the name of their country is in English. If your class has students from different nationalities, encourage them to pronounce every country represented clearly for everyone to hear.

Grammar (SB page 12)

be

Exercises 1 and 2 illustrate a sequence typical of many of the grammar sections in *New Inside Out* – particularly those dealing with verb forms. Exercise 1 establishes and practises the form through a completion task, and then Exercise 2 requires the students to use exactly the same language in a meaningful context. The idea is to give the students at least two opportunities to manipulate the form whilst not losing sight of the meaning. Students should never be in any doubt that grammar exists primarily to 'make meanings'.

1 🔊 1.20

- A table of the present simple of the verb *be* is shown in the margin with both full and contracted forms. Tell the students that in speech you usually use the contracted forms. However, point out that in short answers you say *Yes, I am*, *Yes, he is*, etc., not ~~Yes, I'm~~ and ~~Yes, he's~~.

- Tell the students to look at the information in the margin and use it to complete the questions and answers. Allow them to work in pairs if they wish. Go round monitoring and giving help where necessary.

- When the students have finished, play the recording for them to check their answers. Then play it again for them to repeat after the speakers.

> a) 'Is Anna from Germany?'
> 'Yes, she is.' 'No, she isn't.'
> b) 'Is Rosa from Japan?'
> 'Yes, she is.' 'No, she isn't.'
> c) 'Is Daniel from Poland?'
> 'Yes, he is.' 'No, he isn't.'
> d) 'Are Roberto and Donna from Brazil?'
> 'Yes, they are.' 'No, they aren't.'
> e) 'Are you from Spain?'
> 'Yes, I am.' 'No, I'm not.'
> f) 'Are you and your teacher from Italy?'
> 'Yes, we are.' 'No, we aren't.'

Language notes

Grammar: contractions – *be*

- There are two possible contractions for the negative form of the verb *be* (except for the 'I' form where *I'm not* is the only possibility). For example, *you aren't* or *you're not*, *she isn't* or *she's not*.

- In the negative, there are two ways of contracting the verb *be*. For example *No, he isn't* (contracting *not*) or *No, he's not* (contracting *is*). In *New Inside Out* only *isn't* and *aren't* are used, but accept both forms from your students as both are correct. Note with *I*, only *No, I'm not* is correct.

- Remember that you don't use the contractions in the positive short form answers. You say *Yes, she is*. Not ~~Yes, she's~~.

2

Students work in pairs and take turns to ask each other the questions in Exercise 1. Tell them to base their answers to questions a) to d) on the information given by the flags in Exercise 1. They should give true answers to questions e) and f).

> a) Yes, she is.
> b) No, she isn't.
> c) Yes, he is.
> d) No, they aren't.

3 Pairwork

- The pairwork exercise for this unit is on pages 116 and 121 of the Student's Book. Put the students in pairs and tell them who will be Student A, and who will be Student B.

- While they're doing the pairwork exercise, go round monitoring and giving help. Take note of any errors which may need focusing on later and also any examples of good language use which you can praise. Check answers with the class.

> 1 Claudia Schiffer is from Germany.
> 2 Julio and Enrique Iglesias are from Spain.
> 3 JK Rowling is from Britain.
> 4 Bill and Hillary Clinton are from the USA.
> 5 Gisele Bundchen is from Brazil.
> 6 Roman Polanski is from Poland.

Cultural notes

Claudia Schiffer (born 1970)
German supermodel of the 1990s. She became famous after being on the cover of the magazine *Elle*, and then advertising jeans for Guess. She's also worked for Chanel and has appeared in a few films.

Julio Inglesias (born 1943) and
Enrique Iglesias (born 1975)
Spanish singer Julio Iglesias was popular in the 1970s and 1980s. He was one of the most successful recording artists of all time, and has sold albums in seven languages. His first English language success was *Begin The Beguine* in 1982.

Enrique Iglesias, like his father Julio, is an internationally famous singer, and has recorded songs in four languages. He now lives in America.

JK Rowling (born 1965)
British fiction writer who became famous as the author of the *Harry Potter* series.

Bill Clinton (born 1945) and
Hillary Clinton (born 1947)
Democratic politician Bill Clinton was the President of the United States of America from 1993 to 2001. His wife, Hillary was elected the United States Senator for New York in November 2000, the first woman elected to national office.   ➤

Gisele Bundchen (born 1980)
Brazilian supermodel. She's worked for fashion houses such as Valentino, Versace and Christian Dior. She's also appeared on magazine covers such as *Marie Claire*, *Vogue* and *Elle*.

Roman Polanski (born 1933)
Polish film director, famous for films such as *Rosemary's Baby* (1968), *Chinatown* (1974), and more recently films such as *The Pianist* (2002) and *Oliver Twist* (2005).

4 *Grammar Extra* 2

Ask the students to turn to *Grammar Extra* 2 on page 126 of the Student's Book. Here they'll find an explanation of the grammar they've been studying and further exercises to practise it.

---

1 a) I'm from Brazil.
   b) You're from Germany.
   c) He's from Italy.
   d) She's from Japan.
   e) They're from Spain.
   f) We're international!

2 a) I'm not from Brazil.
   b) You aren't from Germany.
   c) He isn't from Italy.
   d) She isn't from Japan.
   e) They aren't from Spain.
   f) We aren't international!

3 a) Is the Eiffel Tower in Moscow?
   b) Is Big Ben in New York?
   c) Are the Petronas Towers in Cairo?
   d) Is the Brooklyn Bridge in London?
   e) Is the Kremlin in Paris?
   f) Are the Pyramids in Kuala Lumpur?

4 a) No, it isn't. It's in Paris.
   b) No, it isn't. It's in London.
   c) No, they aren't. They're in Kuala Lumpur.
   d) No, it isn't. It's in New York.
   e) No, it isn't. It's in Moscow.
   f) No, they aren't. They're in Cairo.

Grammar (SB page 13)

Prepositions: *in* and *near*

1 🌐 1.21

- Focus the students' attention on the diagrams in the margin which show the difference between the prepositions *in* and *near*. Make sure everyone understands these before you move on. Demonstrate by giving an example of places in your country.
- Play the recording and ask them to underline the correct answers. Do the same for b).
- Check answers with the class and then ask the students to work in pairs and take turns to ask and answer the questions.

- Finally, ask them to take turns asking and answering the question *Where are you from?* using true information about themselves. Go round encouraging everyone to use the prepositions correctly.

---

a) near; in   b) near; in

2

Ask the students to work individually to complete the sentence so it's true for them. Tell students who don't live in a big city to use the word *near* (*I'm from Ostia. It's near Rome in Italy.*). For students who live in Rome, they shouldn't use the word *near* (*I'm from Rome in Italy*).

Speaking (SB page 13)

1

- Read out the conversation in the speech bubbles to the class. Then choose a confident student and demonstrate the conversation using your own towns, cities and countries.
- Then ask the students to mingle and ask three other students where they're from.

2

Choose individual students to ask questions about where other students are from. Encourage those who found out the information about these students in the mingling activity in Exercise 1 to answer. Make sure both questions are practised (*Where is X from?* and *Is X from Y?*).

If your students need further practice, you could use Photocopiable Worksheet *2 Grammar* here.

Vocabulary (1) (SB page 14)

Nationalities

1 🌐 1.22

Focus the students' attention on the flags and nationalities shown in the margin. Explain that the words you use for nationalities are always different from the names of the countries. Play the recording and ask the students to repeat the nationalities. When they have done this chorally, ask individual students to pronounce the words.

Language notes

Vocabulary: *Britain/England/UK*

People often confuse England and Britain.

- England is only one of the three countries that make up Britain. People who come from England are English. Its flag is white with a red cross.

- Britain is made up of England, Scotland and Wales. People from Scotland are Scottish and people from Wales are Welsh. Each country has a separate flag.

- The United Kingdom (the UK) is Britain and Northern Ireland. The people are British and the flag is the Union Jack.

Pronunciation: countries

- In the word *Italy*, the stress is on the first syllable /ˈɪtəli/. However, in the word *Italian*, the stress is on the second syllable /ɪˈtæliən/.

- In the word *Japan*, the stress is on the second syllable /dʒəˈpæn/, and on the third syllable in *Japanese* /dʒæpəˈniːz/.

2 🌐 1.23

- Ask the students to look at the photos and see if they can identify any of the people and objects shown. (See Cultural notes on this page.)

- Ask the students to work in pairs and decide which description is correct for each photo. When they've finished, allow them to compare notes with another pair before playing the recording for them to check their answers. When they've checked, play it again for them to repeat after the speaker.

> a) She's Spanish.
> b) It's Polish.
> c) He's British.
> d) They're Italian.
> e) They're Japanese.
> f) They're German.

Extra activity

- To give further practice of *she is/isn't*, ask the class some questions about the photographs. For example, *Is Penelope Cruz English? Is Prince William from Germany? Are they American?* Get the class to respond chorally.

- Get some of the more confident students to ask the class these or similar questions, and get the class to respond to these.

- If necessary, give the students time to prepare some written questions about the photographs. This will give you time to help the less confident students.

- Then get the students asking and answering these questions in pairs.

Cultural notes

Penelope Cruz (born 1974 – photo a)
Spanish actress Penelope Cruz starred in the films *Jamón Jamón* and *Belle Epoque*, and became famous in Pedro Almodóvar's 1999 film *Todo sobre mi madre* (*All About My Mother*). She then moved to Hollywood where she's starred in the films *Blow*, *All the Pretty Horses* and *Vanilla Sky*. She worked again with Almodovar in the award winning film *Volver* in 2006.

LOT (photo b)
LOT is the national airline of Poland.

Prince William (born 1982 – photo c)
Eldest son of Prince Charles and Princess Diana, Prince William is second in line to the British throne.

Luca Toni and **Alberto Gilardino** (photo d)
Luca Toni (left) and Albertino Gilardino (right) are Italian football players. They played for the Italian national team that won the 2006 World Cup in Germany.

Japanese women (photo e)
The Japanese women pictured in the photo on page 14 are wearing kimono, the national costume of Japan.

VW and BMW (photo f)
The two car badges shown are those of two German car companies – BMW and Volkswagen. BMW stands for Bayerische Motoren Werken.

If your students need further practice, you could use Photocopiable Worksheet *2 Vocabulary* here.

Vocabulary (2) (SB page 14)

Numbers

1 🌐 1.24

Play the recording and ask the students to listen and repeat the numbers. Encourage them to pronounce the ends of all the words clearly, so that they differentiate between numbers that end in *teen* and those that end in *ty*.

Extra activity

To encourage the students to focus on the endings *teen* and *ty* when listening and speaking, tell them that you're going to call out some numbers. If the number ends in *teen*, they should stand up, but if it ends in *ty*, they should remain seated. Call out some different numbers at random. When they understand what to do, ask several students to come to the front of the class and call out numbers for the others to react to.

Language notes

Pronunciation: numbers

- For some students, it's difficult to differentiate between *teen* and *ty*, for example, in *thirteen* and *thirty*. Point out how the position of the stressed syllable changes.

- In British English, you say *one hundred and six*. The word *and* is unstressed and pronounced /ən/ to make the liaison between *hundred* and *six*.

- In American English, you say *one hundred six* – *and* is omitted.

2

Pairwork. Ask the students to practise saying the numbers 1–20 with a partner.

3 🌐 **1.25**

Ask the students to work individually to complete the lines. Then play the recording for them to check their answers.

> a) twenty-three
> b) thirty-six
> c) forty-nine
> d) one hundred and thirteen

4 🌐 **1.26**

- Explain that the speaker on the recording will tell them which numbers to join. The first instruction for a) has been followed for them as an example, but note that there's one more instruction to follow for the numbers in a).
- Play the recording, allowing the students time to follow the instructions. When they've joined up all the numbers correctly, the lines they've put on the diagrams should spell out a mystery number.
- Ask if anyone can identify the mystery number.

> The mystery number is TEN.

> 🌐 **1.26**
> a) Join thirty, sixty-six and fourteen.
>   Join thirteen, thirty and seventy-four.
> b) Join fifteen, fifty and ninety-nine.
>   Join fifteen and twenty-four.
>   Join fifty and eighty-three.
>   Join ninety-nine and one hundred and ninety-nine.
> c) Join eighteen, seventy and seventy-nine.
>   Join eighteen, eighty and one hundred and sixty.
>   Join one hundred and sixty, thirty-eight and twenty-nine.

5

- Demonstrate this activity with a confident student first. Ask the student to give you a number between 1 and 199. Respond with the next three numbers. Then call out another number and encourage the student to respond with the next three numbers.
- When the students all understand what they have to do, put them in pairs and ask them to do the activity. Go round, monitoring and giving help. Take note of any pronunciation difficulties, and use these to give them extra practice at the end of the activity.

Pronunciation (SB page 15)

1 🌐 **1.27**

- Tell students that the symbols in this exercise are symbols for different currencies: the pound sign for the UK, the dollar sign for the USA, Australia, Canada and several other countries, the Euro sign for most of Europe. Ask the students to match the words and signs and check answers with the class.
- Then play the recording and ask the students to repeat the words.

> a) euros – €
> b) dollars – $
> c) pounds – £

2 🌐 **1.28**

- Read the two prices in a) to the class, emphasising the difference between them. Then play the recording and ask the students to circle the prices they hear. Allow them to compare answers in pairs before checking with the class.

> a) $3.50   b) £5.30   c) €70.75   d) $19.99
> e) €80.20   f) €40.40   g) £116.00

- Play the recording again for the students to listen and repeat.

Listening (SB page 15)

1 🌐 **1.29**

- Focus the students' attention on the table and the pictures of the different things. Note that all the prices have been put in US dollars for ease of comparison, not because dollars are used in all these cities. Point out that some of the prices in the table are missing and are labelled a) to d). Tell students to listen to the recording and complete the table with the missing prices.
- Play the recording, several times if necessary. Allow the students to compare answers in pairs before checking with the class.

> a) $3.00   b) $1.50   c) $16.50   d) $177.00

> 🌐 **1.29**
> a) 'How much is a cappuccino in New York?'
>   'Three dollars.'
> b) 'How much is a hamburger in Moscow?'
>   'One dollar fifty.'
> c) 'How much is a cinema ticket in London?'
>   'Sixteen dollars fifty.'
> d) 'How much is a 3-star hotel in Tokyo?'
>   'One hundred and seventy-seven dollars.'

2

- Pairwork. Ask the student to discuss in pairs how much these things cost in their city, and to complete the table.

- When they've finished, allow them to compare their results with another pair before getting feedback from the whole class.

Grammar (SB page 15)

How much ...?

1 🌐 1.30

- In this section, the students will practise using *How much ...?* to ask questions about prices. Begin by focusing their attention on the example question in the margin.

- Ask students to work individually to put the words in the correct order. Check the answers by asking individual students to read out their reordered questions.

- Play the recording for the students to check their answer again, and to repeat the questions after the speakers.

> a) How much is a cappuccino in Rome?
> b) How much is a hamburger in London?
> c) How much is a cinema ticket in Tokyo?
> d) How much is a 3-star hotel in Moscow?

2

Ask the students to work in pairs and to take turns to ask and answer the questions. Remind them that the answers are in the table in Listening Exercise 1. Go round, monitoring and giving help.

3

Ask the students to work with their partners, and to take turns asking and answering more questions about the prices shown in the table in Listening Exercise 1. Go round, monitoring and giving help where necessary.

Useful phrases (SB page 16)

1 🌐 1.31

- These short conversations will help students to ask questions about prices of things in English shops. Explain that they don't need to know the words for all the things on sale; they can use *this* and *these*. Remind them that *this* is used for singular things and *these* for plurals.

- Ask the students to work individually to complete the conversations. Then play the recording for them to listen and check their answers.

> a) this   b) these   c) is   d) are

Language notes

Grammar: *this/these* or *that/those*

The demonstrative pronouns *that* and *those* aren't taught explicitly in *New Inside Out* Beginner. However, if you feel your students can cope, then this would be a good point to introduce them. In the context of a shop, you can easily demonstrate through mime the concept of using *this/these* for things which are close to the speaker. Then contrast *this/these* with *that/those* for things which are more distant from the speaker.

Vocabulary: *castanets*

- *Castanets* (picture b) are an instrument made up of two pieces of wood tied together by string and knocked together. They are considered plural.

2 🌐 1.32

Play the recording for the students to listen and repeat.

3

Pairwork. Ask the students to take turns being both the customer and the shop assistant as they practise the conversations. Go round, monitoring and giving help where necessary. Ask a few confident pairs to perform their conversations for the class.

If your students need further practice, you could use Photocopiable Worksheet *2 Communication* here.

Vocabulary *Extra* (SB page 17)

Countries and nationalities

- Focus the students' attention on the example and establish that *Warsaw* is the name of the city shown in the photo, *Poland* is the name of the country and *Polish* the nationality word.

- Ask the students to look at the other photos and to choose the correct words from the box. Go round, giving help and encouragement.

- Point out that the underlining indicates the syllable of the word that has the strongest stress. Ask for choral and individual repetition to check that they are pronouncing all the words correctly.

> 1 a) Poland   b) Polish
> 2 a) Germany   b) German
> 3 a) Spain   b) Spanish
> 4 a) the USA   b) American
> 5 a) Italy   b) Italian
> 6 a) Japan   b) Japanese
> 7 a) Brazil   b) Brazilian
> 8 a) the UK   b) British

Cultural notes

Warsaw Town Square
Warsaw town square (the Rynek) has been rebuilt after being badly destroyed in the Second World War. The beautifully restored buildings are now cafés, restaurants, shops and galleries. In the centre is the Mermaid Statue – the mermaid is the legendary protector of the city.

The Reichstag, Berlin
The Reichstag was built in the late nineteenth century. It was burnt down in 1933, and further damaged at the end of the Second World War. Apart from the dome, it was reconstructed after the war. After the unification of Germany, the Reichstag once again became the seat of parliament, and the dome was put back on the building.

La Fuente de Cibeles, Madrid
La Fuente de Cibeles (Cybele's Fountain) shows the Greek Goddess of fertility, sitting on a chariot pulled by sea-horses. It was completed in 1782 and is the central feature of the Plaza de la Cibeles.

The Statue of Liberty, New York
The statue was a gift to the people of America from France to commemorate the centennial of the United States. It was completed in Paris in 1884 and stands on Liberty Island, at the mouth of the Hudson River in New York Harbour.

The Leaning Tower of Pisa
The bell tower of the Cathedral in Pisa is famous for the fact that it leans. It started to lean during its construction in the twelfth and thirteenth century. Between 1991 and 2001, the tower was closed to the public, while engineers tried to correct the tilt, as the building was in danger of collapsing.

The Golden Pavilion Temple, Kyoto
Kinkakuji (the Golden Pavilion Temple) was built in 1397. It's been burnt down several times since then and the present structure dates from 1955. Most of the pavilion is covered with pure gold leaf, and it houses relics of the Buddha.

Christ the Redeemer, Rio de Janeiro
The statue of Christ the Redeemer was completed in 1931. It stands on the Corcovada hill, which offers stunning views of the entire city of Rio de Janeiro. Standing at 30 metres tall, it's one of the tallest statues in the world.

Big Ben, London
The clock tower of the Houses of Parliament, commonly known as 'Big Ben', is one of London's most famous landmarks. It was built in 1858 and is 96.3 metres high.

Numbers

1

- Remind the students that in the last unit they matched the words for numbers one to ten with the figures. Ask them to do the same with the numbers from *11* to *100*.

- Ask for choral and individual repetition to check that they're pronouncing all the numbers correctly. Pay special attention to the difference between *13* and *30*, *14* and *40*, etc.

11	eleven	20	twenty
12	twelve	30	thirty
13	thirteen	40	forty
14	fourteen	50	fifty
15	fifteen	60	sixty
16	sixteen	70	seventy
17	seventeen	80	eighty
18	eighteen	90	ninety
19	nineteen	100	one hundred

2

As in the last unit, the students work in pairs to dictate numbers to each other. Demonstrate the activity with a confident student, making sure everyone understands that they have to write the words for the numbers rather than the figures. Then put the students into pairs to continue the activity. Go round, giving help and encouragement. Make sure each student takes a turn at dictating the numbers.

Writing

Workbook page 11

- Punctuation (question mark/full stop)
- Writing short questions and answers

Photocopiable resource materials

Grammar: *Where is it?* (Teacher's notes page 122. Worksheet page 147.)

Vocabulary: *Bingo!* (Teacher's notes page 123. Worksheet page 148.)

Communication: *How much is it?* (Teacher's notes page 123. Worksheet page 149.)

Test CD

See *Test Unit 2* on the CD.

DVD

Programme 1: *Oxford English Centre*

CD-ROM

For more activities go to Unit 2: *International*.

For the best activities for beginner students, see pages xvi–xxi

For practical methodology, from *Classroom interaction* to *Writing*, see pages xxii–xxxv

What can your students do now? See self-evaluation checklists on pages xxxvi–xlvi

3 Relations *Overview*

Section	Aims	What the students are doing
🌐 Listening **SB page 18**	*Listening skills*: listening for specific information	• Listening to a description of a family and matching names to people. • Using family words to complete a family tree.
🌐 Grammar **SB page 18**	*Grammar*: How old ...?	• Asking and answering questions about people's ages.
🌐 Grammar **SB page 19**	*Grammar*: possessive 's/s'	• Completing sentences about family relationships. • Matching descriptions to names.
🌐 Listening **SB page 19**	*Listening skills*: listening for detail	• Listening to a conversation and putting pictures in order. • Listening and underlining the correct word.
🌐 Vocabulary **SB page 19**	*Vocabulary*: family words	• Writing sentences about family relationships.
🌐 Reading **SB page 20**	*Reading skills*: reading for detail	• Matching descriptions to photos. • Matching people to sentences.
🌐 Grammar **SB page 20**	*Grammar*: possessive determiners	• Using possessive determiners to complete sentences.
🌐 Grammar **SB page 21**	*Grammar*: have (present simple)	• Choosing the correct form of the verb *have*.
🌐 Pronunciation **SB page 21**	*Pronunciation*: indefinite articles *a* and *an*	• Practising the pronunciation of *a* and *an* in front of nouns. • Linking words which end in a consonant with those that begin with a vowel.
🌐 Writing **SB page 21**	*Writing skills*: writing a paragraph	• Writing a paragraph about a family member.
🌐 Useful phrases **SB page 22**	*Vocabulary*: phrases which are useful for introducing people	• Listening to a conversation and identifying the people. • Listening and repeating useful phrases for introductions. • Writing and practising introductory conversations.
Vocabulary *Extra* **SB page 23**	*Vocabulary*: revision of words from the unit: family	• Matching pictures with words
Writing **WB page 15**	Punctuation (apostrophes) Describing your family	

Quick revision

- Play the game *Secret number* to review the numbers the students learnt in Unit 2.

- Write a number on the board and get the students to say what it is. Repeat this a few times until the students seem quite confident with numbers.

- Then write a number on a piece of paper, hiding the paper in an exaggerated way so that the students can't see the number. Then write a big question mark in the centre of the board and ask *What's the number?* Keep pointing at the question mark until one of the more confident students calls out a number. Write the number on the board. Gesture that it's incorrect, and indicate with your hands whether it's higher or lower. If it's more than your secret number, write it above the question mark. If it's less, write your number below.

- Encourage the students to suggest other numbers until they find the correct number.

- Repeat this game two or three times.

Listening (SB page 18)

1 🌐 **1.33**

- Focus the students' attention on the illustration. Note that it's a child's drawing of her family. Focus the students' attention on the labels on the illustration and read them out. Explain that the words the child uses to talk about her family members (*Mum, Dad, Grandma, Grandpa*) are informal. The more formal versions are in the list in this exercise, which they have to match to the people's names.

- Read the family words and the list of names, then play the recording and ask the students to match the two.

- Check answers with the class.

> 1 mother (mum) = Helen
> 2 father (dad) = William
> 3 brother = Sam
> 4 sister = Emma
> 5 grandmother (grandma) = Hannah
> 6 grandfather (grandpa) = Tom

> 🌐 **1.33**
>
> *This is my family, and this is me. My name's Luisa.*
> *This is my <u>mum</u>. Her name's <u>Helen</u>.*
> *This is my <u>dad</u>. His name's <u>William</u>.*
> *This is my big <u>brother</u>. His name's <u>Sam</u>, and this is my baby <u>sister</u>. Her name's <u>Emma</u>.*
> *These are my grandparents. My <u>grandma's name is Hannah</u>, and my <u>grandpa's name is Tom</u>.*
> *Oh, and this is our dog. His name's Max.*

2 🌐 **1.34**

- Play the recording for the students to repeat the family words from Exercise 1.

3

- Focus the students' attention on the family tree. Remind them of the symbols for male (♂) and female (♀). Point out the key and the explanation that the equals sign (=) means 'married to'.

- Ask the students to complete the family tree according to the information in Exercise 1.

- Check answers with the class.

> a) Tom   b) Hannah   c) William
> d) Helen   e) Sam   f) Luisa   g) Emma

Extra activity

- Ask the students to draw their own family trees.

- Ask the students to read the text from the listening activity, and then to write a personal version based on their own family tree.

Grammar (SB page 18)

How old ...?

1 🌐 **1.35**

- Focus the students' attention on the question and answer in the margin. They're going to listen to Luisa talking about the ages of the members of her family.

- Play the recording and pause after each question and answer for the students to complete them. Check answers with the class.

a) 'How old are you?'
   'I'm six.'
b) 'How old is your brother?'
   'He's twelve.'
c) 'How old is your sister?'
   'She's one.'
d) 'How old are your mother and father?'
   'They're forty-three.'
e) 'How old is your grandmother?'
   'She's sixty-eight.'
f) 'How old is your grandfather?'
   'He's seventy.'

Language note

Vocabulary: talking about age

When you talk about your age, you can say *I'm 37*.
Or *I'm 37 years old*. But you can't say *I'm 37 years*.

2

Put the students in pairs and ask them to take turns to
ask the questions from Exercise 1. Demonstrate first
with a confident student. You could teach the sentence
I don't have one, so that they can answer questions about
family members that they don't have.

Extra activity

- Ask the students to draw their own family trees
  if you didn't do the previous Extra activity.
- Ask the students to add ages to their family
  tree.
- In pairs, the students ask and answer questions
  about their own family trees.

If your students need further practice, you could use
Photocopiable Worksheet *3 Communication* here.

Grammar (SB page 19)

Possessive 's/s'

1 🔘 1.36

- This exercise focuses on the possessive *'s/s'*. Go
  through the information in the margin making sure
  everyone understands that *brother's* is singular and
  sisters' is plural. Practise the pronunciation, making
  sure that the students realise that the possessive *'s*
  often, but not always, has a /z/ sound.
- Students then work in pairs to complete the
  sentences. Remind them that the information about
  Luisa's family is on the previous page.
- Play the recording for the students to check their
  answers, then play it again for them to repeat.

a) mother (mum)
b) brother
c) grandfather (grandpa)
d) sister
e) father (dad)
f) grandmother (grandma)

Language notes

Grammar: possessive 's

- It isn't usual to say *The house of my brother*. Most
  native speakers would say *My brother's house*.
- To make the possessive form, for a singular
  noun, you add an apostrophe and *s*, (e.g. *My
  friend's brother*.).
- The apostrophe *'s* is pronounced like a plural
  ending, (e.g. *teacher's* /tiːtʃəz/, *teachers* /tiːtʃəz/).
- If the singular ends in an *s* (e.g. *James*), you
  usually add an apostrophe after the *s* (e.g.
  James' brother). This is pronounced /dʒeɪmzɪz/.
  It's also possible to write *James's*, which is
  pronounced the same.

2

Ask the students to work individually to match the
names with the descriptions. Then check answers by
asking individual students to read out the questions
and getting the class to answer them.

a) Sam   b) Emma   c) Helen

If your students need further practice, you could use
Photocopiable Worksheet *3 Grammar* here.

Listening (SB page 19)

1 🔘 1.37

- Focus the students' attention on the photos and tell
  them that these are photos from Luisa's family.
  Explain that they're going to listen to Tom, Luisa's
  grandfather, talking about these photos to a friend,
  and the students have to number the photos in the
  order they hear them on the CD.
- Play the recording, several times if necessary, and ask
  the students for the correct order of the photos.

1 b   2 a   3 c

1.37 (T = Tom; F = Friend)

T: This is in Italy. This is me, and this is my wife.
F: Hannah?
T: Yes, that's Hannah. And this is my daughter getting married.
F: Aah, lovely. What's her name?
T: Helen, and her husband's name is William.
F: And are these your grandchildren?
T: Yes. This is my grandson, Sam.
F: How old is he?
T: He's twelve. And this is Luisa. She's six.
F: And the baby – how old is he?
T: She. That's my granddaughter, Emma. She's one.

2

Play the recording again and ask the students to underline the correct word in each sentence. Check answers with the class.

> a) wife   b) daughter   c) grandson

Vocabulary (SB page 19)

1 🌐 1.38

- Note that some of the family words in the box are used exclusively with male family members, some with female members only and some with both.
- Play the recording for the students to repeat the words.

2

- Go through the examples with the class and then ask the students to work individually on their six sentences. Go round, monitoring and giving help where necessary.
- Check answers with the class, asking a variety of students to read out their sentences. Ask the other students to look at the family tree on page 18, and to check that the sentences which are called out are correct.

3

The students should work on their sentences individually and then compare them with a partner. Go round the class asking various students to read out one or two of their sentences.

Language note

Vocabulary: additional vocabulary

Students, depending on their family situation, may want to express other relationships not covered by the vocabulary taught. If necessary, give them extra vocabulary, such as: *uncle, nephew, niece, stepmother*, etc.

4 Pairwork

- The pairwork exercise for this unit is on pages 116 and 121 of the Student's Book. Put the students in pairs and tell them who will be Student A, and who will be Student B.
- While they're doing the pairwork exercise, go round monitoring and giving help. Take note of any errors which may need focusing on later and also any examples of good language use which you can praise.

Language note

Vocabulary: further vocabulary

The pairwork exercise introduces a new relationship with the word *boyfriend*. This gives more adventurous students the opportunity to explore further vocabulary in this area. Prepare to give them other words, such as *girlfriend, best friend*, etc.

If your students need further practice, you could use Photocopiable Worksheet *3 Vocabulary* here.

Reading (SB page 20)

1 🌐 1.39

- Focus the students' attention on the photos. Play the recording and ask the students to read the two texts as they listen. When they've finished, ask them to match the texts with the photos. Check answers with the class.

> a) 2   b) 1

Language note

Vocabulary: actor

The term *actor* can be used for both men and women. The term *actress* for a female actor does exist, but today *actor* is more commonly used.

Cultural notes

John Travolta (born 1954)
The films *Saturday Night Fever* and *Grease* made American actor John Travolta famous in the 1970s. However, he was unable to find any major acting parts until Quentin Tarantino's *Pulp Fiction* in 1994. Since then he's made a lot of successful films.

Blythe Danner (born 1943)
Blythe Danner was a theatre actress until 1971, when she made her first film *Dr Cook's Garden*. More recently, she's been in the film comedy *Meet the Parents* (2000) and the sequel *Meet the Fockers* (2004). She's also plays Will's mother in the American comedy series *Will and Grace*.

2

Go through the sentences and the people with the class. Then ask the students to work in pairs to match them. Check answers with the class.

> a) 2   b) 3   c) 4   d) 1

Grammar (SB page 20)

Possessive determiners

1 🔘 1.40

- Go through the information on possessive determiners in the margin. Then read the example sentence with the class. Ask the students to complete the remaining sentences.
- Play the recording for students to check their answers. Play it a second time for them to repeat the sentences.

> a) his   b) her   c) his   d) their
> e) My; Our

Language notes

Grammar: review possessive determiners

- In the phrase *John Travolta and his wife*, you use *his* because you're referring back to John Travolta.
- In the phrase *Blythe Danner and her sons*, you use the word *her* because you're referring back to Blythe Danner.
- The gender of *his* and *her* depends upon the person you're referring back to and not the person being described.

2 *Grammar Extra* **3**

Ask the students to turn to *Grammar Extra* 3 on page 126 of the Student's Book. Here they'll find an explanation of the grammar they've been studying and further exercises to practise it.

> **1**
> 1 my   2 your   3 it   4 our   5 their
>
> **2**
> a) parents'   b) mother's   c) father's
> d) sisters'   e) sisters'   f) brother's
>
> **3**
> a) This is their house.
> b) This is her car.
> c) These are his cars.
> d) This is their university.
> e) These are their boyfriends.
> f) These are his girlfriends.

Grammar (SB page 21)

have

1 🔘 1.41

- Focus the students' attention on the example sentence. Ask them to work individually to choose and underline the correct form in each sentence.
- Play the recording for the students to check their answers. Play it a second time for them to repeat the sentences.

> a) have   b) have   c) has   d) have
> e) have   f) has

Language notes

Grammar: *have*

- There are two possible ways of expressing possession in British English – *have/has* or *have got/has got*.
- In *New Inside Out* Beginner, only *have/has* is introduced as this form works in all contexts, i.e. as a main verb to express possession: *I have two brothers*, and as a de-lexicalised verb in expressions such as *He has lunch at 1pm*. This form also has the added advantage of conjugating with *do/does* in the present simple and behaving exactly the same way as all other verbs.

2

Pairwork. Ask the students to discuss in pairs which sentences are true for them, and then to report back to the class.

Pronunciation (SB page 21)

1 🔘 1.42

- Ask the students to listen carefully to the recording. Note the red links between *an* and words beginning with a vowel sound. Explain that all nouns beginning with vowel sounds require *an* not *a* as the indefinite article. Demonstrate that this facilitates the pronunciation by comparing how difficult it is to pronounce *a actor* /ə/ /ˈæktə/ with how easy it is to say *an actor* /ən/ /ˈæktə/. You might want to note that a word beginning with a vowel doesn't necessarily mean a vowel sound, i.e. *a university* /ə/ /ˌjuːnɪˈvɜːsəti/.
- Play the recording again and ask the students to repeat the sentences, paying particular attention to the linked words.

2 🌐 1.43

- Focus the students' attention on the table under the box. Remind them that you use the indefinite article *a* before words that begin with a consonant sound and *an* before those that begin with a vowel sound. Read out the example word in each column, being sure to link *an Audi*.

- Ask the students to put all the words from the box in the correct columns of the table. Encourage them to read the words aloud as they do this, linking any that begin with vowel sounds. Make sure they understand the meaning of all the items in the box. You could refer them back to page 11, where they can find many of the items.

- Play the recording for them to check their answers, then play it again for them to repeat. Encourage them to link words correctly.

> *an* + vowel sound: an Audi; an English dictionary; an Ericsson mobile phone; an IBM computer; an Italian grandmother
>
> *a* + consonant sound: a brother; a dog; a Gucci bag; a passport; a sister

3

Pairwork. Give the students a minute or so to think of their own possessions. Give help with any vocabulary they need. Then ask them to take turns to tell their partner about the things they have. Go round, monitoring and giving help where necessary. Encourage them to link words correctly.

Writing (SB page 21)

Extra activity

- This writing activity is quite complex. For some students, you could do a 'bridge activity' to prepare them for the writing.

- On the board, write these sentences:
  I have a brother. His name is John. He's 23.
  (You can replace the model sentence with true information about yourself if you wish.)

- Get some of the stronger students to make similar sentences about themselves. Ask all the students to write three similar sentences about themselves. Then ask the students to go round the class saying their sentences to each other.

1

- This is a simple writing exercise to get the students started on writing short texts. Read the example with the class so that they get an idea of the sort of text they should produce. They can use this example as a model if they wish, but emphasise that they can choose any family member to write about, and can include any details they wish.

- Allow plenty of time for the students to write their paragraphs. As they do this, go round giving help with vocabulary and checking that the students are constructing their sentences correctly.

2

- Pairwork. Ask the students to read each other's texts. Then encourage them to ask questions about each other's relatives to find out any information that's missing.

- You could elicit the sort of questions they might ask first and put them on the board (*How old is he/she? What is her daughter's name?* etc.).

Useful phrases (SB page 22)

1 🌐 1.44

- Focus attention on the picture and give the students time to look at it, Tell them that the conversations are taking place at a party.

- Play the recording and ask the students to read the conversations as they listen.

- When they've finished, ask students for their answers to the two questions. Don't confirm whether they're correct or not. Then play the recording again for the students to check.

- Note that *Nice to meet you* is a polite response to an introduction and is short for *It's nice to meet you.*

- Ask a couple of pairs of students to roleplay the conversations.

a) Tim   b) Rob

> ### Language notes

Grammar: general review of apostrophe 's

- The apostrophe 's can be confusing for students as it's used for different purposes:
  Contraction of *is*, for example, *He's British. Where's Wally?*
  The possessive form, for example, *Ann's brother. Becky's husband.*

- Point out to students that it's the same form used for different meanings.

2 **1.45**

Play the recording for the students to listen to and repeat the sentences.

3 **1.46**

- Ask the students to look at the illustration and the conversation below it. Ask them to complete the conversation, using the words in the box.

- Play the recording for them to check their answers. Then ask a couple of groups of students to perform the conversation for the class.

1 This	2 Nice	3 meet	4 'm
5 to	6 you		

4

- Put the students in threes and ask them to rewrite the conversation from Exercise 3, using their own names.

- Students should then practise the conversation. Invite confident groups to perform the conversations to the class.

Vocabulary *Extra* (SB page 23)

Family

1

- Focus the students' attention on the list of words and point out that they're all to do with the family. Remind the students that the underlining indicates the syllable of the word that has the strongest stress. Check that the students can pronounce all of the words correctly.

- Ask them to tell each other the names of the brothers, granddaughters, etc., as appropriate.

- Ask the students to look at the pictures and complete the sentences with the correct words from the box.

1) husband	4) brother
2) parents	5) mother
3) granddaughter	6) grandfather

2

- Ask the students to look at the family tree and answer the questions. You could ask the questions around the class, or perhaps get individual students to ask the questions and to choose another student to answer.

a) Charlie.	d) Gary.
b) Delia.	e) Alice and Bill.
c) Fran.	f) Fran.

3

Ask the students to write sentences about their families.

Writing
Workbook page 15
- Punctuation (apostrophes)
- Describing your family

Photocopiable resource materials
Grammar: *Who is he?* (Teacher's notes page 123. Worksheet page 150.)
Vocabulary: *Who's his wife?* (Teacher's notes page 124. Worksheet page 151.)
Communication: *My family* (Teacher's notes page 124. Worksheet page 152.)

Test CD
See *Test Unit 3* on the CD.

DVD
Programme 2: *My family*

CD-ROM
For more activities go to Unit 3: *Relations*.

For the best activities for beginner students, see pages xvi–xxi

For practical methodology, from *Classroom interaction* to *Writing*, see pages xxii–xxxv

What can your students do now? See self-evaluation checklists on pages xxxvi–xlvi

Review A *Teacher's notes*

These exercises act as a check of the grammar and vocabulary that the students have learnt in the introductory unit and the first three units of the Student's Book. Use them to find any problems that students are having, or anything that they haven't understood and which will need further work.

Grammar (SB page 24)

Remind the students of the grammar explanations they read and the exercises they did in the *Grammar Extra* on pages 126 and 127 of the Student's Book.

1

This exercise reviews language from Units 1, 2 and 3.

> a) What's your mother's name?
> b) How old is she?
> c) Where is she from?
> d) What's her nationality?
> e) What's her phone number?
> f) Where is she now?
> a) My mother's name is …
> b) She's … years old.
> c) She's from …
> d) She's …
> e) Her phone number is …
> f) She's in/at … now.

2

This exercise reviews *this* and *these* from Unit 1.

> a) What's this?
>   It's a car.
> b) What are these?
>   They're passports.
> c) What are these?
>   They're buses.
> d) What's this?
>   It's a mobile phone.
> e) What's this?
>   It's a camera.
> f) What are these?
>   They're dictionaries.

3

This exercise reviews present simple of the verb *be* and nationality words from Unit 2.

> a) It's German.   d) It's Japanese.
> b) They're Polish.   e) It's Japanese.
> c) They're American.   f) They're English.

4

This exercise reviews possessive determiners and family words from Unit 3.

> a) my   b) Our   c) Her   d) Their
> e) His   f) your

5

This exercise reviews possessive *'s/s'* and family words from Unit 3.

> a) wife's   b) mother's   c) father's
> d) sons'   e) sister's   f) brothers'

6

This exercise reviews structures used in Units 1, 2 and 3.

> 1 a) My name Tom.
> 2 a) What is?
> 3 a) Where Mario from?
> 4 b) They're from in Spain.
> 5 b) I have twenty years.
> 6 b) She have two children.

If your students need further practice, you could use Photocopiable Worksheet *Review A* here.

Vocabulary (SB page 25)

1

This exercise reviews classroom language from the introductory unit.

a) Listen   b) Practise   c) Ask
d) Look   e) Match   f) Work

2

This crossword reviews numbers *1* to *10* from Unit 1.

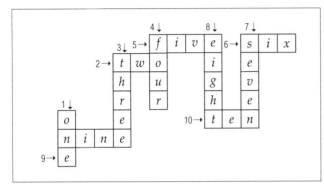

3

This exercise reviews the names of countries from Unit 2.

a) Italy   b) Japan   c) Spain
d) Poland   e) Brazil   f) Germany

4

This exercises reviews units of currency and prices from Unit 2. Remind the students of the different symbols for different currencies.

a) Twelve dollars fifty-five
b) Twenty-four pounds ninety-nine
c) Fifteen euros seventy-five
d) Thirty-seven euros eighty
e) Sixty-nine dollars nineteen
f) One hundred and forty-nine dollars fifty

5

This exercise reviews family words from Unit 3. It's a word puzzle. When it's completed, the boxes will reveal the name of a famous family. Point out to the students that to complete each pair, they need the equivalent family word, but of the opposite sex.

1 daughter   2 father   3 mother
4 husband   5 wife   6 grandmother
7 sister   8 brother   9 son   10 grandson

The famous family: the Simpsons

Pronunciation (SB page 25)

These two exercises review work students did on word stress, using words they met in Units 1–3.

1

Remind the students of the use of large and small stress boxes, which they first saw in Unit 2, page 12, to help them get their intonation right. Here they're being asked to classify words according to how many syllables they have and where the main stress falls. Encourage them to say each word aloud to get a feeling for what sounds right.

(See Exercise 2 for answers)

2 🌐 1.47

Point out the main stresses in the example words which are underlined. Ask the students to do the same for the other words in the table. Play the recording for them to check their answers.

1 and 2

adjective   computer   Japanese
Germany   description   seventeen
granddaughter   possessive
singular   relation

Reading & Listening (SB page 26)

1

• You could ask the students to read the sentences first so that they know what information they're looking for when they read the text.

• When you've checked their answers, ask them to correct the false information.

a) False. (It's in Bath.)
b) True.
c) False. (It has nine rooms.)
d) False. (A room for one night is £85.)
e) True.

2 🌐 1.48

• Go through the choices with the students before they listen to the recording so that they know what information they're listening for. You may need to play the recording several times to allow them to find the answers.

• Note that the character in the Listening activity shares the same name as Arnold Schwarzenegger, the former Mr Universe turned actor who starred in the *Terminator* films, and who became Governor of California in 2003.

a) 1   b) 2   c) 3

> 🔊 **1.48** (R = Receptionist;
>   AS = Arnold Schwarzenegger)
>
> R: *Good afternoon, sir.*
> AS: *Good afternoon. How much is one night at this hotel?*
> R: *£85.*
> AS: *Sorry?*
> R: *One night is £85.*
> AS: *Oh, OK. One night, please.*
> R: *What's your first name?*
> AS: *Arnold.*
> R: *Can you spell that?*
> AS: *A–R–N–O–L–D.*
> R: *And your surname?*
> AS: *Schwarzenegger.*
> R: *Sorry. Can you repeat that?*
> AS: *Schwarzenegger.*
> R: *Schwarzenegger? Can you spell that, please?*
> AS: *S–C–H–W–A–R–Z–E–N–E–G–G–E–R.*
> R: *Sorry. Can you repeat that?*
> AS: *S–C–H–W–A–R–Z–E–N–E–G–G–E–R.*
> R: *Are you American, Mr Schwarzenegger?*
> AS: *Yes, I am. I'm from Los Angeles.*
> R: *Do you have a phone number?*
> AS: *Yes, it's 001–310–863–429.*
> R: *Your passport number please, Mr Schwarzenegger.*
> AS: *It's 489–798–2340.*
> R: *Can your repeat that, please?*
> AS: *489–798–2340.*
> R: *Thank you. Your room number is 103.*

3

Go through the form with the class so that they can see what information is missing. Then play the recording again so that they can complete it. You may need to play it several times.

> Blossoms Hotel
> First name: <u>Arnold</u>
> Surname: <u>Schwarzenegger</u>
> Nationality: <u>American</u>
> City: Los Angeles
> Country: USA
> Phone number: <u>001–310–863–429</u>
> Passport number: <u>489–798–234</u>

Writing & Speaking (SB page 27)

1

Ask the students to look at the Blossoms Hotel form. Explain what a capital letter is, and ask them to look at the form and use it to find examples for the rules on the use of capital letters.

> a) Susan   b) Barclay   c) British
> d) Wellington Street   e) Glasgow
> f) Scotland

2

Go through the questions with the class. You could do an example with them first before asking them to match the questions to the numbered information on the form. Check answers with the class before the students work in pairs to ask each other the questions, and complete the form with their partners' answers.

> a) 3   b) 2   c) 5   d) 4   e) 6   f) 1   g) 7

Photocopiable resource materials

Review A: *The Revision Game* (Teacher's notes page 125. Worksheet page 153.)

Test CD

See *Test Review A* on the CD.

For the best activities for beginner students, see pages xvi–xxi

For practical methodology, from *Classroom interaction* to *Writing*, see pages xxii–xxxv

What can your students do now? See self-evaluation checklists on pages xxxvi–xlvi

4 Favourites *Overview*

Section	Aims	What the students are doing
Vocabulary **SB page 28**	*Vocabulary*: food, drink and sport	• Categorising words in lists.
Grammar **SB page 29**	*Grammar*: the verb *like*	• Listening to a conversation about likes and dislikes. • Completing questions and answers about likes and dislikes.
Reading & Writing **SB page 29**	*Reading skills*: reading for specific information *Writing skills*: writing a short text	• Reading a web profile and writing questions about it. • Writing a web profile for a partner.
Vocabulary (1) **SB page 30**	*Vocabulary*: colours	• Listening and repeating colour words. • Playing games with numbers and colours.
Vocabulary (2) **SB page 30**	*Vocabulary*: adjectives	• Matching descriptions to photos. • Matching adjectives to their opposites.
Pronunciation **SB page 31**	*Pronunciation*: word stress	• Practising word stress with names of countries and cities.
Grammar **SB page 31**	*Grammar*: adjective + noun word order	• Putting words in the correct order. • Combining adjectives and nouns. • Talking about likes and dislikes.
Speaking **SB page 31**	*Conversation skills*: talking about likes and dislikes	• Asking and answering questions about likes and dislikes.
Useful phrases **SB page 32**	*Vocabulary*: phrases which are useful when asking for clarification	• Completing two conversations between waiters and customers. • Listening to and repeating useful phrases. • Practising conversations with a partner.
Vocabulary *Extra* **SB page 33**	*Vocabulary*: revision of words from the unit: food and drink; colours; common adjectives	• Matching pictures with words.
Writing **WB page 19**	Writing a personal web profile	

4 Favourites *Teacher's notes*

Warm up

Ask students to brainstorm as many English words that they know under the categories *Food*, *Drink* and *Sport*.

Vocabulary (SB page 28)

1 🌐 1.49

- Focus the students' attention on the photos. Ask them to identify all the items shown. Then focus their attention on the table underneath and the three columns, *Food*, *Drink* and *Sport*. Ask them to complete the lists.

- Play the recording for them to check their answers. Note that students might not complete the table in the same order as it appears in the recording. Play it a second time for them to repeat the words. Encourage them to pronounce the /ɪŋ/ sound at the end of *swimming* correctly.

> Food: fruit, meat, fish, Italian food,
> Chinese food
> Drink: Coke, wine, coffee, tea
> Sport: swimming, tennis, football

Language note

Vocabulary: *Coke*

Coke is another name for *Coca-Cola*. In a café or bar, when ordering a Coca-Cola, you say: *Can I have a Coke, please?*

2

- Pairwork. Demonstrate the activity with a confident student. Choose a word and encourage the student to say which list it goes in. Then reverse roles.

- When the students understand what they have to do, put them in pairs. As they do the activity, go round checking on individual pronunciation.

Grammar (SB page 29)

1 🌐 1.50

- Ask the students to look at the photo and point out that the conversation takes place in a restaurant. Then focus their attention on the verb *like* in the margin. Read the statements, the question and the two answers aloud. Explain the meaning, if necessary.

- Play the recording for the students to listen and repeat. Encourage them to copy the intonation of the speakers on the recording. You could ask for individual repetition once the students have repeated the conversation chorally.

- Put the students in pairs and ask them to practise the conversation, taking turns to be Ann and Beth.

Language notes

Grammar: *do* auxiliary

- This is the first time students see examples of the auxiliary *do*. Questions and short answers using *like* in the present simple are seen in context in a restaurant conversation. A more formal presentation and practice of other common verbs in the present simple comes in Unit 5 (*I, you, we, they* + *Wh* questions), and Unit 6 (third person singular).

- If you feel that your students would benefit from further explanation at this stage, you could tell them that *do*, in its role as an auxiliary verb, helps to form questions and negatives in the present simple. Other languages form questions and negatives in different ways, without an auxiliary verb.

- As this is the first time students practise short answers using the auxiliary *do*, you may like to explain that *Yes, I do.* and *No, I don't.* sound softer and more natural than simply *Yes* or *No*, but both are correct.

- Point out that *do* + *not* is usually contracted to *don't* in spoken English.

2 🌐 1.51

- Remind the students of the information about *like* in the margin next to Exercise 1. Go through the example with them before asking them to work individually to complete the questions and answers. Go round monitoring and giving help where necessary.

- Play the recording for them to check their answers. Then play it a second time for the students to repeat.

a) 'Do you like Italian food?'
   'Yes, I do.' 'No, I don't.'
b) 'Do you like Chinese food?'
   'Yes, I do.' 'No, I don't.'
c) 'Do you like fish?'
   'Yes, I do.' 'No, I don't.'
d) 'Do you like fruit?'
   'Yes, I do.' 'No, I don't.'
e) 'Do you like coffee?'
   'Yes, I do.' 'No, I don't.'
f) 'Do you like Coke?'
   'Yes, I do.' 'No, I don't.'

a) What's her favourite city?
b) Who's her favourite actor?
c) Who's her favourite singer?
d) What's her favourite sport?
e) What's her favourite food?
f) What's her favourite drink?

a) Cape Town.
b) George Clooney.
c) Shakira.
d) Swimming.
e) Pizza.
f) Malibu and Coke.

3

- Put the students in pairs and ask them to take turns asking and answering the questions for themselves.
- Then give them time to write six more questions. These could be about any likes and dislikes, not just food and drink. Go round, monitoring and giving help. When they've finished, check their answers by getting individual students to ask someone else in the class one of their questions. Alternatively, let the students mingle, asking their questions and taking note of the answers they get. Then, with the whole class, find out what information they learnt about each other's likes and dislikes.

Reading & Writing (SB page 29)

1 🌐 **1.52**

Ask the students to look at the web profile of Nina Frank. Point out that this is information on the internet about a model. Check that the students understand *favourite*. Then play the recording for them to listen to and read the profile.

Cultural note

Nina Frank (born 1980)
Nina Frank is a South African fashion model, presently working in Britain.

2 🌐 **1.53**

- Read the two example questions with the class, then ask them to work individually to write more questions about Nina's favourite things. Remind them that they must use *What* or *Who*.
- Play the recording for them to check their answers. Then play it a second time for them to repeat the questions.

3

Put the students in pairs to take turns asking and answering the questions they've written about Nina.

4

- Remind the students that they'll need to change *her* to *your* when they ask their partner the questions. Read the example with the class before asking them to change the other questions. When they've finished, check that they've all formulated the questions correctly, then put them in pairs to take turns asking and answering the questions about themselves. Tell them that they should take notes of their partner's answers.
- Finally, ask them to write a web profile based on their partner's answers. Tell them they can use the profile of Nina Frank as a model. Get some students to read their profiles out for the rest of the class. Alternatively, display the profiles on the wall for everyone to read.

a) What's your favourite city?
b) Who's your favourite actor?
c) Who's your favourite singer?
d) What's your favourite sport?
e) What's your favourite food?
f) What's your favourite drink?

Vocabulary (1) (SB page 30)

Colours

1 🌐 **1.54**

- The colours on the recording are in the same order as those in the left-hand margin, so encourage the students to look at these as they listen to and repeat the colour words.
- Find out what everyone's favourite colour is and which is the most popular colour in the class.

2

- Focus the students' attention on the illustration with the coloured numbers. Demonstrate the activity with a confident student. Read out a number and get the student to say what colour it is. Then reverse roles.
- Put the students in pairs to continue the activity. Go round, monitoring and giving help. Encourage the students to pronounce the colour words correctly.

3

This exercise takes the colour game one step further. Explain, using the example, that the coloured number chart can be used to do simple equations. Ask the students to make up some simple sums to ask each other. Make sure they also work out the answers. Then put them in pairs to practise asking and answering maths questions.

Extra activity

If your students enjoy this, you could divide them into teams and then call out some more 'maths' questions for them to answer. Give a point to the team that calls an answer out first.

Vocabulary (2) (SB page 30)

1 ● **1.55**

- Focus the students' attention on the photos and ask them what colours they can see in them. Then go through the four descriptions with them and ask them to match them to the photos.

- Play the recording for them to check their answers.

> a) 3   b) 1   c) 4   d) 2

Cultural notes

Red Square, Moscow
Red Square is in the centre the Russian capital. The buildings that surround the square include the Kremlin, Lenin's mausoleum, the Gum department store and St Basil's Cathedral.

La Boca, Buenos Aires, Argentina
La Boca (the mouth) is a colourful and popular tourist area in Buenos Aires, dating back to the end of the 19th century. The main street, the Caminito, is a busy pedestrian street with an arts and craft fair, open-air tango shows, and lots of Italian restaurants.

Oxford Street, London, England
Oxford Street is one of London's main shopping streets and is Britain's busiest high street. Most of the UK's major department stores are there, as well as many chain stores and smaller shops.

Copacabana Beach, Rio de Janeiro, Brazil
Copacabana is one of the world's great beaches. It's five kilometres long, and lies at the foot of the hills of Rio de Janeiro.

2 ● **1.56**

- Explain *opposite* and focus the students' attention on the example (*beautiful* and *ugly*). Ask them to match up the other opposites.

- Play the recording for the students to check their answers. Then play it a second time for them to repeat all the adjectives.

> beautiful – ugly
> big – small
> cheap – expensive
> new – old

3 Pairwork

- The pairwork exercise for this unit is on pages 117 and 122 of the Student's Book. Put the students in pairs and tell them who will be Student A, and who will be Student B.

- While they're doing the pairwork exercise, go round monitoring and giving help. Take note of any errors which may need focusing on later and also any examples of good language use which you can praise. Check answers with the class.

> a) green apples   f) a new building
> b) a Polish passport g) expensive bags
> c) old cars   h) a yellow bus
> d) a black coffee   i) a beautiful fish
> e) a big dog

If your students need further practice, you could use Photocopiable Worksheet *4 Vocabulary* here.

Pronunciation (SB page 31)

1 ● **1.57**

- Read the names of cities in a) and point out that the stressed syllables are underlined. Ask the students to say these words aloud and check that they're getting the stress right.

- Play the recording and ask the students to repeat the words.

2

- Play the recording again and ask the students to underline the stressed syllables in all the other cities and countries in the exercise. Check answers with the class, and tell them that in each line one of the words has a different stress pattern from the other two.

- Point out that in the example Beijing is circled because its stress pattern is different. Ask them to circle the other cities and countries that have different stress. Check answers with the class and play the recording again.

- Ask the students to discuss what their favourite cities or countries are in pairs, and to report back to the class.

> a) <u>Ve</u>nice   <u>Mu</u>nich   (Bei<u>jing</u>)
> b) (<u>Rome</u>)   <u>Flo</u>rence   <u>Mos</u>cow
> c) <u>Se</u>ville   <u>Ber</u>lin   (<u>War</u>saw)
> d) (Ma<u>drid</u>)   <u>Lon</u>don   <u>Pa</u>ris
> e) <u>Ru</u>ssia   <u>France</u>   (<u>Chi</u>na)
> f) <u>Cai</u>ro   <u>To</u>kyo   (Mi<u>lan</u>)

3

Go through the example with the class. Then ask them to work in pairs, and ask and answer similar questions about the other cities in Exercise 1.

> Venice, Rome, Florence and Milan are in Italy.
> Munich and Berlin are in Germany.
> Beijing is in China.
> Moscow is in Russia.
> Seville and Madrid are in Spain.
> Warsaw is in Poland.
> London is in England.
> Paris is in France.
> Cairo is in Egypt.
> Tokyo is in Japan.

Grammar (SB page 31)

Adjective + noun word order

1 🔊 1.58

- Focus the students' attention on the information in the margin. Note that in English adjectives come before the noun, and that adjectives don't change according to the number of nouns being described. Go through the example with the class and ask them to do b) orally. Then ask them to complete the exercise.

- Play the recording for them to check their answers. Then play it again for them to repeat the sentences.

> a) I like black coffee.
> b) I like French films.
> c) I like old buildings.
> d) I like expensive shops.
> e) I don't like British food.
> f) I don't like big cities.

2

- Go through the example to demonstrate how the sentences can be changed to make them true, either by using the negative form of *like* or by changing the adjective.

- Give the students a few minutes to work individually on all the sentences, making them true for themselves. Go round the class asking a variety of students to read out their changed sentences.

3

- Explain that the adjectives and nouns can be combined in a variety of ways. Some (for example, *American*) can be used with all the nouns, others (for example, *red*) are more limited and only make sense with some of the nouns. You may not wish at this point to discuss countable and uncountable nouns and explain why we say *I like white coffee*, but use a plural for *I like old buildings*. However, encourage the students to use the plural forms of the nouns in this exercise where they are given.

- Ask the students to work individually or in pairs to combine the adjectives with the nouns and produce two lists: one of things they like and one of things they don't like. Go round, checking that they've made sensible combinations of adjectives and nouns.

- Get feedback from the class on what things were liked and disliked.

If your students need further practice, you could use Photocopiable Worksheet *4 Grammar* here.

Language notes

Grammar: two adjective word order

- In English, adjectives come before the noun, for example, *a big bus*. You can't say *a bus big*.

- In Exercise 3, when the students are asked to combine adjectives and nouns, because there's no correct solution, the more adventurous may want to combine two adjectives with a noun, for example, *an expensive French restaurant*; *a big American car*.

- When there are two adjectives, the order is:
  – size (*big*)
  – judgement (*beautiful, new, old, expensive, cheap*)
  – colour (*black, red*)
  – origin (*American, French*)

  So, for example, you could say: *A big, old, red, American car*.

4 *Grammar Extra 4*

Ask the students to turn to *Grammar Extra* 4 on page 128 of the Student's Book. Here they'll find an explanation of the grammar they've been studying and further exercises to practise it.

> 1 a) They're expensive cars.
>   b) They're big cities.
>   c) They're Japanese cameras.
>   d) They're brown bags.
>   e) They're ugly buildings.
>   f) They're small hotels.
> 2 a) I have a small apartment.
>   b) I have a new car.
>   c) I have a Brazilian girlfriend.
>   d) I have a big family.
>   e) I have a cheap pen.
>   f) I have an old computer.

Extra activity

- A lot of vocabulary has been introduced in this unit. Some students will need time to assimilate it. One way to do this would be to play *Hangman* to revise the vocabulary and the alphabet. You'll find a full explanation of this technique in the Practical methodology section in the Introduction. Here, however, is another idea. ➤

- Write an anagram of the word *favourites* on the board, e.g. *avrsfoitue*.
- Get the students to guess what the word is. Help them by indicating the first letter is *f*, writing it on the board and adding dashes for each of the other letters. If the students are having problems, give them a second letter and so on until they find the word. When they do find the word, point out where it appears in the text book. (It's the title of this unit.)
- Now get the students to choose a word in the unit, make an anagram from it and then, in turn, write it on the board for the class to guess.

Speaking (SB page 31)

Go through the example questions and answers with the class. Then ask them to work in pairs to ask and answer more questions about each other's likes and dislikes. Insist that they use an adjective with each noun. If they move away from the nouns and adjectives given in the previous section, encourage them to use plurals for countable nouns and singular forms for uncountable nouns.

If your students need further practice, you could use Photocopiable Worksheet *4 Communication* here.

Useful phrases (SB page 32)

1 🌐 1.59

- Ask the students to look at the illustration and say where the conversation takes place (in a restaurant). Tell them that the man is a customer and the woman a waiter. Go through the items on the menu with them and explain any difficult words.
- Play the recording for the students to listen and complete the conversation. Then play it again for them to check their answers.

1 help	2 understand	3 speak

Language note

Vocabulary: *It's a kind of …*

It's a kind of means *It's a sort of* or *It's a type of*. There is no *a/an* after these expressions. So, for example, you can say *A shark is a kind of fish*.

2 🌐 1.60

- Point out that this conversation takes place in the same restaurant. Ask the students to read it and try to complete the conversation. If they have trouble with this, suggest that they look back at the first conversation for some help.
- Play the recording for the students to listen and check their answers. Then play it again for them to repeat.

1 Can
2 help
3 I don't understand
4 Can
5 speak

3 🌐 1.61

Go through the useful phrases with the class. Then play the recording for them to listen and repeat.

4

Pairwork. Put the students in pairs to practise both conversations. Ask them to take turns being the waiter and the customer. Go round monitoring and giving help with pronunciation.

Vocabulary *Extra* (SB page 33)

Food and drink

1

- Focus the students' attention on the list of words and point out that they're all to do with the food and drink. Remind the students that the underlining indicates the syllable of the word that has the strongest stress. Check that the students can pronounce all of the words correctly.
- Ask students to look at the pictures and match each one with one of the words. Point out that the first one has been done for them.

2 coffee	1 pasta
4 fish	5 pizza
7 fruit	6 wine
3 meat	

2

Pairwork. Demonstrate the activity with a confident student. Cover up the words, point to one of the pictures and ask *What's this?* Elicit the answer. Then put the students into pairs to continue the activity. Go round, checking that everyone is pronouncing the words correctly.

Colours

Ask students to match the colours to the correct words.

2 black	8 orange
5 blue	10 pink
3 brown	4 red
6 green	1 white
9 grey	7 yellow

Go through the adjectives with the class and make sure
they can pronounce them. Then ask them to match the
pictures to the adjectives.

6 beautiful	3 expensive
4 big	2 small
1 cheap	5 ugly

Writing

Workbook page 19

Writing a personal web profile

Photocopiable resource materials

Grammar: *Do you like it?* (Teacher's notes page
125. Worksheet page 154.)

Vocabulary: *Categories* (Teacher's notes page 125.
Worksheet page 155.)

Communication: *My favourite* (Teacher's notes
page 126. Worksheet page 156.)

Test CD

See *Test Unit 4* on the CD.

 CD-ROM

For more activities go to Unit 4: *Favourites*.

For the best activities for beginner students,
see pages xvi–xxi

For practical methodology, from *Classroom
interaction* to *Writing*, see pages xxii–xxxv

What can your students do now? See
self-evaluation checklists on pages xxxvi–xlvi

Before the next lesson

Find some photos of famous people your class will
know, and bring them to class for the Quick
revision activity in Unit 5.

5 Life *Overview*

Section	Aims	What the students are doing
Reading SB page 34	*Reading skills*: reading for specific information	• Reading and completing a questionnaire on life expectancy.
Vocabulary SB page 35	*Vocabulary*: collocations with *eat, have, like, live, speak* and *work*	• Completing verb phrases. • Making sentences about lifestyles.
Grammar SB page 35	*Grammar*: present simple with *I, you, we* and *they*	• Completing questions and answers about lifestyles. • Putting questions in the correct order. • Asking and answering questions about lifestyles.
Vocabulary SB page 36	*Vocabulary*: jobs	• Matching jobs with photos. • Matching sentences with jobs.
Pronunciation SB page 37	*Pronunciation*: stress in *Wh* questions	• Practising asking *Wh* questions with the correct stress.
Listening SB page 37	*Listening skills*: listening for detail	• Matching people to real jobs and dream jobs. • Completing questions.
Speaking SB page 37	*Conversation skills*: asking questions about jobs	• Asking questions about real jobs and dream jobs.
Useful phrases SB page 38	*Vocabulary*: phrases which are useful on the telephone	• Matching telephone conversations to pictures. • Listening and repeating useful phrases for telephoning. • Writing and practising new telephone conversations.
Vocabulary *Extra* SB page 39	*Vocabulary*: revision of words from the unit: jobs	• Matching pictures with words.
Writing WB page 23	Preparing a draft, correcting mistakes and writing a final version	

5 Life *Teacher's notes*

Quick revision

- This is a quick review of some of the language the students have learnt so far. Cut out and bring into class some pictures from magazines of famous people they'll know.

- Ask the students questions about these people such as:
  What's his/her name?
  Can you spell that?
  How old is he/she?
  Where is he/she from?
  Do you like (name)?

- Give a photograph to some of the more confident students. Get the students to mill with the more confident students asking the above questions.

Reading (SB page 34)

1

- Explain *life expectancy* (the age that a person can expect to reach before they die) and that this may differ according to your sex, your lifestyle, the country you live in, and a variety of other factors.

- Then ask the students, working individually, to read the questionnaire and complete it. Help with any difficult vocabulary.

- Focus the students' attention on the *How to score* section and ask them to calculate their own scores, and then look at the results section.

2

Pairwork. Ask the students to compare their scores with a partner and to look at the answers they each gave to the questionnaire. Note that higher points were awarded in the questionnaire not only for healthier lifestyles (not smoking, getting plenty of sleep, eating healthy food), but also for leading a contented life (liking your job). Genetics also plays a big role: those with old people in their family score much more highly than people whose family members generally die young, and women have an inbuilt natural advantage over men when it comes to longevity.

Vocabulary (SB page 35)

1 ⊕ 1.62

- Explain that some English verbs are often used in conjunction with other words, producing verb phrases. Check that the students understand the meaning of all the verbs in this exercise, then ask them to match them with the words that they go with. Allow them to work in pairs or compare their results with a partner.

- Play the recording for the students to check their answers. Then play it a second time for them to repeat the sentences.

a) live	b) have	c) work
d) like	e) speak	f) eat

2

Go through the phrases in the box. Then ask students to write sentences using the words from Exercise 1 and the phrases from the box. Allow them to work in pairs. Go round, monitoring and giving help, then check answers by asking students to read out their sentences.

I eat / like healthy food.
I live in a new apartment.
I like my job.
I work outside.
I speak Spanish.
I have two children.

3

Ask the students to work individually to write six sentences about themselves. They should use the verbs from Exercise 1.

If your students need further practice, you could use Photocopiable Worksheet *5 Grammar* here.

Grammar (SB page 35)

Present simple: *I, you, we, they*

1 ⊕ 1.63

- Focus the students' attention on the information about the present simple of the verb *speak* in the margin. Point out the affirmative and negative forms, the question form and the short answers. Remind them that affirmative short answer is *Yes, I do*, not ~~Yes, I speak~~.

- Ask them to complete the short answers in the exercise. Play the recording for them to check their answers. Play it a second time for them to repeat.

> a) 'Do you speak Chinese?'
>   'Yes, I do.' 'No, I don't.'
> b) 'Do you smoke?'
>   'Yes, I do.' 'No, I don't.'
> c) 'Do you and your family live in a city?'
>   'Yes, we do.' 'No, we don't.'
> d) 'Do your friends like football?'
>   'Yes, they do.' 'No, they don't.'
> e) 'Do you eat meat?'
>   'Yes, I do.' 'No, I don't.'
> f) 'Do your parents have a dog?'
>   'Yes, they do.' 'No, they don't.'

2

Put the students in pairs and ask them to take turns asking and answering the questions about themselves.

Extra activity

To give further practice of *do* questions, ask the students to make new questions using the vocabulary in Vocabulary Exercise 1 on page 35.

3 🌐 **1.64**

- Go through the example with the class, then ask the students to put the words in the correct order in the other questions.
- Play the recording for them to check their answers, then play it a second time for them to repeat.

> a) Where do you live?
> b) Where do you work?
> c) What languages do you speak?
> d) What food do you like?
> e) What music do you like?
> f) What sports do you like?

4

Ask the students to work in pairs and to take turns asking and answering the questions. Ask them to report back to the class on what their partner said.

Language note

Grammar: *Wh* questions

- Notice that the grammar section is limited to questions beginning with *Where* and *What* with *do you*. This pattern or word order is fundamental to question forms in English, but this is the first time the students are exposed to it. It's a good idea to draw a table on the board emphasising the word order:

Where		live/work?
What (food)	do you	like?
What (language)		speak?

5 *Grammar Extra* **5**

Ask the students to turn to *Grammar Extra* 5 on page 128 of the Student's Book. Here they'll find an explanation of the grammar they've been studying and further exercises to practise it.

> 1 a) I don't speak Polish.
>   b) I don't smoke.
>   c) I don't drink beer.
>   d) I don't have a car.
>   e) I don't live with my parents.
>   f) I don't work for my father.
>   g) I don't eat meat.
>   h) I don't like English music.
> 3 a) Where do kangaroos live?
>   b) What do penguins eat?
>   c) Where do US Presidents live?
>   d) What language do Brazilians speak?
>   e) What TV programmes do you watch?
>   f) Where do you study English?
> 4 a) Australia.
>   b) Fish.
>   c) In the White House in Washington, D.C.
>   d) Portuguese.

Vocabulary (SB page 36)

1 🌐 **1.65**

- Give the students time to look at the photographs and identify the jobs pictured. Then go through the sentences about jobs in the box. Point out the use of the indefinite article with jobs. Ask the students to match them with the photos.
- Play the recording for them to check their answers. Then play it a second time for them to repeat.

> a) She's a lawyer.
> b) He's a taxi driver.
> c) He's a football player.
> d) He's a pilot.
> e) He's an artist.
> f) She's a musician.

2 🌐 **1.66**

- Ask the students to look at the photos as they listen to the recording, and to repeat the sentences after the speakers. Focus their attention on the underlining, which tells them which syllables are stressed. Encourage them to pronounce journalist /ˈdʒɜːnəlɪst/ correctly.

3 🌐 **1.67**

- Go through the sentences with the class and focus their attention on the words in bold. Point out that you use *in* with places and *for* with company names.

- Ask the students to match the sentences with the jobs in Exercise 2.
- Play the recording for them to check their answers, then play it a second time for them to repeat the sentences.

a) A doctor.	d) A flight attendant.
b) A secretary.	e) A journalist.
c) A shop assistant.	f) A farmer.

Extra activity

If your students have jobs, find out what they are and if they know the English words for them.

4 Pairwork

- The pairwork exercise for this unit is on pages 117 and 122. Put the students in pairs and tell them who will be Student A, and who will be Student B.
- While they're doing the exercise, go round monitoring and giving help. Take note of any errors which may need focusing on later, and also any examples of good language use which you can praise. Check answers with the class.

Example answers:

Student A
a) I'm a shop assistant. I work in a shop.
b) I'm a journalist. I interview people.
c) I'm a football player. I play football for England.
Student B
a) I'm a doctor. I work in a hospital.
b) I'm a farmer. I work outside.
c) I'm a taxi driver. I drive taxis.

If your students need further practice, you could use Photocopiable Worksheet 5 *Vocabulary* here.

Pronunciation (SB page 37)

Several of the pronunciation sections in the book are based on chants. The rhythmic nature of these chants help the students to get their tongues around the new sounds in a fun and memorable way.

1 🌐 1.68

- This exercise focuses on the pronunciation of a variety of *Wh* questions. Point out that the underlining shows the students which syllables and/or words are stressed.
- Play the recording. The first time, ask the students just to listen and notice the words that the speakers stress. Then play it again and ask them to repeat the questions, copying the speakers' stress patterns.
- Go round the class, asking individual students to read out some of the questions. Check that they are stressing the correct words and syllables.

Language notes

Pronunciation: sentence stress

- English is a stress-timed, rather than a syllable-timed, language. This means that the time it takes to say a sentence depends on the number of stressed syllables, not the number of syllables itself.
- This explains why students often think that native speakers of English speak very quickly, or swallow some of their words. It's true! The syllables that aren't stressed are shortened, and the schwa sound /ə/ is very common. For example, in the question *Where do you live?* the unstressed words '*do you*' are pronounced /djə/ – they more or less disappear.
- It may be worth explaining that the words that are stressed are 'content' words or 'key' words of a sentence. They carry the meaning. The words that aren't stressed are 'structure' words. If you take out 'structure' words, you'll probably still understand the meaning of the sentence.
- In *Inside Out*, work on word and sentence stress is given high priority in pronunciation sections. Here in unit 5, students practice *Wh* questions in the form of chants. These chants are designed to help students to notice the 'music' of the language and, of course, to give them a bit of fun. Students should be encouraged to exaggerate the stress patterns.
- For further work on sentence stress, use the tapescripts in the back of the student's book and ask students to underline stressed words as they listen.
- Also, encourage students to underline stressed syllables when writing down new vocabulary.

2

Ask the students to work individually to write two more *Wh* questions. Then ask them to mingle and ask their questions to several different students around the class. Ask them to note the answers they get so that they can report back to the class.

Listening (SB page 37)

1 🌐 1.69

- Explain the difference between a real job (the job you actually do) and a dream job (the job you'd ideally like to do). Focus the students' attention on the photos and explain that these five people were asked what their real jobs are and what their dream jobs are. The students will listen to interviews and put the number of the person next to their real job and their dream job.
- Play the first interview and point out that this one has been done for them. The interviewee is a teacher whose dream job is a musician.

- Play the recording, pausing after each interview for the students to make their choices and put the numbers in the boxes.
- Check answers with the class, then play the recording again. Point out that only one of the interviewees is actually doing his dream job (the actor).

1 teacher – musician
2 lawyer – football player
3 taxi driver – pilot
4 student – DJ
5 actor – actor

🌐 **1.69** (I: Interviewer; M = Man; W = Woman)

1
I: Excuse me. What do you do?
W: I'm a teacher.
I: What's your dream job?
W: Oh, um, musician.
I: Thank you.

2
I: Excuse me. What do you do?
M: I'm a lawyer.
I: And what's your dream job?
M: My dream job? Football player.
I: Thank you.

3
I: Excuse me. What do you do?
M: I'm a taxi driver.
I: What's your dream job?
M: Em, pilot. Yes, pilot.
I: Thank you.

4
I: Excuse me. What do you do?
W: I'm a student.
I: What's your dream job?
W: Oh, I don't know. Em, doctor. No, DJ. No, doctor.
I: Doctor?
W: No, DJ.
I: DJ?
W: Yes, DJ.
I: Thank you.

5
I: Excuse me. What do you do?
W: I'm an actor.
I: What's your dream job?
W: My dream job? Actor!
I: Thank you.

Language note

Vocabulary: *DJ*

A *DJ* /ˈdiːdʒeɪ/ is the abbreviation for *disc jockey*, who is a person who plays music on the radio or in clubs. It's more common to say *DJ* and not *disc jockey*.

2 🌐 **1.70**

See if the students can complete these questions without listening to the recording again. Then play it for them to check their answers and repeat the two questions.

a) What do you do?
b) What's your dream job?

Speaking (SB page 37)

Remind the students of the two questions from the last section which they'll need to find out people's jobs and their dream jobs. Then ask them to mingle and ask three different people what their real jobs and dream jobs are. Tell them to take a note of the people they asked and their answers.

Extra activity

Pairwork. Put the students in pairs and ask them to tell each other about the people they spoke to.

If your students need further practice, you could use Photocopiable Worksheet *5 Communication* here.

Useful phrases (SB page 38)

1 🌐 **1.71**

- Give the students a minute or so to have a good look at the illustrations so they can see what is happening in each one. Then play the recording and ask them to listen to and read the two conversations.
- Ask the students to decide which conversation goes with each picture. When you check answers, ask the students to say what helped them decide. They may simply say that it was the sex of the person making the phone call that gave it away. However, they may also say that the first conversation is more formal. It's an office setting (*British Airways*), the initial greeting is *Good morning* rather than *Hello*, the receptionist is more polite (he says *please*) and both speakers refer to Mr Jones, giving his name and title. The conversation ends with *Thank you* and *Goodbye*. The second conversation is more informal. It's in a home setting, the initial greeting is the informal *Hello*, Janet is referred to by her first name, the person answering the phone doesn't say *please* when she asks the caller to hold, and at the end she says *Thanks* and *Bye*.

a) 1   b) 2

2 🌐 **1.72**

Go through the useful phrases with the class, then play the recording and ask them to repeat after the speakers.

3

- Pairwork. Go through the two situations with the class and tell them that the first one is less formal than the second one. Remind the students that you use slightly more formal language in a business setting than you do when talking to friends. Establish that they should base conversation a) on conversation 2 in Exercise 1, and conversation b) on conversation 1 in Exercise 1.

- Go round, monitoring and giving help as the students write their conversations. Then ask them to practise them in pairs. Go round helping with any pronunciation problems. Take note of a few good pairs who can be asked to perform their conversations for the class.

Vocabulary *Extra* (SB page 39)

Jobs

1

- Focus the students' attention on the list of words and point out that they're all to do with the jobs. Remind the students that the underlining indicates the syllable of the word that has the strongest stress. Check that the students can pronounce all of the words correctly.

- Ask the students to look at the pictures and match each one with one of the jobs. Point out that the first one has been done for them.

3	an actor	4	a lawyer
14	an artist	13	a musician
7	a DJ	15	a pilot
12	a doctor	5	a secretary
1	a farmer	6	a shop assistant
9	a flight attendant	11	a taxi driver
8	a football player	10	a teacher
2	a journalist		

2

Pairwork. Demonstrate the activity with a confident student. Point to one of the pictures and ask *What does he do?* Elicit the answer. Then put the students into pairs to continue the activity. Go round, checking that everyone is pronouncing the words correctly.

Writing

Workbook page 23

Preparing a draft, correcting mistakes and writing a final version

Photocopiable resource materials

Grammar: *Have, live, speak, work* (Teacher's notes page 126. Worksheet page 157.)

Vocabulary: *What's the job?* (Teacher's notes page 126. Worksheet page 158.)

Communication: *Knowing you* (Teacher's notes page 127. Worksheet page 159.)

Test CD

See *Test Unit 5* on the CD.

🌑 **CD-ROM**

For more activities go to Unit 5: *Life*.

For the best activities for beginner students, see pages xvi–xxi

For practical methodology, from *Classroom interaction* to *Writing*, see pages xxii–xxxv

What can your students do now? See self-evaluation checklists on pages xxxvi–xlvi

6 24/7 Overview

Section	Aims	What the students are doing
🌐 Listening SB page 40	*Listening skills*: listening for specific information	• Completing a map of international time zones. • Completing a table with times.
🌐 Grammar SB page 41	*Grammar*: telling the time	• Completing a diagram and a table with times. • Answering questions about times in different time zones.
🌐 Vocabulary SB page 41	*Vocabulary*: the days of the week	• Listening to and repeating the days of the week. • Practising saying the days of the week.
🌐 Vocabulary SB page 42	*Vocabulary*: daily routines	• Listening to and repeating verb phrases for daily routines. • Asking questions about daily routines.
🌐 Reading SB page 42	*Reading skills*: reading for main ideas	• Answering questions about a text on a DJ's day. • Completing the text with the correct verbs. • Marking sentences true or false.
🌐 Grammar SB page 43	*Grammar*: present simple – *he, she, it*	• Completing questions and answers. • Asking and answering questions.
🌐 Pronunciation SB page 43	*Pronunciation*: verbs that have an extra syllable with *he/she/it* present simple	• Listening to and repeating verbs. • Adding verbs to a table.
🌐 Useful phrases SB page 44	*Vocabulary*: phrases which are useful when greeting people	• Listening to phone conversations, answering questions and practising the conversation. • Completing a diagram. • Listening to and repeating useful phrases for saying *Hello* and *Goodbye*. Completing and practising a conversation.
Vocabulary *Extra* SB page 45	*Vocabulary*: revision of words from the unit: the day; daily routine	• Matching pictures with words.
Writing WB page 27	Building a description of a daily routine from notes	

Warm-up

Draw a big analogue clock on the board and teach *one o'clock, two o'clock*, etc. Then call out various times with *o'clock* (avoiding *ten past, a quarter past, half past*, etc. at this stage), and invite individual students to come to the board and draw the hands of the clock in the correct place.

Listening (SB page 40)

1 🌐 **1.73**

• Give the students a couple of minutes to study the map. Focus their attention on the explanation of a.m. and p.m. Point out that *midday* means 12.00 p.m. and teach *midnight* (12.00 a.m.). Ask various students to read out the names of the cities that are labelled. Remind them that the underlining is there to help them get the correct stress.

• Play the recording and ask the students to complete the map with the correct times for the different cities. Allow them to compare their answers in pairs before checking answers with the class, and playing the recording once more for a final check. Encourage them to use a.m. and p.m. correctly.

---

a) San Francisco: 4.00 a.m.
b) Buenos Aires: 9.00 a.m.
c) London: 12.00 p.m.
d) Moscow: 3.00 p.m.
e) Hong Kong: 8.00 p.m.
f) Wellington: 12.00 a.m.

🌐 **1.73**

a) 'What time is it in San <u>Fran</u>cisco?'
   'It's <u>four o'clock in the morning</u>.'

b) 'What time is it in <u>Buenos Aires</u>?'
   'It's <u>nine o'clock in the morning</u>.'

c) 'What time is it in <u>London</u>?'
   'It's midday, <u>twelve p.m.</u>'

d) 'What time is it in <u>Moscow</u>?'
   'It's <u>three o'clock in the afternoon</u>.'

e) 'What time is it in <u>Hong Kong</u>?'
   'It's <u>eight o'clock in the evening</u>.'

f) 'What time is it in <u>Wellington</u>?'
   'It's midnight, <u>twelve a.m.</u>'

Language notes

Vocabulary: the 24-hour clock

• The 24-hour clock isn't widely used in Britain, except for talking about travel times.

• It's quite acceptable to say that you're catching a plane at *14.30* (pronounced as *fourteen thirty*), but you'd arrange a meeting with a friend for that same time at *two thirty* or *half past two*.

2 🌐 **1.74**

• Remind the students of the meaning of a.m. and p.m. and explain that you can say *in the morning* instead of a.m., and *in the afternoon* or *in the evening* instead of p.m. (When *afternoon* changes to *evening* is very much a matter of personal usage, but generally around five or six o'clock most people start to use *evening*.)

• Go through the example with the class and then ask them to complete the table.

• Play the recording for them to check their answers, then play it a second time for them to repeat the times after the speaker.

---

a) It's four o'clock in the morning.
b) It's nine o'clock in the morning.
c) 12.00 p.m.
d) It's three o'clock in the afternoon.
e) It's eight o'clock in the evening.
f) 12.00 a.m.

---

3 🌐 **1.75**

Focus the students' attention back on the map and ask them to look at the other cities which are marked on it. Play the recording for them to repeat the names of these cities. Encourage them to copy the speakers' pronunciation. Ask for individual repetition of the names of the cities afterwards.

🌐 **1.75**

Mexico <u>Ci</u>ty
New <u>York</u>
Bra<u>si</u>lia
<u>Ven</u>ice
Jo<u>han</u>nesburg
<u>Bang</u>kok
<u>To</u>kyo
<u>Syd</u>ney

Grammar (SB page 41)

The time

1 🔘 **1.76**

- Focus the students' attention on the information in the margin. Point out the question and the use of *past* as in *half past,* and *to* as in *quarter to.* Explain that you can also say *quarter past,* but not half to.

- Ask the students to look at the clock. Ask them to work in pairs to complete the times. Go round, monitoring and giving help if necessary.

- Play the recording for them to check their answers. Then play it again for them to repeat the times.

> f) It's twenty-five past.
> i) It's twenty to.
> j) It's quarter to.
> l) It's five to.

2 🔘 **1.77**

- Focus the students' attention on the illustrations of clock displays and point out that these are digital rather than analogue clocks as in Exercise 1. Explain that there's another way to talk about times without using *past* or *to.* Go through a) and b) with the class, explaining that *two thirty* and *half past two* are both ways of saying the same thing; the same with *seven fifty* and *ten to eight.*

- Ask the students to work in pairs to complete the times. Allow them to compare their answers with another pair before playing the recording for them to check. Focus their attention on the first time in e): *five-oh-five.*

- Play the recording a second time for the students to repeat all the times.

> a) It's half past two.
> b) It's seven fifty.
> c) It's three thirty-five.
> d) It's quarter past ten.
> e) It's five past five.
> f) It's twelve forty-five.

3

Pairwork. The students take turns to say a time with their partner, saying the same time in a different way. Go through the examples in the speech bubbles first so that the students are clear what they have to do.

4

- Refer the students back to the time zone map on page 40. Read through the questions with the class, then ask them to work individually or in pairs to work out the answers.

- Check with the class before asking them to make up similar questions to ask a partner.

> a) 1.30 a.m.   b) 11.40 p.m.   c) 9.10 a.m.

Vocabulary (SB page 41)

Days of the week

1 🔘 **1.78**

Focus the students' attention on the days of the week in the margin. Play the recording and ask them to repeat the names of the days after the speaker. Point out the pronunciation of Wednesday /ˈwenzdeɪ/ and make sure that the students don't try to pronounce the *d* in the middle.

2

Pairwork. Ask the students to try to do this as quickly as possible. See who can provide the following three days the fastest. As they do this, go round, checking that they're pronouncing all the days correctly.

Vocabulary (SB page 42)

1 🌐 **1.79**

Focus students' attention on the pictures. Tell them that the illustrations show the kinds of things people do every day: their daily routine. Give the students time to identify the different actions and read the captions. Then play the recording and ask them to listen and repeat the verb phrases.

2

Pairwork. In pairs, the students take turns asking and answering questions about what time they do certain things. Go through the example in the speech bubbles with the class first, and point out that the questioner asks not only about the time of day, but also the day of the week. Encourage the student to do the same when they formulate their questions. If your students need extra support, elicit a few of the questions they'll need to ask about the actions in Exercise 1 before they start the activity.

If your students need further practice, you could use Photocopiable Worksheet 6 *Vocabulary* here.

Reading (SB page 42)

1 🌐 **1.80**

Ask the students to look at the photo and then read and listen to the text about DJ Judge Jules, ignoring the gaps for now. Play the recording. Ask the students to answer the questions. Check answers with the class.

> a) He works in a recording studio and in clubs.
> b) Gatecrasher in Liverpool.

Cultural note

Judge Jules (born 1965)
Judge Jules (real name Jules O'Riordan) is a DJ who works on the radio and around clubs in the UK, and on holiday islands such as Ibiza, Corfu, Cos and Cyprus. For more information go to www.judgejules.net

2

Point out that the verbs that complete the text are *get, go* and *have*. Ask the students to decide which one to put in which gap. Play the recording again for them to check their answers.

On weekends			
1 get	2 go	3 have	4 go
On Saturdays			
5 go	6 go	7 have	
On Sundays			
8 get	9 have	10 have	

3

Ask the students to go back over the text to find out if the sentences are true or false. Check answers with the class and ask them to correct the false sentences.

> a) True.
> b) True.
> c) False. (He goes to work in a recording studio.)
> d) False. (On Saturdays he goes to work in the evening. He works all night in a club.)
> e) True.
> f) True.

If your students need further practice, you could use Photocopiable Worksheet 6 *Communication* here.

Grammar (SB page 43)

Present simple: he, she, it

1 🌐 **1.81**

- Focus the students' attention on the information in the margin about the use of the present simple with *he, she* and *it*.
- Read the question and answers in a) with the class, and then ask the students to complete the other questions and answers.
- Play the recording for them to check their answers, then play it a second time for them to repeat after the speakers.

> a) 'Does he go to the gym on weekdays?'
>   'Yes, he does.' 'No, he doesn't.'
> b) 'Does he have children?'
>   'Yes, he does.' 'No, he doesn't.'
> c) 'Does he go to bed in the evening on Saturdays?'
>   'Yes, he does.' 'No, he doesn't.'
> d) 'Does he work in clubs all round the world?'
>   'Yes, he does.' 'No, he doesn't.'
> e) 'Does he like his job?'
>   'Yes, he does.' 'No, he doesn't.'
> f) 'Does he get home in the evening on Sundays?'
>   'Yes, he does.' 'No, he doesn't.'

Language notes

Grammar: third person s

- Studies of native speakers show that the third person *s* is one of the last items of language to be assimilated correctly by some young native speaker learners.
- Some of your students may need a great deal of practice before they can produce this form without error.
- Note that the omission of the third person 's' rarely leads to a breakdown of communication.

2

Pairwork. The students take turns to ask and answer the questions in Exercise 1, basing their answers on the information about Judge Jules in the text on page 42.

> a) Yes, he does.
> b) Yes, he does.
> c) No, he doesn't. (He goes to bed in the afternoon.)
> d) Yes, he does.
> e) Yes, he does.
> f) No, he doesn't. (He gets home in the morning.)

3 _Grammar Extra_ 6

Ask the students to turn to _Grammar Extra_ 6 on page 128 of the Student's Book. Here they'll find an explanation of the grammar they've been studying and further exercises to practise it.

> 1
> a) does   b) finishes   c) gets   d) goes
> e) has   f) likes   g) studies   h) watches
> 2
> a) Do   b) Does   c) Does   d) Do
> e) Does   f) Do
> 4
> 'I <u>get up</u> at 4.30 a.m. I <u>go</u> to work at 5.30 a.m. and I <u>finish</u> work at about 1.00 p.m. I <u>get</u> home at 2.00 p.m. and <u>have</u> lunch at 3.00 p.m. I <u>go</u> to the gym in the afternoon. I <u>have</u> dinner at 7.00 p.m. and I <u>go</u> to bed at about 9.30 p.m.'

4 Pairwork

- The pairwork exercise for this unit is on pages 117 and 122 of the Student's Book. Put the students in pairs and tell them who will be Student A, and who will be Student B.

- While they're doing the exercise, go round monitoring and giving help. Take note of any errors which may need focusing on later, and also any examples of good language use which you can praise.

> **Student A: Questions**
> a) Do you get up early?
> b) Do you work in an office?
> c) Do you have lunch in a restaurant?
> d) Do you finish work at 5.00 p.m.?
> e) Do you go shopping on Saturdays?
> f) Do you like Sundays?
>
> **Student B: Questions**
> a) Do you get up at 7.00 a.m.?
> b) Do you work outside?
> c) Do you have lunch at home?
> d) Do you finish work at 7.00 p.m.?
> e) Do you go to the gym on Saturdays?
> f) Do you like Mondays?

If your students need further practice, you could use Photocopiable Worksheet _6 Grammar_ here.

Pronunciation (SB page 43)

1 🌐 1.82

- Focus the students' attention on the table and point out the difference between the verbs in the first column and those in the second. Play the recording and ask the students just to listen to the pronunciation of the verbs. Ask them to notice the extra syllable in the verbs in column B.

- Play the recording a second time for the students to repeat. Encourage them to pronounce the extra syllable in the column B verbs.

2 🌐 1.83

- Before you play the recording, ask the students, in pairs, to read the verbs in the box aloud, and try to decide which column of the table in Exercise 1 they should go in.

- Play the recording for them to listen and repeat. Ask them to add the verbs to the correct place in the table. Check answers with the class.

> | A | B |
> |---|---|
> | like – likes | teach – teaches |
> | read – reads | watch – watches |
> | take – takes | |
> | work – works | |

Useful phrases (SB page 44)

1 🌐 1.84

Focus the students' attention on the illustration for a few moments before you tell them what's happening: someone has made an international phone call, forgetting that the person he's calling is in a different time zone. Play the recording and ask the students to read the conversation as they listen. Then elicit the answers to the questions.

> a) It's 8.30 a.m. in New York.
> b) It's 11.30 p.m. in Sydney.

2 🌐 1.85

- Ask the students why they think Mr Edwards responds to John's _Good evening_ with _Goodnight_ in the recording in Exercise 1. (He's ending the phone call – _Goodnight_ is a way of saying _Goodbye_ – and emphasising the fact that it's night time, and too late for John to be calling him.)

- Ask the students to complete the diagram and then explain that you can say _Good morning_, _Good afternoon_ or _Good evening_ at the beginning of a conversation to mean the same as _Hello_, but that _Goodnight_ always means _Goodbye_.

- Play the recording for the students to listen and repeat the phrases.

a) Hello.	b) Goodbye.

3

Pairwork. Focus students' attention on the illustration, and ask them to write a similar telephone conversation using the conversation in Exercise 1 as a model. Go round, monitoring and giving help where necessary. When they've finished, ask them to practise their conversation, taking turns to be Mrs Harper and Jenny. Take note of a few good conversations to be performed for the class.

Vocabulary *Extra* (SB page 45)

The day

- Focus the students' attention on the list of words and point out that they're all to do with the times of day. Remind the students that the underlining indicates the syllable of the word that has the strongest stress. Check that the students can pronounce all of the words correctly.

- Ask the students to look at the pictures and match each one with one of the times of day. Point out that the first one has been done for them.

3	morning	1	evening
6	midday	2	midnight
4	afternoon	5	night

Daily routine

1

- Focus the students' attention on the list of words and point out that they're all to do with the daily routines. Remind the students that the underlining indicates the syllable of the word that has the strongest stress. Check that the students can pronounce all of the words correctly.

- Ask the students to look at the pictures and match each one with one of the words. Point out that the first one has been done for them.

9	finish work	4	have a shower
7	get home	8	relax
5	get up	1	study
3	go to bed	6	watch TV
2	go to work		

2

Ask the students to look at the table and to work individually to put the items from Exercise 1 in the right columns for them. Allow them to compare results in pairs or small groups to see whether any of their answers are different. They can then report back to the class.

Writing

Workbook page 27

Building a description of a daily routine from notes

Photocopiable resource materials

Grammar: *The same time* (Teacher's notes page 127. Worksheet page 160.)

Vocabulary: *Time of day* (Teacher's notes page 128. Worksheet page 161.)

Communication: *A day in a job* (Teacher's notes page 128. Worksheet page 162.)

Test CD

See *Test Unit 6* on the CD.

DVD

Programme 3: *My life*

CD-ROM

For more activities go to Unit 6: 24/7.

For the best activities for beginner students, see pages xvi–xxi

For practical methodology, from *Classroom interaction* to *Writing*, see pages xxii–xxxv

What can your students do now? See self-evaluation checklists on pages xxxvi–xlvi

Review B *Teacher's notes*

These exercises act as a check of the grammar and vocabulary that the students have learnt in Units 4, 5 and 6 of the Student's Book. Use them to find any problems that students are having, or anything that they haven't understood and which will need further work.

Grammar (SB page 46)

Remind the students of the grammar explanations they read and the exercises they did in the *Grammar Extra* on pages 128 and 129 of the Student's Book.

1

This exercise reviews the use of *I like* and *I don't like* for personal preferences. When you've checked answers, ask the student to tick the sentences that are true for them and compare with a partner.

> a) I don't like big cities.
> b) I like old films.
> c) I don't like small dogs.
> d) I like expensive pens.
> e) I don't like cheap wine.
> f) I like black coffee.

2

The students questions should be based on the sentences in Exercise 1. Check answers and then put the students in pairs to ask and answer the questions.

> a) 'Do you like big cities?'
>   'Yes, I do.' / 'No, I don't.'
> b) 'Do you like old films?'
>   'Yes, I do.' / 'No, I don't.'
> c) 'Do you like small dogs?'
>   'Yes, I do.' / 'No, I don't.'
> d) 'Do you like expensive pens?'
>   'Yes, I do.' / 'No, I don't.'
> e) 'Do you like cheap wine?'
>   'Yes, I do.' / 'No, I don't.'
> f) 'Do you like black coffee?'
>   'Yes, I do.' / 'No, I don't.'

3

Remind the students of the *Wh* questions they studied in Unit 5. Ask them to complete the questions and check their answers before they ask and answer them in pairs.

> a) Where   b) What   c) Where   d) What
> e) Who   f) What

4

Focus the students' attention on the example and remind them of the two ways of saying the time that they practised in Unit 6. If necessary, refer them back to page 41.

> a) 6   b) 5   c) 2   d) 1   e) 3   f) 4

5

Remind the students of the verbs for daily routines that they studied in Unit 6.

> 1 works   2 gets   3 has   4 goes
> 5 has   6 works   7 has   8 finishes
> 9 gets   10 goes

6

If the students get any of these wrong, refer them back to the relevant sections of the units.

> 1 a) 'Do you like pizza?' 'Yes, I like.'
> 2 b) I like films Spanish.
> 3 a) We no speak Chinese.
> 4 a) It's fifteen past one.
> 5 b) Does she likes music?
> 6 b) My mum get up at 6 a.m.

Vocabulary (SB page 47)

1

When the students have chosen their 'odd words out', ask them to explain their choices if they can.

> a) swimming (the others are types of food)
> b) meat (the others are sports)
> c) wine (the others are food items)
> d) fruit (the others are drinks)
> e) tea (the other are dishes)

2 and 3

Remind the students that they studied colour words in Unit 4. If necessary, refer them to the margin illustration on page 30 of the Student's Book.

Black and white are the two colours in 9.

4

When the students have completed the statements, they should compare them with a partner.

a) I (don't) eat meat.
b) I (don't) like jazz.
c) I (don't) have a sister.
d) I (don't) work for a company.
e) I (don't) live with my parents.
f) I (don't) speak Italian.

5

All these jobs were taught in Unit 5, page 36.

a) taxi driver   b) doctor   c) lawyer
d) artist   e) journalist   f) flight attendant

6

When the students have completed the questions, ask them to work in pairs and take turns asking and answering them.

a) get up
b) have a shower
c) go to work
d) have lunch
e) get home
f) go to bed

If your students need further practice, you could use Photocopiable Worksheet *Review B* here.

Pronunciation (SB page 47)

1

Remind the students of the use of large and small stress boxes to help them get their intonation right. Ask individual students to read out the words in the four columns of the table and make sure that they're using the correct stress. Then ask them to add the words from the box to the table. Encourage them to say each word aloud as they do the exercise so that they can get a feeling of what sounds right.

2 ⊕ 1.86

Ask the students to underline the stressed syllables. They needn't underline anything in the one-syllable words. When they've finished, play the recording for them to check their answers. Then play it a second time for them to repeat the words.

1 and 2
A: France, gets, smokes
B: <u>taxi</u>, <u>watches</u>, <u>Wednesday</u>
C: Bra<u>zil</u>, Ma<u>drid</u>, o'<u>clock</u>
D: ex<u>pen</u>sive, mu<u>sic</u>ian, re<u>lax</u>es

Reading & Listening (SB page 48)

1 ⊕ 1.87

Ask the students to read the text as they listen to the recording. Then ask them to underline the correct information. Check answers with the class.

a) 1   b) 3   c) 3   d) 2   e) 1

Cultural note

Dan Hovey (born 1958)
Dan Hovey is considered one of the best jazz guitarists in New York. He's toured extensively in the US and performs in clubs in New York with his own group.

2 ⊕ 1.88

The conversation isn't printed on the page, so the students will have to listen carefully to get the information they need. You may need to play the recording several times.

a) True.
b) True.
c) False. It's three o'clock in the afternoon in London. It's ten o'clock in the morning in New York.
d) True.
e) False. She's Italian.
f) True.

1.88 (P = Paula; D = Dan)

P: *Hello? Is that Dan Hovey?*
D: *Yes. Who is this?*
P: *Hi, I'm Paula Fox. <u>I work for 'Blue Jazz' music magazine in London</u>.*
D: *Oh. OK. What time is it in London, Paula?*
P: *Er, it's three o'clock in the afternoon.*
D: *Well, Paula <u>it's ten o'clock in the morning here</u>.*
P: *Oh … er, sorry, Dan. Look, can I ask you some questions for the magazine?*
D: *Er, yes, OK.*
P: *Where do you live?*
D: *Here, in New York.*
P: *OK. And where do you <u>work</u>?*
D: *<u>In a jazz club – 'The Night Life'</u>.*
P: *OK. What <u>languages</u> do you speak?*
D: *Er, <u>English, and Italian</u>. <u>My wife's Italian</u>, you see.*
P: *Oh. And who's your <u>favourite musician</u>?*
D: *<u>Chet Baker</u>.*
P: *Oh, could you spell that, please?*
D: *C-H-E-T, B-A-K-E-R.*
P: *Uh huh. And what's your <u>favourite colour</u>?*
D: *Er, um … <u>red</u>.*
P: *What's your <u>favourite city</u>? <u>Do you like London</u>?*
D: *Er, <u>yes, I do</u>. But <u>I love New York</u>!*
P: *Oh. And what's your <u>favourite food</u>?*
D: *<u>Steak</u>.*
P: *OK. And finally, what time do you get up?*
D: *11.30.*
P: *Oh, yes, sorry! Thank you, Dan. Goodbye.*
D: *Goodbye, Paula.*

3

Go through the information with the class before you play the recording again so that they know what information they're listening for.

Name: Dan Hovey
Lives: in New York
Works: in a jazz club (*The Night Life*)
Speaks: English and Italian
Favourite musician: Chet Baker
Favourite colour: red
Favourite city: New York
Favourite food: steak

Writing & Speaking (SB page 49)

1

Go through the examples and the gapped rules with the class. Make sure everyone understands the meaning of the plus and minus signs (affirmative and negative statements). Check answers with the class.

a) + / + I play my guitar and I listen to music.
   – / – I don't like coffee and I don't like tea.
b) + / – I like cats but I don't like dogs.
   – / + I don't like classical music but I love jazz.

2

Do the first item as an example with the whole class and then ask the students to do the others. Go round, monitoring and giving help where necessary. Check answers with the class.

a) but   b) and   c) and   d) but   e) and
f) but

3

Go through the example with the whole class to make sure everyone understands what they have to do. As the students do the exercise, go round, monitoring and giving help where necessary. Check answers with the whole class.

a) I watch TV and I relax.
b) I like tea but I don't like coffee.
c) I have one sister and I have one brother.
d) I speak English and I speak Chinese.
e) I don't have a dog but I have a cat.
f) I play the piano and I play the guitar.

4

This is a guided writing exercise. The students can use the text about Dan Hovey on page 48 of the Student's Book as a model. Give help where necessary.

5

Ask the students to look at the form first so that they know what information about their partners they'll have to get. This will help them formulate the correct questions. If your students need extra help, go through the questions they'll need to ask for each piece of information required on the form first with them.

6

This could be set for homework. If you do it in class, go round, giving help where necessary. You could display the Star profiles on the wall of the classroom for other students to read, or select a few to be read out in class.

Photocopiable resource material

Review B: Song – *Friday, I'm In Love* (Teacher's notes page 129. Worksheet page 163.)

Test CD

See *Test Review B* on the CD.

For the best activities for beginner students, see pages xvi–xxi

For practical methodology, from *Classroom interaction* to *Writing*, see pages xxii–xxxv

What can your students do now? See self-evaluation checklists on pages xxxvi–xlvi

7 NYC *Overview*

Section	Aims	What the students are doing
⊕ Vocabulary **SB page 50**	*Vocabulary*: places and features of cities	• Matching photos with places in New York City. • Listening to and repeating words to do with places and features of cities. • Listing famous places in students' own city or country.
⊕ Reading **SB page 51**	*Reading skills*: reading for specific information	• Reading what three British people say about living in New York. • Matching people with descriptions. • Completing descriptions with *in* and *near*.
Writing **SB page 51**	*Writing skills*: writing a description	• Writing a description of where students live and work. • Identifying descriptions.
Reading & Writing **SB page 52**	*Reading skills*: reading for detail *Writing skills*: writing sentences	• Choosing one thing to do in New York from a webpage. • Completing sentences about things to do in a city
⊕ Grammar **SB page 52**	*Grammar*: *there is* and *there are*	• Completing information about Central Park. • Writing sentences about home cities.
⊕ Pronunciation **SB page 53**	*Pronunciation*: chants	• Listening to and practising chants using *there is* and *there are*. • Writing and practising new chants with *there is* and *there are*.
⊕ Grammar **SB page 53**	*Grammar*: *Is there?* and *Are there?*	• Completing questions and answers. • Asking and answering questions. • Completing a table.
⊕ Useful phrases **SB page 54**	*Vocabulary*: phrases which are useful when asking about locations	• Matching British and American words. • Listening to two British tourists in New York. • Completing conversations. • Listening to and repeating useful phrases for asking directions. • Writing and practising a conversation with a partner.
Vocabulary *Extra* **SB page 55**	*Vocabulary*: revision of words from the unit: town and country	• Matching places in a picture with words.
Writing **WB page 31**	Linking sentences with *and* and *but* Describing a city	

Quick revision

Remind the students of the abbreviations they looked at when they studied the alphabet in Unit 1. Ask them if they can remember what *NYC* stands for (New York City). Ask them if they know of any other cities that are referred to by their initials. They may be able to name Los Angeles (LA), Washington, DC (DC), and Kuala Lumpur (KL).

Vocabulary (SB page 50)

1 🌐 2.01

- Give the students plenty of time to look at the photos. Allow them to do the matching activity in pairs and to compare results with another pair before you play the recording for them to check their answers.

- Play the recording a second time for them to repeat the names. Encourage them to pronounce the /dʒ/ sound in *bridge* correctly. Point out that the sound at the beginning of *Chrysler* is /k/ rather than /tʃ/. Also highlight the /ɪ/ sound in *building*. When the students have repeated the names chorally, ask for individual repetition to make sure that they're pronouncing them correctly.

> 1 The Chrysler Building
> 2 Grand Central Station
> 3 Central Park
> 4 Times Square
> 5 The Metropolitan Museum
> 6 Brooklyn Bridge
> 7 The Statue of Liberty

Cultural notes

The Chrysler Building
The Chrysler Building was built in 1930 for the Chrysler car company. It's 1,048 feet high and was, until the construction of the Empire State Building, the tallest building in the world. It's still the world's tallest brick building.

Grand Central Station
Grand Central Station is the largest train station in the world. It has 44 platforms serving 67 train tracks. It contains restaurants, fast-food outlets, newsstands, a food market, part of the New York Transit Museum and over forty shops.

Central Park
Central Park is an 843-acre public park in the middle of New York City. It was created in 1853. There are several artificial lakes, two ice-skating rinks, sports areas, as well as several children's playgrounds. It's popular with joggers, cyclists and rollerbladers.

Times Square
Time Square is full of brightly-lit advertising hoardings, theatres, nightclubs and bars.

The Metropolitan Museum of Art
The Metropolitan Museum of Art, situated just off Central Park, is the largest art museum in New York City. It has a huge permanent collection of modern and classical works of art from all over the world, and has special exhibitions throughout the year.

Brooklyn Bridge
Brooklyn Bridge crosses the East River from Brooklyn to Lower Manhattan. It's 2,000 metres in length, and at the time of its completion in 1883, it was the longest suspension bridge in the world.

The Statue of Liberty
The statue was a gift to the people of America from France to commemorate the centennial of the United States. It was completed in Paris in 1884 and stands on Liberty Island, at the mouth of the Hudson River in New York Harbour.

2

Ask the students to work in pairs to draw up a list of famous places that they know of in New York. As a whole-class, find out how many places have been listed. The following are some suggestions of places in New York: Ground Zero, JFK airport, the Guggenheim Museum, Trump Tower, Fifth Avenue, Greenwich Village, Bloomingdales, Tiffany's.

3 🌐 2.02

- Play the recording for the students to repeat the words. Ask for individual pronunciation of the words afterwards to check that the students have the correct pronunciation.

- Ask the students to find examples in the photos. When checking answers, encourage them to use the formula set out in the example speech bubbles (*There's a ... in photo (6).*)

```
a bridge: 6
a building: 1, 2, 3, 4, 5 and 6
a lake: 3
a museum: 5
a park: 3
a river: 6
a square: 4
a station: 2
a statue: 7
a theatre: 4
```

4

Ask the students to work on their own on their lists, as they'll be using the lists for pairwork in the next exercise. Go round, giving help and encouragement.

5

Pairwork. The students take turns to say the name of one of the famous places on their lists. The other student has to say what it is. Go through the examples with the class first, so that they're clear what they have to do.

If your students need further practice, you could use Photocopiable Worksheet 7 *Vocabulary* here.

Reading (SB page 51)

1 🌐 **2.03**

- Focus attention on the photographs of the three people and explain that they're all British people who live in New York City. Point out the lines that show on the map where each of them lives.

- Ask the students to read the descriptions as they listen to the recording. For now, all they have to do is match the descriptions to the people. You may need to play the recording more than once. Check answers with the class.

```
a) 3 (Rick)   b) 2 (Betty)   c) 1 (Emma)
```

Cultural notes

East Village
The East Village lies to the east of Greenwich Village. It has many art galleries and is famous for its music venues. Many important bands and singers started out in the East Village clubs, including Madonna, Blondie, Talking Heads and Patti Smith.

Washington Square Park
The centre and heart of Greenwich Village, Washington Square Park is one of the best-known parks in New York City. It's surrounded by New York University and so is a popular meeting place for students.

Greenwich Village
Greenwich Village is a largely residential neighbourhood on the west side of southern Manhattan. Greenwich Village, known by its inhabitants as 'The Village' is famous for its colourful, artistic residents. The area has lots of restaurants, bars, clubs and theatres.

2

- Remind the students that they studied the prepositions *in* and *near* in Unit 2 (page 13). Point out that text *a* already has the prepositions in place (in bold). Ask them to complete the other two texts.

- Play the recording again for them to check their answers.

```
Description b
1 in   2 near   3 in   4 near   5 in
Description c
1 in   2 in   3 in   4 near   5 in   6 near
```

Writing (SB page 51)

1

Focus the students' attention on the example and explain that they can use the texts in the previous section as a model. Tell them to write their descriptions on a blank sheet of paper and remind them that they mustn't put their names on their texts. Give them plenty of time to write and, as they do so, go round, giving help and encouragement.

2

Collect in the students' descriptions and shuffle them. Then distribute them around the class. Ask the students to read the description they've received, and to try to work out who wrote it. Choose students to read out the texts that they've received, and to say who they think wrote them. The people they name should then say whether or not they're correct.

Reading & Writing (SB page 52)

1

- Focus the students' attention on the webpage and give them plenty of time to familiarise themselves with it. Tell them that it's a webpage advertising things to do in New York City. Ask the students to read the text silently to themselves. Then choose confident students to read sections of it aloud.

- Ask each student to choose the best thing to do in New York. Then put them in pairs or small groups to compare their choices. Then, as a whole class, find out what the top attraction was.

Extra activity

In Vocabulary Exercise 2 on page 50, the students named other famous places in New York. Ask them to write more things to do in New York, following the pattern in the reading text. For example, *Go to the top of the Statue of Liberty. Go down Broadway. Go to the Guggenheim museum.*

Language notes

Vocabulary: *go down/up, go out*

• The verb *go* combines with many particles to form some of the most common phrasal and prepositional verbs. These are so frequently used in English that it's a good idea to start introducing them to students at this early stage.

• *To go down a street* has the idea of going from a higher place to a lower one (Uptown and Downtown in Manhattan get their names because Uptown is on a hill.) If you walk in the opposite direction, you *go up* the street.

• *To go out* here means to spend an evening outside the home with some form of entertainment, for example, at a restaurant, a cinema, or in a bar. You can use it to invite someone to do something with you, for example, *Do you want to go out on Saturday night?*

Cultural notes

Broadway

Broadway is a wide avenue in New York City. One famous stretch near Times Square is known as the Theater District. It's the home of many Broadway theatres, which put on a variety of plays, particularly musicals.

Fifth Avenue

Fifth Avenue, the most expensive street in the world, runs through the centre of central Manhattan. Many famous buildings are on this street, such as the Empire State Building, as well as famous museums such as the Metropolitan Museum of Art and the Guggenheim Museum. It's also a popular shopping area.

The Empire State Building

At 102 storeys high, the Empire State Building was the world's tallest building from 1931 to 1972. Now that the World Trade Center has been destroyed, it's once again the tallest building in New York City.

SoHo

SoHo (SOuth of HOuston Street) is a residential area in Manhatten with a large artistic community, and a large number of restaurants and bars.

2

• Refer the students back to the way the sentences were completed in the text in Exercise 1. Then give them plenty of time to think of ways of completing the sentences for a city in their country. Go round, monitoring and giving help, where necessary.

• When the students have finished, put them in pairs and ask them to compare their results.

Grammar (SB page 52)

there is / there are

1 🌐 2.04

• Point out the information about *there is* and *there are* in the margin, and ask the students to look back at the text on this page and underline all the examples of *there is* and *there are*. Point out that *there is* is used with singular nouns and *there are* with plurals.

• Ask the students to complete the information about Central Park.

• Play the recording for them to check their answers, then play it a second time for them to repeat the sentences.

a) There's	d) There are
b) There are	e) There's
c) There are	f) There are

2

This could be done for homework. If you choose to do it in class, go round while the students are writing and help with any individual problems.

> *Example:*
> There's a school.
> There are some bars.
> There's a café near my house.

If your students need further practice, you could use Photocopiable Worksheet 7 *Communication* here.

Pronunciation (SB page 53)

1 🌐 2.05

• Remind the students of the work they did on linking words in Unit 3, when words that end in a consonant link with words that begin with a vowel. Ask them to practise saying *There's a* and *There are*, linking the two words together each time.

• Tell them that they're going to hear the sentences A and B in a chant. Ask them to listen to the recording and repeat the two chants.

2

Allow the students to work in pairs to write their chants. They should practise saying it aloud in their pairs. Go round and note any particularly good ones which you can ask the students to perform for the class.

Grammar (SB page 53)

Is there? / Are there?

1 ⊕ 2.06

- Focus the students' attention on the question forms *Is there?* and *Are there?* in the margin. Check that they can pronounce these questions correctly by asking three students to read the first question and the two answers aloud, and another three to read the second question and the answers. Encourage them to use correct pronunciation.

- Ask the students to work individually to complete the questions and answers.

- Play the recording for them to check their answers. Then play it a second time for them to listen and repeat.

> a) 'Is there a station near your house?'
>   'Yes, there is.' 'No, there isn't.'
> b) 'Are there any restaurants near your house?'
>   'Yes, there are.' 'No, there aren't.'
> c) 'Is there a museum in your city?'
>   'Yes, there is.' 'No, there isn't.'
> d) 'Is there a park near your house?'
>   'Yes, there is.' 'No, there isn't.'
> e) 'Are there any hotels in your city?'
>   'Yes, there are.' 'No, there aren't.'
> f) 'Is there a church near your house?'
>   'Yes, there is.' 'No, there isn't.'

2

Put the students in pairs and ask them to take turns asking and answering the questions for themselves.

3 Pairwork

- The pairwork exercise for this unit is on pages 118 and 123 of the Student's Book. Put the students in pairs and tell them who will be Student A, and who will be Student B.

- While they're doing the exercise, go round monitoring and giving help. Take note of any errors which may need focusing on later and also any examples of good language use, which you can praise.

Possible answers	Student A's photo	Student B's photo	Similar/ Different?
buildings	✓	✓	Similar
buses	✓	✗	Different
cars	✗	✓	Different
a church	✓	✓	Similar
people	✓	✓	Similar
a river	✓	✗	Different
shops	✗	✗	Different
a square	✗	✓	Different
a statue	✗	✓	Different
a street	✓	✓	Similar

4

Go through the words in the box and check that everyone understands them and can pronounce them correctly. Then ask the students to complete the table. They should do this individually and then compare their completed tables with a partner.

Extra activity

Do a chain memorisation activity based on *There is/are* and the vocabulary in the table of Exercise 4. Write on the board *There's a beach in my city and …*, and encourage a confident student to finish the sentence. Then ask another student to repeat the sentence and add another element.

You will find a full explanation of this technique in the Practical methodology section in the Introduction.

Cultural note

Manhattan

New York City is made up of five boroughs of which Manhattan island is the best known. It's the cultural and financial centre of the city, and most of New York's famous sights and buildings can be found here.

If your students need further practice, you could use Photocopiable Worksheet *7 Grammar* here.

5 *Grammar Extra* 7

Ask the students to turn to *Grammar Extra* 7 on page 130 of the Student's Book. Here they'll find an explanation of the grammar they've been studying and further exercises to practise it.

> 1 a) There are seven days in a week.
>   b) There are twenty-six letters in the English alphabet.
>   c) There are sixty minutes in an hour.
>   d) There are fifty states in the USA.
>   e) There are twenty-four hours in a day.
>   f) There are eleven players in a football team.
>
> 2 a) there are ~~any~~ / some dictionaries.
>   b) there's a / ~~an~~ map of Britain.
>   c) there are ~~any~~ / some Italian students.
>   d) there's ~~a~~ / an old CD player.
>   e) there's a / ~~an~~ computer.
>   f) there are ~~any~~ / some photos.
>
> 3 a) there aren't any dictionaries.
>   b) there isn't a map of Britain.
>   c) there aren't any Italian students.
>   d) there isn't an old CD player.
>   e) there isn't a computer.
>   f) there aren't any photos.

Language notes

Grammar: some/any

- In this unit, students are introduced to *there is* and *there are* to talk about things that exist. They learn that *there are* is followed by *some* + a plural noun, and that in questions and negatives, *Are there* and *There aren't* are followed by *any* + a plural noun.

- At this level, it's probably not appropriate to go into any more detail on the uses of *some* and *any*.

- In Unit 8 Useful Phrases, students come across the phrase *Would you like some tea?*. It would appear to contradict the rule that the students have learnt in Unit 7, i.e. that *some* is used in affirmative sentences, *any* in negatives and questions. In fact, *some* is used in situations where the question isn't a real question, but a request or an invitation, and the answer *yes* is expected. Encourage students to learn these as complete phrases.

Useful phrases (SB page 54)

1 ⊕ 2.07

- Ask the students if they know of any words that are different in American and British English. They may know *movie* (American English) and *film* (British English), *elevator* (American English) and *lift* (British English), etc. Put a few suggestions on the board, but don't pre-empt the exercises in this section too much.

- Focus the students' attention on the photos and ask them which flag is the US flag (the stars and stripes), and which the British flag (the Union Jack). Ask them to read out the captions in American English. Point out the example in British English, then ask them to read out the British English equivalents in the box and to match them to the pictures. You may need to point out that many British words for shops (such as *chemist's*) end in the possessive *'s*. This is because they're short for *chemist's shop*, *baker's shop*, etc.

- Play the recording for them to check their answers. Then play it a second time for them to listen and repeat the words.

> a) a chemist's
> b) a cashpoint
> c) an underground station
> d) a toilet

Language notes

American and British English

- There are differences between British and American English both in terms of vocabulary and grammar. However, few of these cause any major problems of understanding between speakers of the two types of English.

- In terms of vocabulary, in addition to the words given in the unit and the Teacher's notes, students may be interested to learn the following differences between British and American usage.

British	American
petrol station	gas station
petrol	gas
lorry	truck
pavement	sidewalk
motorway	freeway
fortnight	two weeks
trousers	pants

2 ⊕ 2.08

- Give the students a couple of minutes to look at the illustrations and try to decide what the situation is in each conversation.

- Ask them to read the conversations as they listen to the recording. At this stage all they need to do is to identify what each tourist asks for. Check answers with the class.

> A chemist's and a toilet.

3

Ask the students to try to complete the gaps in the conversations without listening to the recording again. Then play it for them to check their answers.

> | 1 there | 2 near | 3 pharmacy | 4 Excuse |
> |---|---|---|---|
> | 5 there | 6 near | 7 Sorry | 8 Near |

4 ⊕ 2.09

- Point out that *Excuse me* is a polite way of attracting someone's attention, particularly when you want to ask them a question.

- Play the recording for the students to repeat the phrases. Then ask them to say the first phrase, substituting a variety of other things in place of *chemist's*. For example, *Excuse me, is there a park near here? Excuse me, is there a museum near here?* etc.

5

- Pairwork. The students work together to write a new conversation about a cashpoint/an ATM or an underground/a subway station. Remind them that they can use the conversations in Exercise 2 as models. Go round giving help and encouragement where necessary.

- When they've finished, ask them to practise their conversations, taking turns to be the tourist and the American. Select some pairs to perform their conversations for the class.

Vocabulary *Extra* (SB page 55)

Town and country

1

- Focus the students' attention on the list of words and point out that they're all to do with the town and country. Remind the students that the underlining indicates the syllable of the word that has the strongest stress. Check that the students can pronounce all of the words correctly.

- Ask the students to look at the pictures and match each one with one of the words. Point out that the first one has been done for them.

14	an airport	11	a park
3	a bar	7	a restaurant
15	a beach	4	a school
12	a bridge	8	a square
5	a church	10	a station
2	a cinema	9	a statue
13	a lake	1	a theatre
6	a museum		

2

Pairwork. Demonstrate the activity with a confident student. Cover the words, point to one of the pictures and ask *What's this?* Elicit the answer. Then put the students into pairs to continue the activity. Go round, checking that everyone is pronouncing the words correctly.

Writing

Workbook page 31

- Linking sentences with *and* and *but*
- Describing a city

Photocopiable resource materials

Grammar: *Old town, New town* (Teacher's notes page 129. Worksheet page 164.)

Vocabulary: *Famous places* (Teacher's notes page 130. Worksheet page 165.)

Communication: *My town* (Teacher's notes page 130. Worksheet page 166.)

Test CD

See *Test Unit 7* on the CD.

 CD-ROM

For more activities go to Unit 7: *NYC*.

For the best activities for beginner students, see pages xvi–xxi

For practical methodology, from *Classroom interaction* to *Writing*, see pages xxii–xxxv

What can your students do now? See self-evaluation checklists on pages xxxvi–xlvi

8 Houses *Overview*

Section	Aims	What the students are doing
⊙ Reading **SB page 56**	*Reading skills*: reading for general information	• Matching a plan of the interior of Paul McCartney's childhood home to the correct photo of the house. • Reading about Paul McCartney's childhood home and completing a description of the house.
⊙ Listening & Vocabulary **SB page 57**	*Listening skills*: listening for specific information *Vocabulary*: rooms and furniture	• Listening and numbering rooms in the order they are mentioned. • Labelling objects in a room. • Completing sentences with names of rooms. • Writing sentences about Paul McCartney's house.
⊙ Reading **SB page 58**	*Reading skills*: reading for specific information	• Reading an article and matching people with places. • Matching questions and answers. • Talking about places that students love or hate.
⊙ Grammar **SB page 59**	*Grammar*: object pronouns	• Completing answers to questions using pronouns. • Asking for and giving opinions about things students love and hate.
⊙ Vocabulary **SB page 59**	*Vocabulary*: ordinal numbers	• Listening to and repeating ordinal numbers. • Completing sentences. • Talking about people in an apartment building.
⊙ Pronunciation **SB page 59**	*Pronunciation*: th – /ð/ and /θ/	• Practising the pronunciation of the letters *th*. • Completing a table according to the pronunciation of *th*.
⊙ Useful phrases **SB page 60**	*Vocabulary*: phrases which are useful with visitors when offering drinks	• Listening to a conversation and answering questions. • Listening and repeating useful phrases when talking to visitors. • Writing and practising a new conversation offering someone a drink.
Vocabulary *Extra* **SB page 61**	*Vocabulary*: revision of words from the unit: rooms; furniture	• Matching pictures with words.
Writing **WB page 35**	Punctuation (commas) Describing the rooms in a house	

8

Houses *Teacher's notes*

1 hall	2 Upstairs	3 Paul's bedroom
4 toilet	5 living room	

Warm-up

The first two sections of this unit are concerned with Paul McCartney's childhood home. Before you start the unit, you could find out what the students know about Paul McCartney and the Beatles. Write *the Beatles* on the board and ask students who they are, and then write *Paul McCartney* on the board and ask who he is.

Cultural note

The Beatles & Paul McCartney (born 1942)
Paul McCartney, John Lennon, George Harrison and Ringo Starr came from Liverpool in the north of England. They formed the band the Beatles, which became the most famous pop group of the 1960s. Paul McCartney and John Lennon wrote some of the best-known songs in rock and pop music, including *Yesterday*, *Hey Jude* and *Let it Be*.

After the break-up of the Beatles in 1970, McCartney formed the band Wings. He still writes music and performs in concerts.

John Lennon was shot dead in New York in December 1980, and George Harrison died of cancer in December 2001.

Reading (SB page 56)

1 🌐 2.10

- Focus the students' attention on the photos of the two houses and allow the students time to look carefully at them. Point out that one was his home when he was a child, and one is a home that he owns now.

- Give the students plenty of time to look at the picture as it's quite complicated. Ask them to match it to one of the houses in the photos.

- Play the recording for them to listen and repeat the words.

> a) 20 Forthlin Road, Liverpool

2 🌐 2.11

Play the recording and ask the students to read the text as they listen. Give them a few minutes to complete the text with the words from Exercise 1. Check answers with the class.

Language note

Vocabulary: *a number one hit*

A number one hit is a top selling record in the popular music charts. The song *Love me do* was the Beatles' first single, but it actually only made it to number 17 in the chart. *Please, please me*, their second single, got to number one.

Listening & Vocabulary (SB page 57)

1 🌐 2.12

- Explain that the students are going to listen to another description of Paul McCartney's house. They have to listen and number the rooms in the order they are mentioned. Point out that number 1 (the kitchen) has been done for them.

- Play the recording – you may need to play it more than once. Then check answers with the class.

1: c) the kitchen	4: f) Paul's bedroom
2: b) the dining room	5: e) the bathroom
3: a) the living room	6: d) the toilet

> 🌐 2.12
>
> *This is 20 Forthlin Road in Liverpool, Paul McCartney's family home.*
>
> *This is the <u>kitchen</u>. There's a washing machine, a sink and a cooker.*
>
> *This is the <u>dining room</u>. There's a table with six chairs. Can you imagine dinner with the McCartney family in this room? On the walls there are photos of the family. There's a photo of Paul. He's playing his guitar.*
>
> *This is the <u>living room</u>. There's a television – one of the first. There's an armchair and a sofa. There's also a lamp and an old carpet.*
>
> *There are three small bedrooms. This is <u>Paul's bedroom</u>. This is his bed and this is his chair.*
>
> *This is the <u>bathroom</u>. There's a bath, but there isn't a shower. And this is the <u>toilet</u>.*

2   2.13

- Pairwork. The students work together to try to name all the items in the illustration. Allow them to compare their answers with another pair before playing the recording for them to check.
- Play the recording a second time for them to repeat all the words.

a) a washing machine	h) a sofa
b) a sink	i) a lamp
c) a cooker	j) a carpet
d) a table	k) a bed
e) chairs	l) a bath
f) a television	m) a shower
g) an armchair	n) a toilet

If your students need further practice, you could use Photocopiable Worksheet 8 *Vocabulary* here.

3   2.14

- Focus the students' attention on the three photos of rooms in Paul McCartney's house. Read the example sentence and ask the students to find the cooker. Then ask them to find the other items in the exercise and complete the sentences.
- Play the recording for them to check their answers. Then play it a second time for them to repeat the sentences.

a) the kitchen
b) the living room
c) Paul's bedroom
d) the living room
e) the kitchen
f) the living room

4

The students could work in pairs to write more sentences. Alternatively, you could get them to work individually to write sentences, and then have them write them out again with gaps for a partner to complete.

5 Pairwork

- The pairwork exercise for this unit is on pages 118 and 123 of the Student's Book. Put the students in pairs and tell them who will be Student A, and who will be Student B.
- While they're doing the exercise, go round monitoring and giving help. Take note of any errors which may need focusing on later and also any examples of good language use which you can praise.

If your students need further practice, you could use Photocopiable Worksheet 8 *Grammar* here.

Reading (SB page 58)

1   2.15

- Focus the students' attention on the six photos of places. Ask them if they can identify these places (a supermarket, a bed, a gym, Paris, a kitchen, an airport). Teach any words they don't know.
- Focus the students' attention on the photos of the three people. Ask them about their jobs. Then tell them to read the article as they listen to the recording. Ask them to match the people with the places. Check answers with the class.

a) 4, 6   b) 5, 1   c) 2, 3

2

Go through the example with the class and then ask the students to match the other questions and answers. Allow them to compare in pairs before you check with the class. Note that answers 2 and 5 are the same, so questions a) and e) can be matched with either of them.

a) 2   b) 4   c) 6   d) 3   e) 5   f) 1

3

Give the students a few minutes to think of places that they love or hate. Help the students with any vocabulary that they need. Then put them in pairs to take turns telling their partner about the places they love and hate. Point out the use of *but* in the example sentence to contrast something that the speaker loves with something they hate.

Grammar (SB page 59)

1   2.16

- If your students are unfamiliar with the Sugarbabes, David Beckham (a British footballer, currently playing for LA Galaxy, USA) or Hillary Clinton (wife of former President of the USA Bill Clinton), you may want to substitute more familiar items when the students practise asking and answering the questions in pairs. Alternatively, teach the expression *I don't know him/her/it*, which also comes up in the *Grammar Extra* exercises.
- Go through the information on subject and object pronouns in the margin, putting some example sentences using them on the board.
- Ask them to complete the questions and answers. Go round checking and giving help if necessary.
- Play the recording for them to check their answers. Then play it a second time for them to repeat.

a) them   b) it   c) it   d) them   e) him   f) her

2

Put the students in pairs to take turns asking and answering the questions.

3

- Ask the students to work individually to make their lists. Go round, giving help and encouragement.
- Focus the students' attention on the example speech bubbles and point out that *What do you think of ...?* is a useful way to ask someone's opinion about something or someone.

Language notes

Grammar: U2 are plural

- Note that the band U2 are referred to as *they* here.
- In British English, you can consider companies, teams, etc. as being either an entity (and singular), or a group of people (and plural). For example, *The government is ...*, *The government are ...* But you generally refer to bands like U2 as *they*.

4 *Grammar Extra* 8

Ask the students to turn to *Grammar Extra* 8 on page 130 of the Student's Book. Here they'll find an explanation of the grammar they've been studying and further exercises to practise it.

---

1 a) she, me
   b) them, they
   c) me, him
   d) She, her
   e) him, us
   f) we, them

2 a) What do you think of the Beatles?
      I like them. I don't like them. They're OK.
      I don't know them.
   b) What do you think of Brad Pitt?
      I like him. I don't like him. He's OK.
      I don't know him.
   c) What do you think of Mariah Carey?
      I like her. I don't like her. She's OK.
      I don't know her.
   d) What do you think of rugby?
      I like it. I don't like it. It's OK.
      I don't know it.
   e) What do you think of Woody Allen?
      I like him. I don't like him. He's OK.
      I don't know him.
   f) What do you think of hip hop?
      I like it. I don't like it. It's OK.
      I don't know it.

If your students need further practice, you could use Photocopiable Worksheet *8 Communication* here.

Vocabulary (SB page 59)

Ordinal numbers

1 🌐 **2.17**

- Remind the students that they've already learnt the cardinal numbers (*one*, *two*, *three*, etc.). Elicit the numbers from one to ten. Then focus their attention on the list of ordinal numbers in the margin.
- Play the recording for the students to listen and repeat.
- Go round the class, calling on students at random to supply the ordinal numbers from *first* to *tenth*. Pay particular attention to the pronunciation of the *th* sound at the ends of some of the numbers. Students may have difficulty with *fifth* /fɪfθ/, *sixth* /sɪkθ/ and *eighth* /eɪtθ/. They'll be doing more work on the *th* sound in the Pronunciation section below.
- Ask the students if they can think of situations when they might use these (talking about floors in a building, winning positions in a competition, dates, etc.).

2 🌐 **2.18**

- Give the students a minute or two to look at the picture. Point out that this shows the door buzzers in an apartment block with the names of the people who live on each floor. Explain that *the Smiths* is a way of referring to a family – Mr and Mrs Smith may well have children. However, this is not necessarily so. We could equally well refer to Mr and Mrs Robinson as *the Robinsons*, even if they have no children.
- Ask the students to work in pairs to complete the sentences using ordinal numbers.
- Play the recording for them to check their answers, then play it a second time for them to repeat the sentences. Encourage them to pronounce *Smiths* /smɪθs/ correctly.

---

a) second   b) third   c) first   d) fifth
e) fourth

Cultural note

British English: *ground floor* = American English: *first floor*

Note that in British English, you have a *ground floor*, and that the floor above it is called the *first floor*. In American English, the British English *ground floor* is called the *first floor*, and the British English *first floor* is called the *second floor*.

3

- Find out how many of your students live in apartment buildings and if they know the names of any other people who live there. Put them in pairs to tell each other about the people in their building, or an apartment building they know. Go through the example with the class before they begin.

- If apartment buildings are not common in your country, or your students don't live in one, or know any people who do live in one, then ask them to talk about an office block, a school or any other place which has a number of different floors. Students might say, for example, *My office is on the third floor.*

Pronunciation (SB page 59)

1 🌐 2.19

- Remind the students of the sound of the letters *th* at the end of some of the ordinal numbers (*fourth, fifth, sixth,* etc.). Ask them if they know of any other way in which the letters *th* can be pronounced. Remind them of the words *the, their* and *them,* which they already know. Make sure they can all distinguish between the two different sounds by giving them a couple of examples. See Language notes below.

- Play the recording and ask them to listen and repeat the four sentences. Tell them to ignore the rest of the table for the time being. Encourage them to pronounce the /ð/ and /θ/ sounds correctly, and ask for individual pronunciation of the sentences to check.

Language notes

Pronunciation: *voiced* versus *unvoiced*

- One way to make your students more aware of the difference between voiced and unvoiced sounds is to get them to touch their throats as they are practicing. They should be able to feel the vibration as they make voiced sounds.

- You can give extra practice by giving them the words that they have already met and asking them to classify them into voiced and unvoiced. For example:

  Voiced: *the their them that there this these they*
  Unvoiced: *thing third thirty think thank thirteen three Thursday*

2

- Focus the students' attention on the two columns of the table. Point out the phonemic symbols used to distinguish between the two sounds made by the letters *th*. Read out the first sentence (*The Smiths live in Bath.*). Demonstrate that *the* has the first sound, so it goes in the column under /ð/, and *Smiths* and *Bath* have the second sound and go under /θ/.

- Ask the students to work individually to put the words with *th* in the other sentences into the correct columns of the table. Encourage them to say the words aloud as they do this. Allow them to compare their answers in pairs before checking with the class.

> a) /ð/: The; /θ/: Smiths, Bath
> b) /ð/: Their, the; /θ/: fourth
> c) /ð/: their; /θ/: third, sixth, birthday
> d) /θ/: birthday, Samantha

Useful phrases (SB page 60)

1 🌐 2.20

- Focus the students' attention on the illustration and explain what the situation is (the young man is visiting the woman's house; she's welcoming, but he looks embarrassed).

- Read the two questions with the class so that they know what information they're looking for, then play the recording and ask them to read the conversation as they listen.

- Ask the students to answer the questions. Point out that Jo is probably a friend of Bryan's.

> a) A cup of tea, a cup of coffee and a glass of water.
> b) He wants Jo.

Extra activity

You could then ask a pair of confident students to read and act out the conversation for the class. Encourage them to copy the intonation on the recording and play the parts in character – Mrs Gregg being overly welcoming, and Bryan feeling uncomfortable and impatient.

2 🌐 2.21

- Play the recording and ask the students to repeat the useful phrases. Point out that *Would you like ...?* can be used in a variety of situations when you're offering things to people.

- Ask for individual reading of the phrases and check that the students are pronouncing them correctly.

3

- Pairwork. Go through the various drinks illustrated with the class and encourage them to pronounce all the words correctly. Tell them that you can use *Would you like ...?* with all of these. Then put the students into pairs to write new conversations using these drinks. Go round, giving help and encouragement. Take note of any particularly good conversations which you can ask the students to perform for the class.

- When the students have written their conversations, ask them to practise them, taking turns to play the different roles.

Vocabulary *Extra* (SB page 61)

Rooms

- Focus the student's attention on the list of words and point out that they're all to do with rooms. Remind the students that the underlining indicates the syllable of the word that has the strongest stress. Check that the students can pronounce all of the words correctly.
- Ask the students to look at the pictures and match each one with one of the words. Point out that the first one has been done for them.

> 2　the bedroom
> 4　the dining room
> 3　the kitchen
> 5　the living room
> 1　the bathroom

Furniture

1

- Focus the students' attention on the list of words and point out that they're all to do with furniture. Remind the students that the underlining indicates the syllable of the word that has the strongest stress. Check that the students can pronounce all of the words correctly.
- Ask the students to look at the pictures and match each one with one of the words. Point out that the first one has been done for them.

> 7　an armchair
> 10　a bath
> 4　a bed
> 11　a carpet
> 1　a chair
> 12　a cooker
> 2　a lamp
> 14　a shower
> 13　a sink
> 9　a sofa
> 5　a table
> 3　a television
> 6　a toilet
> 8　a washing machine

2

Pairwork. Demonstrate the activity with a confident student. Cover the words, point to one of the pictures and ask *What's this?* Elicit the answer. Then put the students into pairs to continue the activity. Go round, checking that everyone is pronouncing the words correctly.

Writing

Workbook page 35

- Punctuation (commas)
- Describing the rooms in a house

Photocopiable resource materials

Grammar: *Our flat* (Teacher's notes page 131. Worksheet page 167.)

Vocabulary: *Password!* (Teacher's notes page 131. Worksheet page 168.)

Communication: *Do you like him?* (Teacher's notes page 131. Worksheet page 169.)

Test CD

See *Test Unit 8* on the CD.

DVD

Programme 4: *My house*

CD-ROM

For more activities go to Unit 8: *Houses.*

For the best activities for beginner students, see pages xvi–xxi

For practical methodology, from *Classroom interaction* to *Writing*, see pages xxii–xxxv

What can your students do now? See self-evaluation checklists on pages xxxvi–xlvi

9 Diet *Overview*

Section	Aims	What the students are doing
🔘 Reading **SB page 62**	*Reading skills*: reading for specific information	• Reading and listening to an article about a man's unusual diet. • Discussing meals with a partner.
🔘 Vocabulary **SB page 63**	*Vocabulary*: food and drink	• Completing a chart with food and drink words. • Talking to a partner about eating habits.
🔘 Grammar **SB page 63**	*Grammar*: How often ...?	• Matching time expressions. • Putting words in order to make sentences. • Asking and answering questions.
🔘 Reading **SB page 64**	*Reading skills*: reading for detail	• Reading a weblog and identifying correct information. • Talking about international food.
🔘 Grammar **SB page 65**	*Grammar*: adverbs of frequency	• Matching sentence halves. • Completing sentences.
🔘 Pronunciation **SB page 65**	*Pronunciation*: /ɪ/ and /iː/	• Practising distinguishing between sounds. • Completing a table.
🔘 Useful phrases **SB page 66**	*Vocabulary*: phrases which are useful when ordering in a café	• Listening to a conversation and completing it. • Listening and repeating useful phrases for buying a coffee. • Writing and practising new coffee shop conversations.
Vocabulary *Extra* **SB page 67**	*Vocabulary*: revision of words from the unit: food and drink	• Matching pictures with words.
Writing **WB page 39**	Linking sentences with *and* and *or* Describing daily meals	

Diet *Teacher's notes*

Quick revision

- Play *Five of the best* to revise some vocabulary the students have seen in previous units and the alphabet.
- Write *kitchen* on the board. Point out to the students that this is a *room*. Ask the students to name five other rooms. Write these on the board, sometimes asking the students to spell the word.
- Do the same thing for some of the following categories: sports, food, colours, verbs, places, nationalities, countries, clothes, days, months.

Reading (SB page 62)

🎧 **2.22**

- Explain that *diet* /ˈdaɪət/ can mean simply 'the things you eat', but is often used to refer to an eating plan undertaken in order to lose weight. Teach *I'm on a diet*.
- This article is about an American diet called the 3-hour diet. For more information, go to www.3hourdiet.com
- Go through the sentences with the class and make sure they understand them. You could ask them in which sentence you can eat a meal at 7 a.m., 10 a.m., 1 p.m., 4 p.m., etc. Then play the recording and ask the students to read the article as they listen.
- Check the answer to the question and go through any difficult vocabulary with the class. Ask them if they think that the 3-hour diet is a good idea and whether they think it would help someone to lose weight. Would they like to try it?
- Focus the students' attention on the food pictures. Go through the various items with them and find out who likes what in the class. Find out what their favourite foods are.

> Sentence *b* is true.

Extra activity

- Pairwork. Choose a confident student and ask what time they have breakfast, lunch and dinner. Then put the students in pairs to practise asking and answering questions about meal times. Go round monitoring and giving help, and take note of any pronunciation problems. Encourage the students to pronounce *breakfast* /ˈbrekfəst/ correctly.
- Teach the word *snacks* /snæks/ and find out how many students eat snacks between meals. In pairs, they ask each other what snacks they eat and at what time.

Language note

Vocabulary: *diet*

The word *diet* can be a false friend in some languages. It doesn't mean eating no food at all. It means restricting what you eat in order to lose weight or for other health reasons.

Vocabulary (SB page 63)

1 🎧 **2.23**

- Elicit a few suggestions for each category from the class and explain alphabetical order. The students may find it easier to note down the words they want to put in each category, and then determine the order to put them in the table.
- Allow the students to compare charts in pairs before playing the recording for them to check their answers. Play it a second time for them to repeat, and ask for individual repetition of difficult-looking words such as *biscuits* /ˈbɪskɪts/, *cereal* /ˈsɪəriəl/, *lettuce* /ˈletɪs/ and *steak* /steɪk/.

> Drinks: beer, coffee, cola, milk, orange juice, tea
> Breakfast: bread, cereal, eggs
> Lunch/Dinner: chips, fruit, green beans, a hamburger, ice cream, meat, potatoes, salad
> Snacks: biscuits, cake, chocolate

2

* Pairwork. Go through the example dialogue in the speech bubbles with the class. Then invite a confident student to say what they have for breakfast and to ask you what you have. Respond with something other than orange juice. Then put the students into pairs and tell them to take turns asking each other what they have for the various meals. Encourage them to formulate this as in the example; by offering information about themselves first, followed by *What about you?* Go round, giving help and encouragement.

* As a whole class, find out if anyone has anything unusual for any of the meals.

If your students need further practice, you could use Photocopiable Worksheet *9 Vocabulary* here.

Grammar (SB page 63)

How often ...?

1 🌐 2.24

* Point out the question in the margin: *How often do you drink coffee?* and the answer *Every day*. Go round the class asking a number of students the same question, perhaps varying the drink each time. Make sure they understand the difference between *How often?* and *When?* Ask them *When do you drink coffee?*

* Go through column A with the class. Remind them of the meaning of *a.m.* and *p.m.* Tell them that in b) *Mon* is short for *Monday*, and get them to say the full names of the other days of the week.

* Point out all the expressions with *every* in column B, and ask them to match them up with the possibilities in column A. Allow them to compare answers in pairs before playing the recording for them to check. Play it a second time for them to repeat.

> a) 3: Every three hours.   d) 1: Every Saturday.
> b) 4: Every day.   e) 2: Every week.
> c) 6: Every morning.   f) 5: Never.

2 🌐 2.25

* Look at the example with the class. The other sentences follow the same pattern, but with different verbs so they should be quite simple for the students to work out.

* Allow students to compare answers in pairs before playing the recording for them to check. Play it a second time for them to repeat the sentences.

> a) How often do you drink coffee?
> b) How often do you drink beer?
> c) How often do you drink tea?
> d) How often do you eat hamburgers?
> e) How often do you eat fruit?
> f) How often do you eat chocolate?

3

Pairwork. Ask the students to take turns asking and answering the questions.

4 Pairwork

* The pairwork exercise for this unit is on pages 118 and 123 of the Student's Book. Put the students in pairs and tell them who will be Student A, and who will be Student B.

* While they're doing the exercise, go round monitoring and giving help. Take note of any errors which may need focusing on later, and also any examples of good language use, which you can praise. Note any pairs whose work is particularly good so you can ask them to perform their conversations to the class.

Reading (SB page 64)

1 🌐 2.26

- Go through the statements with the class so that they know what information they're looking for in the text. Explain any unknown words and encourage the students to pronounce *delicious* /dɪˈlɪʃəs/.

- Play the recording and ask the students to read the text as they listen. Then give them a few minutes to make their choices and underline the answers they think are correct. Allow them to compare results in pairs before checking answers with the class.

> a) loves   b) says   c) never cooks
> d) has   e) is   f) doesn't spend

Extra activity
Find out if your students have ever eaten Thai food and whether they like it. Do they have a favourite dish?

Cultural notes
Bangkok
Bangkok is the capital of Thailand. It's one of the biggest cities in the world, with a population of around 10 million. Tourist sites include the Grand Palace and the Temple of the Emerald Buddha.

Thai food
The food in the south of Thailand is spicy with many curry dishes, some of them extremely hot. In the north there's more meat. Some of the best Thai food can be bought from the many stalls in the crowded streets of Bangkok. Thai food is very popular in Britain.

2

- Remind the students that the words for nationalities are different from the words for countries. Elicit the countries that all these nationality words corresponds to (*China, France, India, Italy, Japan, Spain, Thailand*), and check that they can pronounce the country and nationality words correctly.

- Read out the example speech bubbles and choose a few confident students to practise the question and answer with. Then put the students in pairs to take turns telling each other about their favourite international food. Encourage them to give examples of the dishes or types of food that they like, as well as the nationality of the food. If necessary, stop the activity and elicit a few names of dishes that they might talk about for each of the nationalities given, for example, China: *noodles, shark's fin soup*; India: *curry*; Japan: *sushi, sashimi*; Spain: *paella, tapas*, etc.

- Finally, encourage the students to report back to the class on what kind of food their partner likes.

Grammar (SB page 65)
Adverbs of frequency

1 🌐 2.27

- Focus the students' attention on the table in the margin showing adverbs of frequency. Point out that these are on a cline from 0% to 100%. Read the example sentences below and ask for a few more examples from the class, e.g. *I never eat meat, I sometimes drink wine.*

- Go through the two columns with the students and remind them of the text they read about Mike on page 64 of the Student's Book. Read out the example and ask them to match the other sentence halves. They can look back at the text on page 64 to find the correct information.

- Allow them to compare results in pairs or small groups before playing the recording for them to check. Play it a second time for them to repeat the sentences. Point out that adverbs of frequency are often stressed.

> a) 2: Mike never cooks at home.
> b) 5: Mike sometimes has a cup of coffee for breakfast.
> c) 3: Mike always has noodles for dinner.
> d) 1: Mike usually drinks beer with his dinner.
> e) 4: Mike doesn't usually spend more than $4 a day.

Language note
Grammar: adverbs of frequency
Adverbs of frequency come before a main verb: *She always has coffee for breakfast.*

Adverbs of frequency come after *be*: *She's always happy.*

2

- The students should work individually to complete the sentences. When they've completed the sentences, focus their attention on the example speech bubbles and get a confident student to read the first one aloud. Respond with the second one, emphasising the adverb of frequency to show how the second speaker contrasts with the first.

- Put the students in pairs to compare their answers and practise telling each other about their food habits. You may like to teach *Me, too* and *Me, neither*, so that students who agree with their partner's statements can have something to say.

3 *Grammar Extra* 9

Ask the students to turn to *Grammar Extra* 9 on page 130 of the Student's Book. Here they'll find an explanation of the grammar they've been studying and further exercises to practise it.

---

1   a) Don usually gets up at 7 a.m.
    b) Sue always has a big breakfast.
    c) Rick sometimes goes to the gym.
    d) Dana usually takes her children to school.
    e) Kate doesn't usually have dinner before
       8 p.m.
    f) Jack never goes to bed before midnight.

If your students need further practice, you could use Photocopiable Worksheet *9 Grammar* here.

Pronunciation (SB page 65)

1 🌐 2.28

Play the recording and ask the students to repeat the questions. Listen carefully to see if they're making the difference between the /ɪ/ and /iː/ sounds.

Extra activity

When they've finished, say the two sounds and make sure they can hear the difference. Write *drink* on the left-hand side of the board and *eat* on the right. Say these words aloud again and then call out a series of words at random which contain the two sounds (e.g. *dish, tea, dinner, biscuits, three, week, milk, six, green, lettuce, cream*). Ask the students to raise their left hands if the sound is /ɪ/ and their right hands if the sound is /iː/. Gradually say the words quicker and quicker and see if they can keep up.

2 🌐 2.29

- Explain the use of the phonemic symbols and add them to the board next to the words *drink* and *eat*. Ask them to put the words in Exercise 1 in the correct columns. Encourage them to say the words aloud as they do this.

- Play the recording for the students to check their answers, then play it a second time for them to repeat all the words. Ask for individual repetition around the class of any words that they have difficulty with.

/ɪ/: drink, fish, chips, milk
/iː/: eat, meat, beans, tea

Useful phrases (SB page 66)

1 🌐 2.30

- The conversation here takes place in a café. First, focus the students' attention on the menu at the top. Give them time to look at it and explain any difficult vocabulary to them. Make sure they all understand *small*, *medium* and *large* by drawing different sized cups on the board, and that they can pronounce the words. Ask them what they'd order from the menu if they were in the coffee shop right now.

- Play the recording and ask the students to read the conversation as they listen. Then play it again and ask them to complete the gaps. Allow them to compare answers in pairs before checking with the class.

- Play the recording again for a final check.

---

1   Small, medium … large
2   Large, please
3   Sugar
4   No, thanks
5   Chocolate on top
6   Yes, please

---

2 🌐 2.31

- Point out where the useful phrases appear in the conversation in Exercise 1. Point out who says each one. You may need to explain that *Anything else?* is short for *Do you want / Would you like anything else?* and that *Here you are* is something you often say when you give something to someone else, particularly something that they've asked for. It has nothing to do with where the person is. Point out that *Just a minute, please* can be used in a variety of situations when you want someone to wait for a short time.

- Play the recording and ask the students to listen and repeat the phrases. Then ask for individual repetition around the class, encouraging them to use the correct pronunciation.

3

- Groupwork. Put the students into groups of three and ask them to write a similar conversation using different items from the menu above. Go round, giving help and encouragement.

- When the students have finished, ask them to practise their conversations. As you monitor this, take note of any particularly good ones that can be performed for the class. When groups perform for the class, encourage them to act out the situation so that the waiter, is behind a desk, the person ordering is facing the waiter and the customer's companion is seated at a desk nearby. This will help the customer to raise their voice when trying to find out exactly what their companion wants.

If your students need further practice, you could use Photocopiable Worksheet *9 Communication* here.

Vocabulary *Extra* (SB page 67)

Food and drink

1

- Focus the students' attention on the list of words and point out that they're all to do with food and drink. Remind the students that the underlining indicates the syllable of the word that has the strongest stress. Check that the students can pronounce all of the words correctly.

- Ask the students to look at the pictures and match each one with one of the words. Point out that the first one has been done for them.

4	beer	20	ice cream
13	biscuits	7	milk
11	bread	15	noodles
5	cake	18	orange juice
2	cereal	6	potatoes
17	chips	10	salad
19	chocolate	16	sandwich
21	cola	3	soup
14	egg	12	sugar
8	green beans	9	water
1	hamburger		

2

Ask the students to work individually to produce their lists, then to compare answers in pairs or small groups. They can then report back to the class on any differences.

Writing

Workbook page 39

- Linking sentences with *and* and *or*
- Describing daily meals

Photocopiable resource materials

Grammar: *Are you healthy?* (Teacher's notes page 132. Worksheet page 170.)

Vocabulary: *Do you eat it?* (Teacher's notes page 132. Worksheet page 171.)

Communication: *Small or large?* (Teacher's notes page 133. Worksheet page 172.)

Test CD

See *Test Unit 9* on the CD.

⊕ CD-ROM

For more activities go to Unit 9: *Diet*.

For the best activities for beginner students, see pages xvi–xxi

For practical methodology, from *Classroom interaction* to *Writing*, see pages xxii–xxxv

What can your students do now? See self-evaluation checklists on pages xxxvi–xlvi

Review C *Teacher's notes*

These exercises act as a check of the grammar and vocabulary that the students have learnt in Units 7, 8 and 9 of the Student's Book. Use them to find any problems that students are having, or anything that they haven't understood and which will need further work.

Grammar (SB page 68)

Remind the students of the grammar explanations they read and the exercises they did in the *Grammar Extra* on pages 130 and 131 of the Student's Book.

1

This exercise reviews the use of *there is* and *there are* in affirmative and negative statements and questions. Make sure that the students contract *there is* to *there's* in speech, but that they understand what the full form is. Remind them that you use *some* in affirmative statements (*There are some nice shops*), but this tends to change to *any* in questions (*Are there any nice shops?*).

> a) There are
> b) There's
> c) There's
> d) There are
> e) There's
> f) There are
>
> a) Are there any good restaurants?
> b) Is there a park?
> c) Is there a theatre?
> d) Are there any hotels?
> e) Is there a museum?
> f) Are there any nice shops?
>
> Students' own answers.
> Yes, there is / there are.
> No, there isn't / there aren't.

2

This is a simple matching exercise to check that the students can match the person to the right present simple verb form, and can use *it* and *them* correctly.

> a) 2   b) 3   c) 6   d) 5   e) 1   f) 4

3

This should be fairly fresh in the students' minds. Check that they've put the adverbs of frequency in the right order before they complete the sentences.

> 1 always   2 usually   3 sometimes
> 4 not usually   5 never

4

Remind the students of the work they did on *How often?* questions in Unit 9. Check that they've formed the questions correctly before they move on to practise asking and answering them in pairs.

> a) How often do you eat apples?
> b) How often do you drink milk?
> c) How often do you have a snack?
> d) How often do you eat Chinese food?
> e) How often do you drink Thai beer?
> f) How often do you buy fresh fruit?

5

This exercise gives the students an opportunity to identify mistakes, a skill that will be useful when they come to check their own work. They have the advantage here of seeing what the correct sentence should be in each case.

> 5
> 1 a) ~~There some nice bars near my house.~~
> 2 a) ~~Is there bank near here?~~
> 3 b) ~~'Does she like dogs?' 'Yes, she loves it.'~~
> 4 b) ~~How often you eat fish?~~
> 5 a) ~~I have always breakfast in bed.~~
> 6 a) ~~He no usually drinks beer.~~

If your students need further practice, you could use Photocopiable Worksheet *Review C* here.

Pronunciation (SB page 68)

1

Remind the students of the use of large and small stress boxes to help them get their intonation right. Go through the examples with the class, reading them aloud and getting some of the students to say them. Then ask them to complete the table. Encourage them to say the words aloud. Check that they know the meanings of all the words when you check answers with the class. Remind them that they can find all these words in Units 7–9.

(See Exercise 2 for answers.)

2 🌐 **2.32**

- Ask the students to underline all the stressed syllables in the words in the table. Point out the underlining in the example words. Play the recording for them to check their answers, then ask individual students to say which letters they underlined.

- Play the recording a second time for them to listen and repeat. Ask for individual repetition around the class of any words that are difficult.

> A: <u>bis</u>cuit, <u>buil</u>ding, <u>cho</u>colate, <u>mi</u>nute
> B: <u>ce</u>real, <u>pos</u>sible, <u>Sa</u>turday, <u>the</u>atre
> C: de<u>li</u>cious, fan<u>tas</u>tic, mu<u>se</u>um, po<u>ta</u>to

Vocabulary (SB page 69)

1

Point out that the photos are clues for the words that fit in the crossword. Allow the students to work in pairs to complete the crossword if they wish.

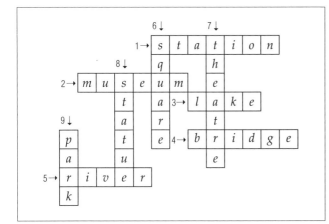

Cultural notes

Waterloo Station, London
This is the largest and one of the busiest of London's mainline stations. Eurostar trains to France and Belgium go from here.

The Louvre, Paris
The Louvre Museum is one of the largest museums in the world. Among the thousands of famous paintings housed in the Louvre is Leonardo da Vinci's *Mona Lisa*. *The Venus de Milo* sculpture can also be found there.

Lake Torrens, Adelaide, Australia
Lake Torrens is a 5,700 kilometre-square lake in South Australia in the Lake Torrens National Park.

Golden Gate Bridge, San Francisco
The Golden Gate Bridge was opened in May 1937 and was the longest bridge in the world for 27 years. The bridge is painted bright orange.

The River Seine, Paris
The Seine is one of the major rivers of north-western France, and flows through the city of Paris, where it's a major tourist attraction.

Old Town Square, Prague
Prague's Old Town Square dates back to the late 12th century. Originally it was the central marketplace for Prague. It now has numerous shops, restaurants and pavement cafés.

Wyndam's Theatre, London
Wyndham's Theatre is in central London, near Leicester Square. The theatre has put on many plays starring famous British actors.

Buddha statue
This statue of the Buddha is in Ayuthaya Park, Thailand. Ayuntha was once the capital of Thailand, and the park is now UNESCO World Heritage site.

St James's Park, London
St James's Park is the oldest Royal park in London. It's surrounded by the Houses of Parliament, St James' Palace and Buckingham Palace. National celebrations often take place in this park.

2

Remind the students that they studied ordinal numbers in Unit 8. Warn them to be careful with the spelling of *eighth*. When checking answers, encourage them to pronounce the ordinal numbers correctly.

1st	first	6th	sixth
2nd	second	7th	seventh
3rd	third	8th	eighth
4th	fourth	9th	ninth
5th	fifth	10th	tenth

3

This could be made into a fun activity by reading out each of the words and asking the students to stand up if they think the word is American, and remain seated if they think it's British. If they do this with no problems, throw in some other words (*lift/elevator*, *pavement/sidewalk*, *film/movie*, etc.) which you may have discussed when you discussed British and American words in Unit 7.

British	American
cashpoint	ATM
chemist's	pharmacy
toilet	restroom
underground	subway

4

Remind the students that they studied words for items of furniture in Unit 8. Check answers by calling on individual students to read out words and spell them; this will also give practise in saying the letters of the alphabet.

> a) bedroom: bed, lamp, carpet
> b) dining room: table, chairs
> c) kitchen: cooker, sink
> d) living room: sofa, armchair
> e) bathroom: bath, toilet

5

Point out that *potato* is the odd word out in *a)* because both the other items are drinks. When checking answers, ask the students to say why each one is the odd word out.

> a) potato (the others are drinks; potato is a food item)
> b) breakfast (the others are food items; breakfast is a meal)
> c) noodles (the others are meals; noodles is a food item)
> d) drink (the others are food items)
> e) menu (the others are food items; a menu is a list of what is available in a café or restaurant)
> f) snack (the others are specific food items; snack is a term for anything eaten between meals)

Reading & Listening (SB page 70)

1 🌐 2.33

- Focus attention on the photo of Linda and the details of her dream home. Explain that this is a website that attempts to match people with the sorts of homes they want. Go through Linda's requirements for her dream home with the class, and make sure they all understand exactly what sort of home she wants.

- Focus attention on the photos of the homes. Tell the students that these are three homes for sale in New York. Ask them to read the descriptions as they listen to the recording.

- Put the students in pairs to discuss which of the homes best matches what Linda wants. Don't reveal the correct answer at this stage, but check that the students are having discussions along the right lines.

> The Central Park apartment (2) is good for Linda. The others are not good because: the Queens house (3) is very big and not central, and the Greenwich Village apartment (1) is OK, but it has a small kitchen and it isn't near a park.

2 🌐 2.34

Tell the students that they're going to hear Linda talking to an estate agent called Nick Sutton. Explain that the job of an estate agent is to sell homes. Play the recording and ask them if they chose the correct home in Exercise 1.

> The estate agent describes the Central Park apartment.

> 🌐 2.34 (L = Linda; N = Nick)
> L: Hello. Nick Sutton?
> N: Yes.
> L: I'm Linda Sondstrum.
> N: Ah, Linda. Thanks for coming in. Would you like a cup of coffee?
> L: Er, can I have cup of tea, please? Sorry, <u>I don't really like coffee</u>.
> N: Of course. Now, I think I have a place for you. <u>It's a third-floor apartment in Manhattan.</u>
> L: Great!
> N: <u>There are two bedrooms and two bathrooms. One room has a bath. The other room has a shower.</u>
> L: OK.
> N: <u>There's a large kitchen with a new cooker.</u>
> L: Fantastic!
> N: And <u>it's very near Central Park</u>!
> L: Oh, that's wonderful.
> N: <u>Grand Central Station is only ten minutes away.</u> Oh, and <u>there are lots of really good restaurants and cafés, near the apartment</u>. What do you think?
> L: I love it! … Now, how much is it?
> N: OK, well, it is in a fantastic location …

3

Go through the sentences with the class to check that they understand them and know what they're listening for. Then play the recording again and ask them to decide if they're true or false. Check answers with the class.

> a) False. (She likes tea.)
> b) False. (It's on the third floor.)
> c) True.
> d) False. (There is one bath and one shower.)
> e) True.
> f) True.

Writing & Speaking (SB page 71)

1

- Focus the students' attention on the photos on this page and ask if they'd like to live in any of them. Ask the class to vote for the one they'd most like to live in. The different kinds of homes illustrated are apartments, a villa and a cottage.

- Remind the students of the requirements for Linda's dream home which they read about on the previous page. Check that they remember what accommodation type means, and elicit some of the possibilities (*apartment, house, bungalow,* etc.). Encourage the students to work individually to complete their forms. Then put them in pairs to compare their results. Go round and see if there are any interesting dream homes to present to the rest of the class.

2

Go through the example description with the class. Remind them that they can use the texts on the previous page as a model. Encourage them to include as much detail as possible. This could be set for homework and the results displayed in the classroom for everyone to read.

Photocopiable resource material

Review C: *The Revision Game* (Teacher's notes page 133. Worksheet page 173.)

Test CD

See *Test Review C* on the CD.

For the best activities for beginner students, see pages xvi–xxi

For practical methodology, from *Classroom interaction* to *Writing*, see pages xxii–xxxv

What can your students do now? See self-evaluation checklists on pages xxxvi–xlvi

10 Clothes Overview

Section	Aims	What the students are doing
🌐 Listening & Vocabulary SB page 72	*Listening skills*: listening for specific information *Vocabulary*: colours and clothes	• Completing descriptions of clothes with colours. • Listening and matching names with models. • Asking questions about clothing.
🌐 Reading SB page 73	*Reading skills*: reading for detail	• Reading texts about clothes and matching them to photos. • Completing a table with information from texts.
🌐 Grammar SB page 73	*Grammar*: present continuous	• Completing questions and answers. • Answering questions.
🌐 Pronunciation SB page 74	*Pronunciation*: intonation with *ing* words	• Listening and repeating chants with *ing* words. • Writing and practising a chant.
🌐 Listening SB page 74	*Listening skills*: listening for specific information	• Matching pictures and descriptions. • Matching people and actions.
Speaking SB page 75	*Conversation skills*: talking about what you are doing	• Completing and practising conversations.
🌐 Vocabulary SB page 75	*Vocabulary*: verb phrases with *do, play, read* and *make*	• Completing verb phrases. • Completing diagrams. • Practising using verb phrases.
🌐 Useful phrases SB page 76	*Vocabulary*: phrases which are useful when buying clothes	• Listening to a conversation and matching it to a picture. • Listening and repeating useful phrases for buying clothes. • Writing and practising new clothes shop conversations.
Vocabulary *Extra* SB page 77	*Vocabulary*: revision of words from the unit: clothes	• Matching pictures with words.
Writing WB page 43	Writing a postcard	

10 Clothes *Teacher's notes*

Quick revision

Remind the students that they studied colour words in Unit 4. Ask them how many colours they can identify in the classroom. Steer them towards talking about the colours of other students' clothes.

Language note

Pronunciation: clothes

The word *clothes* can be difficult for some students to pronounce. You say /kləʊðz/. Note also that *clothes* has no singular, instead you usually say something to wear. For example, *I'm going to buy something to wear to the party.*

Listening & Vocabulary (SB page 72)

1 🌐 **2.35**

- Focus the students' attention on the four fashion models. Go through the colours in the box and ask the students to use them to complete the descriptions of the clothes the models are wearing. Check answers by asking individual students to read out the items. Explain any unknown words and help them with the pronunciation of words like *trousers* /ˈtraʊzəz/, *skirt* /skɜːt/, *shirt* /ʃɜːt/ and *suit* /suːt/.
- Play the recording for the students to listen and check. Then play it a second time for them to repeat.

> a) 1 a black jacket, 2 a yellow T-shirt,
>   3 blue trousers, 4 black shoes
> b) 1 a blue hat, 2 a green top, 3 a brown skirt,
>   4 red boots
> c) 1 a red dress, 2 black shoes
> d) 1 a grey suit, 2 an orange tie, 3 a white shirt,
>   4 black and white trainers

Language notes

Vocabulary: T-shirt / tee shirt

Some words in English have alternative spelling, as spelling has not been standardized. *T-shirt* is one example. Both are commonly used.

Vocabulary: *trousers*, etc. are plural

Like the word *lederhosen* in Unit 2, items of clothing with two legs are plural: *trousers, jeans, pyjamas, shorts, knickers, underpants, pants*. However, you can talk about *a* (singular) *pair of jeans, a pair of shorts, a pair of trousers*, etc.

2 🌐 **2.36**

Play the recording for the students to match the names of the models with the photos.

> Jasmine – c   Jason – d
> Kate – b   Leon – a

> 🌐 **2.36**
>
> *Jasmine is wearing a red dress and black shoes.*
>
> *Kate is wearing a blue hat, a green top, a brown skirt and red boots.*
>
> *Jason is wearing a grey suit, an orange tie, a white shirt and black and white trainers.*
>
> *Leon is wearing a black jacket, a yellow T-shirt, blue trousers and black shoes.*

3

- Remind the students of the work they did on adverbs of frequency and the question *How often?* in Unit 9. Get a confident student to ask you the question in the example speech bubble (*How often do you wear brown shoes?*) and give the answer. Then ask another question back, for example, *How often do you wear a white shirt?*
- Go through the chart headings *Every day, Sometimes* and *Never* with the class and make sure that they understand them. Then put the students in pairs to take turns asking and answering questions about how often they wear certain items.

If your students need further practice, you could use Photocopiable Worksheet *10 Vocabulary* here.

Reading (SB page 73)

1 🌐 **2.37**

- Focus the students' attention on the photos and ask them if they think these are the kinds of clothes these people wear every day. Point out that they probably wear them for special occasions, but not every day.

- Play the recording and ask the students to read the three texts as they listen. You may need to play the recording more than once. Then ask the students to match the texts with the photos. Check answers with the class and explain any unknown vocabulary.

- Ask the students if they had/have to wear a *uniform* /juːnɪfɔːm/ at school. Find out if any of the students come from a country which has a national costume, and ask them to describe it.

a) 3   b) 1   c) 2

Language notes

Vocabulary

costume

The term *costume* is usually used to describe rather unusual clothing, such as that worn for a fancy-dress party, a carnival or a fiesta.

The term *national costume* is used to describe the traditional clothing of a country. Most people only wear it for special occasions these days.

parasol

A *parasol* (text c) is like an umbrella, but it protects you from the sun rather than from the rain.

Pronunciation: *a uniform*

You use *a* before a consonant sound, even if it starts with a vowel. For example, *a uniform* /ˈjuːnɪfɔːm/, *a university* /juːnɪˈvɜːsɪti/, and *an* before a vowel sound, even if it starts with a consonant. For example, *an hour* /ˈaʊə/, *an honour* /ˈɒnə/.

Cultural notes

Venice Carnival costumes

The carnival in Venice began in 1296 and traditionally brought people of all classes together. Since the 1980s, the Carnival has been held for two weeks every year. Many of the palaces in Venice have masked balls.

Kimono

A kimono is the traditional woman's costume of Japan. In general, kimono is only worn for special occasions such as weddings, funerals and special days such as Adult's Day, which celebrates a woman's 20th birthday.

Traditional Spanish costumes

Andalucian festivals include traditional flamenco music, dancing and costumes. Women wear dresses that are brightly coloured with lots of frills.

2

Ask the students to work in pairs to complete the table. Go round, giving help and encouragement. Check answers with the class.

	Job	Clothes they usually wear	Clothes in the photo
Lola and Ana	receptionists	blue skirts and white tops	traditional clothes
Paolo	a policeman	a uniform	a costume
Elisa	a teacher	trousers and a jacket	a costume
Yuko	a student	jeans	a kimono

Grammar (SB page 73)

Present continuous

1 🌐 2.38

- Focus the students' attention on the information about the present continuous in the margin. Ask them to read out the different forms and the example sentences. Then ask them to look back at the texts in the previous section and underline any examples of the present continuous. Tell them that these are used to describe what the people are wearing at the present moment, and that the present simple is used to describe what they usually wear. Go around the class asking individual students what they are wearing. Encourage them to use the present continuous in their replies.

- Focus the students' attention on the questions and answers. Go through the first one or two with the class and then ask them to complete the rest. Monitor and help where necessary.

- Play the recording for the students to check their answers. Then play it a second time for them to repeat.

a) 'Are Lola and Ana wearing blue skirts?'
   'Yes, they are.' 'No, the aren't.'
b) 'Are they dancing?'
   'Yes, they are.' 'No, they aren't.'
c) 'Is Paolo wearing a uniform?'
   'Yes, he is.' 'No, he isn't.'
d) 'Are Paolo and Elisa having a great time?'
   'Yes, they are.' 'No, they aren't.'
e) 'Is Yuko wearing jeans?'
   'Yes, she is.' 'No, she isn't.'
f) 'Is she holding a parasol?'
   'Yes, she is.' 'No, she isn't.'

If your students need further practice, you could use Photocopiable Worksheet *10 Grammar* here.

Language notes

Grammar: present simple versus present continuous

- The difference between the present simple and the present continuous can be confusing for students even at an advanced level. However, here the difference is clear. You use the present simple to talk about what you do regularly, every day, and you use the present continuous to talk about what you are doing now.

- Further uses and differences will be met at higher levels. For the moment, beginners just need lots of practice of the structure.

2

The students can do this in pairs, taking turns to ask a question and to find the correct answer in the photos. Check answers with the class.

a) No, they aren't.
b) Yes, they are.
c) No, he isn't.
d) Yes, they are.
e) No, she isn't.
f) Yes, she is.

Extra activity

- Play *Who is it?* Describe what one of the students is wearing. The students have to decide who you are describing.

- To make this more fun, start with a description that could apply to several of the students, for example, *This student is wearing jeans. Who is it?* Then give more detail until the students guess who it is.

- Then describe other students for the class to guess.

- Let the more confident students describe what their classmates are wearing too.

3 Pairwork

- The pairwork exercise for this unit is on pages 119 and 124. Put the students in pairs and tell them who will be Student A, and who will be Student B.

- While they're doing the exercise, go round monitoring and giving help. Take note of any errors which may need focusing on later and also any examples of good language use which you can praise. Note any pairs whose work is particularly good so you can ask them to perform their conversations to the class.

4 *Grammar Extra* 10

Ask the students to turn to *Grammar Extra* 10 on page 132 of the Student's Book. Here they'll find an explanation of the grammar they've been studying and further exercises to practise it.

1
A: speak – speaking; do – doing; play – playing
B: have – having; make – making; write – writing
C: sit – sitting; run – running; get up – getting up

2
A: go – going; learn – learning; read – reading; sleep – sleeping; study – studying; work – working
B: come – coming; dance – dancing; take – taking
C: stop – stopping

4
a) What's he doing? He's running.
b) What are they doing? They're dancing.
c) What's he doing? He's having a shower.
d) What are they doing? They're playing football.
e) What's she doing? She's reading.
f) What's she doing? She's getting up.

Pronunciation (SB page 74)

1 ⊕ 2.39

- Point out that the underlining indicates the syllable of the words that is stressed the most. Point out that in the *ing* verbs, it's the first syllable that is stressed.

- Play the recording and ask the students to repeat the chants. Encourage them to copy the intonation of the speakers.

2

- Point out that the first two questions of the three chants in Exercise 1 involved pairs of verbs with opposite meanings. Go through the pairs of verbs in the box and explain any the students don't know. Then ask them to choose pairs of verbs to create a new chant. They could do this in pairs if they wish. Go round, monitoring and giving help.

- Finally, ask the students to practise their chants, perhaps performing them for the rest of the class.

Listening (SB page 74)

1

- Focus the students' attention on the pictures and establish that each one shows someone who is receiving a phone call from someone else.

- Read out the three descriptions and ask the students to match the descriptions to the pictures.

a) 2   b) 3   c) 1

2 ⊕ 2.40

- Ask the students to look at the pictures in Exercise 1 again. Explain that in each case, the person being telephoned is going to tell the other person what they're doing. However, they aren't going to tell the truth!

- Play the recording. Ask the students to match the pictures (showing what the people are <u>really</u> doing) with the sentences in which they <u>say</u> what they're doing.

---

a) 3   b) 1   c) 2

🔵 2.40

a) (H = Husband; W = Wife)

H: Hello, Kate.
W: Oh, hello, darling.
H: Where are you?
W: Oh, um, I'm in a shop.
H: What are you doing?
W: I'm buying fish for dinner.

b) (L = Liz; D = Don)

L: Hello, Don.
D: Oh, hi, Liz.
L: What are you doing?
D: I'm making dinner.
L: Ah, good.

c) (M = Mother; S = Son)

M: Hello.
S: Hi, Mum.
M: What are you doing?
S: I'm doing my homework.
M: Good boy.

Speaking (SB page 75)

1

- Focus the students' attention on the first picture and the completed conversation. Ask the students what other things the person could have said in response to the question *Where are you going?*
- Pairwork. Ask the students to look at the second and third pictures and the conversations and to discuss how to complete them. You could check that they've formed the two questions correctly before they move on to deciding how to answer them.
- Go round, monitoring and giving help. Take note of any particularly interesting or amusing conversations which you can ask the students to perform later.

---

a) Where are you going? I'm going to London.
b) What are you making? I'm making …
c) What are you listening to? I'm listening to …

2

Pairwork. In the same pairs, the students practise their conversations. Ask some of them to perform them for the class.

Vocabulary (SB page 75)

1 🔵 2.41

- Remind the students that in Unit 5 they looked at some verb phrases; verbs that are commonly used in conjunction with other words. Ask them to look at diagram a). Read out the sentences *do the housework* and *do the washing* with the class.
- Read out the other verbs, *play*, *read* and *make*. Ask the students to work in pairs and decide which goes in which diagram.
- Play the recording for them to check their answers, then play it a second time for them to repeat the verb phrases.

---

a) do   b) make   c) play   d) read

Language notes

Vocabulary: *do* versus *make*

- *Do* and *make* are combined with nouns to talk about actions you perform.
- *Do* is often used when the action is a noun ending in -*ing*. For example, *do the shopping, do the cooking, do some sightseeing*, etc. It's also used to talk about daily activities or jobs. For example, *do homework / housework / the ironing / the dishes / a job*.
- *Make* is often used to talk about an activity that creates something. For example, *make food / a cup of tea / a mess*.
- However, there are a number of fixed expressions using *do* and *make* that don't fit into these categories. For example, *do business / make your bed*. Encourage the students to learn these as complete phrases.

2

Go through the phrases in the box and ask the students to make more verb phrases with *do, play, read* or *make*. Allow them to compare results in pairs before you check answers with the class.

---

a) do your homework
b) make dinner
c) play on a PlayStation
d) read a newspaper

3

- Demonstrate the activity by choosing one of the activities and miming it in front of the class. Ask a student *What am I doing?* and elicit an answer using the present continuous. For example, *You're doing the housework.*
- Put the students in pairs to continue the activity. Go round, giving help and encouragement.

If your students need further practice, you could use Photocopiable Worksheet *10 Communication* here.

Useful phrases (SB page 76)

1 🌐 2.42

* Focus the students' attention on the pictures and ask them what type of shops they are: a) a sports shop, b) men's clothes shop and c) a women's clothes shop. Explain that in each shop a customer is deciding what clothes to buy. Then play the recording and ask the students to say which picture matches the conversation.

* Point out some of the useful language demonstrated in the conversation. We often use *I'm looking for* (*a dress*) when someone asks if they can help. It's gentler and more polite than *I want* (*a dress*). Explain *prefer* and make sure the students can pronounce it with the correct intonation /prɪˈfɜː/.

> Picture c

Language notes

Grammar: stative verbs *like*, *prefer*, etc.

* Some verbs are never or rarely used in the progressive form. Some of the common non-progressive verbs refer to mental or emotional states rather than actions, e.g. *believe, like, prefer, love*. You say *I believe it* not *I'm believing it*.

* However, in the case of the verb *love*, McDonalds is in the process of creating its own language with the slogan *I'm lovin' it*, which deliberately plays on the fact that this is non-standard English.

2 🌐 2.43

Play the recording for the students to listen and repeat the useful phrases. Check that they're copying the intonation of the speakers, and ask for individual repetition of the phrases afterwards.

3

* Pairwork. In pairs, the students write similar conversations for one of the other pictures in Exercise 1. Go round giving help and encouragement. Give help with any extra vocabulary that they need (for example, they may ask how to describe the stripes on the trainers).

* When they've finished, ask them to practise their conversations. Select a few pairs to perform theirs for the class.

Vocabulary *Extra* (SB page 77)

Clothes

1

* Focus the students' attention on the list of words and point out that they're all to do with clothes. Remind the students that the underlining indicates the syllable of the word that has the strongest stress. Check that the students can pronounce all of the words correctly.

* Ask the students which of the items are worn by men, which by women and which by both.

* Ask them to look at the pictures and match each one with one of the words. Point out that the first one has been done for them.

7	boots	12	a shirt	13	a top
3	a dress	14	shoes	2	trainers
11	a hat	1	a skirt	10	trousers
8	a jacket	6	a suit	5	a T-shirt
4	jeans	9	a tie		

2

Pairwork. Demonstrate the activity with a confident student. Cover the words, point to one of the pictures and ask *What's this?* Elicit the answer. Then put the students into pairs to continue the activity. Go round, checking that everyone is pronouncing the words correctly and using *It's* and *They're* appropriately.

Writing

Workbook page 43

* Writing a postcard

Photocopiable resource materials

Grammar: *I'm wearing blue jeans* (Teacher's notes page 133. Worksheet page 174.)

Vocabulary: *Crossword* (Teacher's notes page 134. Worksheet page 175.)

Communication: *What am I doing?* (Teacher's notes page 134. Worksheet page 176.)

Test CD

See *Test Unit 10* on the CD.

DVD

Programme 5: *The Red Carpet*

🌐 CD-ROM

For more activities go to Unit 10: *Clothes*.

For the best activities for beginner students, see pages xvi–xxi

For practical methodology, from *Classroom interaction* to *Writing*, see pages xxii–xxxv

What can your students do now? See self-evaluation checklists on pages xxxvi–xlvi

11 Events *Overview*

Section	Aims	What the students are doing
Vocabulary **SB page 78**	*Vocabulary*: months and years	• Practising asking about months using ordinal numbers. • Completing a table of famous birthdays. • Matching years in numbers with years in words. • Dictating years to a partner.
Listening **SB page 79**	*Listening skills*: listening for detail	• Listening and repeating dates. • Matching dates to events. • Making a list of important events and dates.
Grammar **SB page 80**	*Grammar*: be (past simple)	• Completing questions and answers. • Asking and answering questions.
Reading **SB page 80**	*Reading skills*: reading for gist	• Reading about people who went to the Live 8 concerts and identifying feelings. • Choosing the correct answers to complete sentences.
Vocabulary **SB page 81**	*Vocabulary*: positive and negative adjectives	• Matching reactions to the Live 8 event to the appropriate person. • Completing sentences.
Pronunciation **SB page 81**	*Pronunciation*: stress in adjectives	• Listening and repeating adjectives. • Categorising adjectives according to stress patterns.
Useful phrases **SB page 82**	*Vocabulary*: phrases which are useful when buying tickets	• Listening to a telephone conversation and identifying what the customer wants. • Completing a conversation with dates, times and numbers. • Listening to and repeating useful phrases for buying tickets. • Writing and practising a new conversation.
Vocabulary *Extra* **SB page 83**	*Vocabulary*: revision of words from the unit: common adjectives	• Matching pictures with words.
Writing **WB page 47**	Building a description of an event from notes	

Warm-up

Write today's date on the board. Read it out to the class, saying, for example, *Today is the third of February*. Point out that yesterday was the second of February. In subsequent classes, begin by asking a different student each time what the date is.

Vocabulary (SB page 78)

Months

1 🌐 2.44

- Focus the students' attention on the list of months in the margin. Remind them that the underlining shows which syllable of a word should be stressed.

- Play the recording and ask the students to listen and repeat the months. Pay particular attention to the pronunciation of ones that they're likely to have difficulty with, such as *January* /ˈdʒænjuəri/, *February* /ˈfebruəri/ and *August* /ˈɔːgəst/. Ask for individual pronunciation of all the months.

- Focus the students' attention on the speech bubbles and read the question, prompting a student to give you the answer. Remind them that they studied ordinal numbers in Unit 8 and ask another question, for example, *What's the second month?* Then put them in pairs to continue the activity. Go round monitoring and checking that they're all pronouncing the names of the months correctly.

2 🌐 2.45

- Look at the table of famous names with the class. Ask them if they know all the people pictured and what they are famous for. (See Cultural notes opposite.)

- Ask a student when Bono's birthday is. Point out the use of *the* and *of* in dates. Ask another student when Paul McCartney's birthday is. Then ask them to complete the table putting the other birthdays into words.

- Play the recording for them to listen and check. Then play it a second time for them to repeat. Have a final check by asking around the class *When's (Ronaldo's) birthday?*

> a) the tenth of May
> b) the eighteenth of June
> c) the fifth of August
> d) the sixteenth of August
> e) the twenty second of September
> f) the fourteenth of November

Language notes

Vocabulary: dates

- Point out that months are written like days of the weeks, with a capital letter.

- Variants do exist, but in standard British English you write *10ᵗʰ May*, but you say *the tenth of May*. However, in American English you write *May 10*, and you say *May tenth*.

- In British English, when you write the date in figures, you write *10/5/2007*. However, because in American English you say the month first, you write *5/10/2007* when referring to *10ᵗʰ May*.

Cultural notes

Bono (born 1960)
Bono is the lead singer of the Irish rock band U2. He performed in the original Band Aid, and then at Live Aid the following year, and at Live 8 in 2005. He's involved in campaigning for third-world debt relief and raising awareness of the problems of Africa.

Paul McCartney (born 1942)
Paul McCartney, John Lennon, George Harrison and Ringo Starr came from Liverpool in the north of England. They formed the band the Beatles, which became the most famous pop group of the 1960s. Paul McCartney and John Lennon wrote some of the best-known songs in rock and pop music, including *Yesterday*, *Hey Jude* and *Let it Be*.

After the break-up of the Beatles in 1970, McCartney formed the band Wings. He still writes music and performs in concerts.

Neil Armstrong (born 1930)
American Astronaut Neil Armstrong was the commander of Apollo 11, America's first attempt to land a manned vehicle on the Moon. On 20ᵗʰ July he became the first person to walk on the Moon.

Madonna (born 1958)
Madonna, is one of the most successful recording artists of all time, with songs such as *Material Girl* and *Into the Groove*. She's also appeared in a number of films, including *Desperately Seeking Susan* and *Evita*. In 2000, she married British film director Guy Ritchie.

➤

Ronaldo (born 1976)
Ronaldo played in the Brazilian football team that won the World Cup in 2002, and holds the record for the most goals scored by a player in World Cup matches. He currently plays for Real Madrid.

Prince Charles (born 1948)
Prince Charles is the eldest son of Queen Elizabeth II and Prince Philip. He was married to Lady Diana Spencer, who was killed in a car crash in Paris in 1997. They had two sons, William and Harry. Prince Charles is now married to Camilla Parker-Bowles.

3

- Ask several students when their birthdays are. Then ask them to write five birthdays in their family in the style shown. When they've finished, focus their attention on the speech bubble and read it out. Then get a student to ask you when your birthday is. Reply using the same formula: *My birthday is the … .*

- Put the students in pairs and ask them to tell each other about the birthday's on their list. Go round, monitoring and giving help. Encourage them to pronounce the dates correctly.

4 🌐 2.46

- Look at the example with the class and read out the date (1969). Then ask them to match the other years in numbers with the equivalent words.

- Play the recording for them to check their answers. Then play it a second time for them to listen and repeat. Ask for individual repetition of the years. Check that they're pronouncing the final syllable of *nineteen* clearly and differentiating it from *ninety*. Also check that *thousand* is pronounced correctly (/ˈθaʊzənd/).

> a) 3: nineteen sixty-nine
> b) 5: nineteen seventy-five
> c) 2: nineteen eighty-nine
> d) 6: nineteen ninety-seven
> e) 1: two thousand and five
> f) 4: two thousand and six

5

- Ask the students to write down five different years in numbers. They should do this individually and not let anyone else see what they have written.

- Put the students into pairs and ask them to dictate their years to a partner, again without showing them what they have written. The partner should write down the date they hear. Afterwards, they should compare what they've written to check that it's the same. They then change roles. Go round, monitoring and giving help where necessary.

If your students need further practice, you could use Photocopiable Worksheet *11 Vocabulary* here.

Extra activity

Ask the students to mill. Get them to tell each other their date of birth, and to organise themselves in a line from the youngest to the oldest, or from January to December if there are students in the class who are reluctant to say their age.

Language note

Vocabulary: pronunciation of *2010* onwards

It's as yet unclear what method of pronunciation will be generally used to refer to the years *2010* onwards. Some will prefer to continue with the present method and say *two thousand and ten*. Others will prefer to use the pre *2000* method and say *twenty-ten*. The latter seems to be the preferred British method as the BBC are using it. Also the Olympics in London in 2012 are referred to as the *Twenty-twelve Olympics*.

Listening (SB page 79)

1 🌐 2.47

Focus the students' attention on the dates in the box and ask several students to read them out. Then play the recording for them to listen and repeat.

2 🌐 2.48

- Focus the students' attention on the four photos. Ask them if they remember any of these events and can tell the class anything about them. Did they watch any of them on television? Point out the television viewing figures given in the captions and teach them how to say the large numbers. Ask students *Which event did most people watch?* (The 2006 World Cup Final).

- Then ask if they can match some of the dates from the box in Exercise 1 with these events. Allow them to discuss this in pairs or small groups, and then get them to report back to the class on their decisions. Do not confirm any answers at this stage.

- Play the recording for the students to check their answers. Find out which pair or group got the most correct answers.

> a) 9th July 2006
> b) 2nd July 2005
> c) 6th September 1997
> d) 20th July 1969

🌐 2.48

a)

*Welcome to 'Spectacular Television Events'.
Our first event is an important football match. On
9ᵗʰ July 2006, Italy won the World Cup in Germany.
Three and a half billion people watched the match on
television. France lost the match on penalties.*

b)

*Our next event is Live 8. On 2ⁿᵈ July 2005, three
billion people watched the Live 8 concerts on
television. Paul McCartney, U2, Stevie Wonder,
Björk and Coldplay were some of the big names at
Live 8 concerts around the world.*

c)

*The death of Princess Diana was a tragic event. On
6ᵗʰ September 1997, two and a half billion people
watched her funeral on television. Prince William
was fifteen years old, and Prince Harry was only
twelve.*

d)

*And finally, were you born when the first man
landed on the Moon? On 20ᵗʰ July 1969 Neil
Armstrong said the famous words, 'That's one small
step for man, but one giant leap for mankind'. Five
hundred million people watched the historic event on
television.*

Cultural notes

The World Cup final 2006
Italy beat France 5–3 in a penalty shoot-out in the
2006 World Cup final in Berlin, Germany.

Live 8
Live 8 was a series of ten simultaneous music
concerts around the world. The concerts took
place in July 2005 as part of the 'Make Poverty
History' campaign. More than 1,000 musicians
performed at the concerts. For more information,
go to www.live8live.com

Princess Diana's funeral
Princess Diana was killed in a car crash in Paris in
the early hours of August 31ˢᵗ 1997. Her funeral
took place a week later. It's estimated that more
than a million people lined the London streets to
say goodbye.

The first Moon landing
In July 20ᵗʰ 1969, Neil Armstrong and Buzz Aldrin
became the first astronauts to set foot on the Moon.

3

• Pairwork. If your students are of different
nationalities, you could try to pair them up so that
the students in each pair are from the same country.
If not, they can simply make two lists and help each
other with suggestions and questions.

• Ask the pairs to report back to the class on their lists.

Grammar (SB page 80)

be: past simple

1 🌐 2.49

• Focus the students' attention on the information
about the past simple of the verb *be* in the margin.
Explain that you use this tense to talk about things
that happened in the past, and go through the forms
with them. Ask several students the question
Were you at the Live 8 concert? and elicit the answers
Yes, I was or *No, I wasn't*. Then choose an event that
some of them may well have attended and ask about
that. You could simply ask *Were you at school
yesterday?* Encourage some of them to ask similar
questions. Encourage them also to use the correct
pronunciation of *were* /wɜː/ and make sure that they
know the difference between *were* and *where* /weə/.
Teach the negative form *weren't*.

• Focus the students' attention on the questions and
answers and go through the example with them.
Then ask them to complete the rest. Go round,
monitoring and giving help.

• Play the recording for the students to check their
answers, then play it a second time for them to listen
and repeat the questions and answers.

> a) 'Were you at secondary school in 2002?'
>   'Yes, I was.' 'No, I wasn't.'
> b) 'Were you at work yesterday?'
>   'Yes, I was.' 'No, I wasn't.'
> c) 'Was it sunny yesterday?'
>   'Yes, it was.' 'No, it wasn't.'
> d) 'Was your mother born before 1963?'
>   'Yes, she was.' 'No, she wasn't.'
> e) 'Were you and your friends in town
>   yesterday?'
>   'Yes, we were.' 'No, we weren't.'
> f) 'Were your parents at university in 1975?'
>   'Yes, they were.' 'No, they weren't.'

Language note

Vocabulary: *was born*

You use the past simple tense of the verb *to be born*
when you give your date or place of birth: *I was
born in London in 1987.*

2

Pairwork. Put the students in pairs and get them to take
turns asking and answering the questions in Exercise 1,
giving answers that are true for them. Monitor and help,
encouraging them to use the correct pronunciation.

3 Pairwork

• The pairwork exercise for this unit is on pages 119
and 124 of the Student's Book. Put the students in
pairs and tell them who will be Student A, and who
will be Student B.

- While they're doing the pairwork exercise, go round monitoring and giving help. Take note of any errors which may need focusing on later, and also any examples of good language use which you can praise. Check answers with the class.

---

1 Ronaldinho: He was born on 21st March 1980. He was born in Porto Alegre in Brazil.
2 J K Rowling: She was born on 31st July 1965. She was born in Chipping Sodbury in England.
3 Johnny Depp: He was born on 9th June 1963. He was born in Kentucky in the USA.
4 Antonio Banderas: He was born on 10th August 1960. He was born in Malaga in Spain.

Cultural notes

Ronaldinho (born 1980)
Brazilian football player who is considered one of the best footballers in the world. He currently plays for Barcelona. He was in the Brazilian national team that won the World Cup in 2002, and also played for Brazil in the 2006 World Cup.

JK Rowling (born 1965)
British fiction writer who became famous as the author of the *Harry Potter* series.

Johnny Depp (born 1963)
Johnny Depp's film debut was in *Nightmare On Elm Street* (1984). He then acted in the popular TV series *21 Jump Street*, before starring in the film *Edward Scissorhands* (1990), directed by Tim Burton. His most popular films to date are probably the *Pirates of the Caribbean* trilogy.

Antonio Banderas (born 1960)
Born in Malaga, Spain, Antonio Banderas started acting in theatre and television in Madrid. In the 1980s, he became famous when he acted in a number of films directed by Pedro Almodovar. He then moved to Hollywood and started appearing in American films such as *Desperado* (1995), *The Mask of Zorro* (1998) and *The Legend of Zorro* (2005).

4 *Grammar Extra* 11

Ask students to turn to *Grammar Extra* 11 on page 132 of the Student's Book. Here they'll find an explanation of the grammar they've been studying and further exercises to practise it.

---

1 a) I was at home yesterday afternoon. / I wasn't at home yesterday afternoon.
   b) I was in bed at 7 a.m. this morning. / I wasn't in bed at 7 a.m. this morning.
   c) It was sunny yesterday. / It wasn't sunny yesterday.
   d) *The Simpsons* were on television yesterday evening. / *The Simpsons* weren't on television yesterday evening.
   e) My mother was a student in 1978. / My mother wasn't a student in 1978.
   f) My parents were born in this country. / My parent weren't born in this country.

3 a) No, he wasn't. He was a writer.
   b) No, she wasn't. She was born in England.
   c) No, he wasn't. He was a scientist.
   d) No, she wasn't. She was an actor.
   e) No, they weren't. They were born in Spain.
   f) No, he wasn't. He was Italian.

Reading (SB page 80)

1 🌐 2.50

- Remind the students that they saw a photo of one of the Live 8 concerts on the previous page. Explain that there were several concerts held around the world on the same day. Focus the students' attention on the photos and explain that each of these people attended one of the Live 8 concerts, and that they're talking about their experience.

- Go through the questions with the class and make sure that they understand *excited*, *happy* and *lucky*.

- Play the recording and ask the students to read the text as they listen. Then elicit the answers to the questions.

---

a) Japanese people were excited.
b) Olga Ekareva was happy.
c) Amy Ronson was lucky.
d) Juliette Auguste wasn't happy.

---

2 🌐 2.51

- Explain affirmative and negative if the students don't know these terms. Read out the example with the class. Then ask them to look back at the texts in Exercise 1 to find whether the verbs should be affirmative or negative.

- Allow the students to compare results in pairs before playing the recording for them to check their answers. Play it a second time for them to repeat the correct sentences.

---

a) were   b) weren't   c) wasn't   d) was
e) was   f) was

If your students need further practice, you could use Photocopiable Worksheet *11 Grammar* here.

Vocabulary (SB page 81)

1 🌐 2.52

- Ask the students to look at the photos of Andy and Cathy. Ask them: *Who is happy? Who is unhappy?* Ask two of the stronger students to read the example reactions. Encourage them to put expression into their voices. Then ask students to match the other reactions to the appropriate person.

- Play the recording for the students to check their answers, then play it a second time for them to listen and repeat.

> Andy: 'It was amazing/excellent/fantastic/
> great/wonderful.'
> Cathy: 'It was awful/boring/terrible.'

2 🌐 2.53

Ask the students to look back at the opinions on page 80 and to find which adjective should go in each gap. Allow them to discuss their answers in pairs before you play the recording for them to check. Play it a second time for them to listen and repeat the sentences.

> a) amazing   b) awful   c) excellent
> d) great   e) wonderful   f) fantastic

3

- Make sure that the students understand and can pronounce all the words in the first box. Take care with *restaurant* (/'restərɒnt/). Ask a student to read out the examples.

- Ask the students to work individually to make sentences for themselves.

- Put the students in pairs to compare their sentences. Encourage them to ask each other for further details and to report back to the class.

Pronunciation (SB page 81)

1 🌐 2.54

- Explain to the students that all these adjectives represent quite strong feelings about the things they are describing. Encourage them to reflect this strength of feeling in their intonation when they say them. Demonstrate by saying *amazing* in an excited tone and in a boring tone, and explain why the latter is inappropriate.

- Play the recording and ask the students to listen and repeat the adjectives. Point out that the adjective *delicious* is generally only used for food.

2 🌐 2.55

- Remind the students of the function of the small and large stress boxes. Ask a student to read out the two example words, *excellent* and *amazing*. Focus their attention on the underlining, which indicates the stressed syllable. Then ask the students to put the adjectives in the box in Exercise 1 into the correct columns according to their stress pattern, and to underline the stressed syllables.

- Allow the students to compare answers in pairs before playing the recording for them to check their answers. Play it a second time for them to repeat all the adjectives.

> A: <u>ex</u>cellent, <u>te</u>rrible, <u>won</u>derful
> B: a<u>ma</u>zing, de<u>li</u>cious, ex<u>pen</u>sive, fan<u>tas</u>tic, im<u>por</u>tant

Useful phrases (SB page 82)

1 🌐 2.56

- Focus the students' attention on the Arts Centre events page and ask what events are taking place. Students are going to listen to a telephone conversation in which someone is booking a ticket for one of the events.

- Go through the three statements and the options with the class. Then play the recording and ask them to underline the correct answers. You may need to play the recording more than once. Check answers with the class.

> a) *Shrek*
> b) two tickets
> c) by credit card

Cultural note

Shrek

Shrek is a computer-animated film. It won an Oscar for Best Animated Feature. It's the third most successful movie of all time, behind *Titanic* and the original *Star Wars*.

2

- Ask several students to read out the dates, times and numbers in the box.

- Play the recording again and ask the students to read the conversation as they listen, and complete it with the correct information.

- Play the recording again for them to check their answers.

1 Friday 13th March
2 6.30
3 Two
4 £20
5 4899 2424 1836 5800
6 January 2012

3 **2.57**

Ask the students to find the useful phrases in the conversation in Exercise 2. Play the recording and ask them to listen and repeat the phrases.

4

Pairwork. As the students write their conversations, go round, giving help and encouragement. When they've finished, get them to practise them aloud. Take note of any particularly good conversations and ask the students involved to perform them for the class.

If your students need further practice, you could use Photocopiable Worksheet *11 Communication* here.

Vocabulary *Extra* (SB page 83)

Common adjectives

1

• Focus the students' attention on the list of words and point out that they're all to do with common adjectives. Remind the students that the underlining indicates the syllable of the word that has the strongest stress. Check that the students can pronounce all of the words correctly.

• Ask the students to look at the pictures and match each one with one of the words. Point out that the first one has been done for them.

3	awful	7	great
8	boring	10	happy
2	delicious	4	important
9	fantastic	6	lucky
5	good	1	terrible

2

• Explain positive and negative, and ask the students to work in pairs to decide which of the adjectives in Exercise 1 should go in which column.

• You may like to point out the hierarchies of the adjectives in this section: *terrible* is worse than *awful*; *great* is better than *good*, but not as good as *fantastic*.

Positive (✓): delicious, fantastic, good, great, happy, important, lucky
Negative (✗): awful, boring, terrible

Writing
Workbook page 47
Building a description of an event from notes

Photocopiable resource materials
Grammar: *It's a lie!* (Teacher's notes page 135. Worksheet page 177.)
Vocabulary: *What are the numbers?* (Teacher's notes page 135. Worksheet page 178.)
Communication: *Going out* (Teacher's notes page 136. Worksheet page 179.)

Test CD
See *Test Unit 11* on the CD.

CD-ROM
For more activities go to Unit 11: *Events*.

For the best activities for beginner students, see pages xvi–xxi
For practical methodology, from *Classroom interaction* to *Writing*, see pages xxii–xxxv
What can your students do now? See self-evaluation checklists on pages xxxvi–xlvi

Hero *Overview*

Section	Aims	What the students are doing
Vocabulary **SB page 84**	*Vocabulary*: sports	• Listening to and repeating the names of sports. • Adding *go* or *play* to the names of sports.
Speaking **SB page 84**	*Conversation skills*: asking *How often?* questions about sport	• Asking questions about how often a partner does certain sports. • Talking about favourite sports and sporting heroes.
Reading **SB page 85**	*Reading skills*: reading for specific information	• Reading a text about cycling star Lance Armstrong. • Ordering events in Armstrong's life. • Completing sentences with dates.
Grammar **SB page 86**	*Grammar*: past simple (regular verbs)	• Completing a table of verbs. • Completing sentences. • Making sentences about yesterday.
Pronunciation **SB page 86**	*Pronunciation*: present and past verb forms	• Listening to and repeating present and past verb forms. • Categorising verbs according to their past simple endings.
Grammar **SB page 87**	*Grammar*: past simple (irregular verbs)	• Listening to and repeating past simple forms of irregular verbs. • Completing a text.
Listening **SB page 87**	*Listening skills*: listening for detail	• Listening to a text about famous people and noting the order in which they are mentioned. • Completing past simple sentences. • Matching sentences to famous people. • Talking about heroes in history.
Useful phrases **SB page 88**	*Vocabulary*: phrases which are useful on special occasions	• Matching greetings cards to special occasions. • Completing conversations with appropriate messages. • Listening to and repeating useful phrases for special occasions. • Writing and practising a new conversation. • Talking about special occasions.
Vocabulary *Extra* **SB page 89**	*Vocabulary*: revision of words from the unit: verb phrases	• Matching pictures with words.
Writing **WB page 51**	Building a personal life history from notes	

Quick revision

- This game is a quick review of ordinal numbers and dates, and pre-teaches *was born* which appears in the Reading activity.

- Write on the board the following six dates: *14th August 1966, 16th May 1953, 26th October 1965, 21st June 1982, 14th November 1948, 28th April 1974.*

- Put the students into pairs. Ask them to look at the picture of Pierce Brosnan on page 6 in their book and decide when he was born and write it down. Then do the same with the other people in the list below.
  Pierce Brosnan (page 6) – 16th May 1953
  Halle Berry (page 6) – 14th August 1966
  Penelope Cruz (page 14) – 28th April 1974
  Prince William (page 14) – 21st June 1982
  Prince Charles (page 24) – 14th November 1948
  DJ Judge Jules (page 42) – 26th October 1965

- Ask the students to give you the dates they have put for each person and give the correct answer. The winners are the pair with the most correct answers.

Vocabulary (SB page 84)

1 🌐 **2.58**

- Ask individual students to read out the names of the sports in the box. Make sure that they use the underlining to tell them which syllables are stressed. Then play the recording and ask them to listen and repeat them. Ask if any students do these sports.

- Focus attention on the photos and give the students a couple of minutes to discuss in pairs which person does which sport. Check answers with the class.

a) Lance Armstrong: cycling
b) Pelé: football
c) Maria Sharapova: tennis
d) Ellen MacArthur: sailing
e) Tiger Woods: golf
f) Michael Jordan: basketball

Language note

Vocabulary: sports with *go/play/do*

More adventurous students, or students who aren't complete beginners, may suggest other sports that they play, or heroes from other sports. If they do, some of the sports may not collocate with *play* or *go*, but be used with *do*:

go: *sailing, swimming, riding, running, walking,* etc.
play: *tennis, golf, table tennis, badminton, football,* etc.
do: *gym, aerobics, karate, judo,* etc.

Cultural notes

Lance Armstrong (born 1971)
Lance Armstrong is most famous for winning the Tour de France cycle race a record seven consecutive times from 1999 to 2005. (But don't tell the class this, as it's the answer to Reading exercise 1 on page 85.) He achieved this despite being treated for cancer in 1996. Armstrong retired from racing at the end of the 2005 Tour de France.

Pelé (born 1940)
Pelé is a former Brazilian football player widely regarded as the finest player the world has ever seen. Over the course of his career, Pelé scored over a thousand goals and won three World Cups.

Maria Sharapova (born 1987)
At the age of 17, Russian tennis player Maria Sharapova became Wimbledon women's singles champion – the first Russian champion.

Ellen MacArthur (born 1976)
Ellen MacArthur is best known as a solo long-distance yachtswoman who, on February 7, 2005, broke the world record for the fastest solo circumnavigation of the globe.

Tiger Woods (born 1975)
Tiger Woods is widely considered to be one of the greatest golfers of all time. Woods, who is of mixed race, is credited with prompting a major surge of interest in the game of golf among minorities and young people in the United States.

Michael Jordan (born 1963)
Michael Jordan is considered by many to be the greatest basketball player of all time. Jordan ended his career of 15 seasons with a regular-season scoring average of 30.12 points per game.

2 ⊕ 2.59

- Explain that the verbs you use to talk about doing different sports can vary. For example, you *play* cricket, you *go* swimming, you *do* karate. Tell the students that it's a good idea when they note down new vocabulary to make a note of the verbs that are used with them. Here the students only have to decide between *go* and *play*. They may spot that the sports that end in *ing* are the ones you use *go* with. If not, point this out when you check their answers.

- Play the recording for the students to check their answers, then play it a second time for them to repeat.

play basketball	play golf
go cycling	go sailing
play football	play tennis

Speaking (SB page 84)

1

Remind the students that they learnt how to make *How often?* questions in connection with food in Unit 9. Ask two pairs of students to read out the example speech bubbles. Then put the students in pairs to practise asking and answering *How often?* questions about sport. Go round, giving help and encouragement.

2

- Have a quick show of hands to see what everyone's favourite sport is. Give help with vocabulary if any of the students are interested in unusual sports.

- Explain the meaning of *hero* and ask if any of the sportspeople in the photos on this page are the students' sporting heroes? If not, who are their sporting heroes? Ask them to discuss in pairs.

Language note

Vocabulary: *hero/heroine*

A *hero* is a person admired for doing something exceptional or brave. Here the word *hero* is used to refer to both male and female heroes. A feminine word *heroine* exists, but its usage is generally limited to fictional characters in a film or a book.

Reading (SB page 85)

1 ⊕ 2.60

- Focus the students' attention on the main photo and tell them it's Lance Armstrong, the famous American cyclist. Brainstorm any information the students may know about him and write it on the board.

- Play the recording and ask the students to read the article as they listen. Tell them that the only piece of information they have to find is how many times Lance Armstrong won the Tour de France. Check answers with the class and go over any difficult vocabulary.

He won the Tour de France seven times.

2

Ask the students to go back over the article and find the information that will help them to put the events in order. Allow them to do this in pairs, and to compare their results with another pair before you check answers with the class.

1 b	2 e	3 d	4 a	5 c

3 ⊕ 2.61

- Remind the students that they learnt how to say dates in Unit 11 and get one of them to say the first date (1971). Then ask them to go back over the article and find the dates to complete the stages of Armstrong's life. Check answers with the class, asking individual students to read out each of the stages.

- Play the recording for them to check again. Play it a second time for them to repeat the sentences.

a) 1971	b) 1978	c) 1988	d) 1992
e) 1996	f) 1997	g) 1998	h) 2005

If your students need further practice, you could use Photocopiable Worksheet *12 Grammar* here.

Grammar (SB page 86)

Past simple

1

- Tell the students that they're going to do some more work on the past simple tense. Remind them that they learnt the past tense of the verb *be* in Unit 11. Focus their attention on the information about *work* in the margin. Read out the past simple form and explain that it's the same for all persons (*I, you, he, we,* etc.). Tell the students that *work* is known as a regular verb.

- Ask the students to look at the headings in the box and the table of spelling rules for regular verbs. Point out the example verbs in each column and explain that the columns represent the different endings for regular verbs in the past simple.

- Ask the students to complete the table with the correct headings from the box. Check answers with the class before moving on to the next stage of the exercise.

a) Add *ed* / *d*
b) Delete *y* and add *ied*
c) Add consonant + *ed*

- Allow the students to work in pairs to decide which of the verbs in the box should go in which column of the table. Do a couple with the class first as an example. When they add the verbs to the table, they should write in the past simple forms next to them.

- Go round, checking that everyone has understood the principles of the different spellings and giving extra help to anyone having difficulty. Encourage them to record new verbs with the past simple forms next to them. Check answers with the class.

> a) Add *ed / d*: talk – talked, live – lived, arrive – arrived, complete – completed, cook – cooked, finish – finished, join – joined, like – liked, phone – phoned, recover – recovered, retire – retired, use – used, walk – walked, watch – watched
> b) Delete *y* and add *ied* study – studied, try – tried
> c) Add consonant + *ed*: stop – stopped, plan – planned

Language notes

Grammar: regular past simple endings

- Verbs that end in a consonant, such as *talk*, add *ed*.
- Verbs that end with an *e*, such as *live*, simply add *d*.
- Verbs that end with a vowel followed by *y*, such as *play*, simply add *ed*.
- Verbs that end in a consonant and *y*, such as *study*, change the *y* to an *i* and add *ed*.
- Verbs that end in one stressed vowel then one consonant, such as *stop* or *plan*, double the consonant and add *ed*.
- Verbs that end in one stressed vowel then *w* or *y*, such as *allow* or *stay*, simply add *ed*.

2 🌐 **2.62**

Ask the students to work individually to complete the sentences. Then allow them to compare their results in pairs before you play the recording for them to check their answers. Play it a second time for them to repeat the sentences.

> a) liked   b) joined   c) finished
> d) recovered   e) started   f) retired

3 🌐 **2.63**

- Go through the example sentence with the class. Then ask students to use the prompts to complete the other sentences. Play the recording for them to check their answers, then play it again for them to repeat the sentences.
- Ask the students to tick the sentences that are true for them. If any are false, ask them if they can make some true sentences about what they did yesterday.

> a) I used a computer.   d) I listened to music.
> b) I walked to work.   e) I cooked the dinner.
> c) I planned a holiday.   f) I studied English.

Pronunciation (SB page 86)

1 🌐 **2.64**

Play the recording and ask the students to repeat the present and past forms of the verbs. Then ask for individual repetition around the class.

> All the verbs in list B have an extra syllable in the past form.

Language notes

Pronunciation: *ed* endings

- The *ed* ending on regular past simple verbs ending in /t/ or /d/ is pronounced with an extra syllable (/ɪd/). For example, *started, waited, ended*.
- For all other regular past simple verbs there's no extra syllable. After unvoiced sounds: /k/, /p/, /f/, /s/, /ʃ/ and /tʃ/, *ed* is pronounced /t/. For example, *stopped, walked, watched*. After voiced sounds, *ed* is pronounced /d/. For example, *arrived, changed, used*.

2 🌐 **2.65**

- Ask the students to say the past simple forms of the verbs out loud. This will give them a feel for what sounds right. If they can't say a past simple form without adding an extra syllable, then the verb belongs in list B.
- Play the recording for them to check their answers, then play it a second time for them to repeat the verbs.

> | **A** | **B** |
> |---|---|
> | help – helped | start – started |
> | stop – stopped | wait – waited |
> | ask – asked | hate – hated |
> | join – joined | point – pointed |
> | pass – passed | want – wanted |
> | play – played | |
> | watch – watched | |

Grammar (SB page 87)

Past simple: irregular verbs

1 🌐 **2.66**

- Remind the students that so far they've looked at the past simple tense of the verb *be* and some regular verbs. Explain that some English verbs are irregular (*be* is one of them), and their past simple forms don't follow any kind of rule.
- Focus the students' attention on the information about the verb *go* in the margin. Tell the students that though they'll have to learn each of the irregular past forms individually, they don't change according to the person. Remind them that they used *went* in Unit 11 when they talked about the last concert, party, etc., that they went to.

- Play the recording and ask the students to listen and repeat the infinitive and past simple forms of the verbs.
- Ask them to work in pairs to identify which past simple form in each line has a different sound from the others. Encourage them to say the words aloud so that they get a feel for what sounds right. Check answers with the class.

> a) do – did
> b) know – knew
> c) get – got
> d) write – wrote
> e) take – took
> f) give – gave

Extra activity

- Use chanting to help students memorise the past forms. Say the infinitive form of one of the verbs in Exercise 1, and get the students to chant out the past simple form. Repeat until the students seem confident.
- Then change: give the past form and ask the students to chant the infinitive form.

Language notes

Grammar: teaching irregular verbs

- There are approximately 180 irregular verbs. Some of these are very rare, but many others are very useful and students need to learn them at some stage.
- Some people learn a list by heart. Others think you'll just gradually acquire them over time. However, one useful method is for students to note down new irregular verbs when they meet them in sentences rather than as individual words.

If your students need further practice, you could use Photocopiable Worksheet 12 Vocabulary here.

2 Pairwork

- The pairwork exercise for this unit is on pages 119 and 124. Put the students in pairs and tell them who will be Student A, and who will be Student B.
- While they're doing the pairwork exercise, go round monitoring and giving help. Take note of any errors which may need focusing on later, and also any examples of good language use, which you can praise. Check answers with the class.

> A: Ellen MacArthur
> B: Pelé
> C: Michael Jordan
> 1: Maria Sharapova
> 2: Diego Maradona
> 3: Muhammed Ali

3 *Grammar Extra* 12

Ask the students to turn to *Grammar Extra* 12 on page 132 of the Student's Book. Here they'll find an explanation of the grammar they've been studying and further exercises to practise it.

> 1
> 1 worked   2 lived   3 stop   4 studied
> 5 liked   6 completed   7 try   8 listen
> 2
> a) said   b) saw   c) bought   d) got
> e) went   f) had

4 🌐 2.67

- Ask the students if they've ever heard of Juan Sebastián Elcano. If not, explain that he was a sixteenth-century Spanish explorer. Focus their attention on the map of his travels round the world.
- Ask them to read the text and complete it with the past simple of the verbs in brackets. You could point out that some of the verbs are regular and some are irregular. Allow the students to work in pairs if they wish. Go round helping anyone who is having difficulty with forming the simple past tense.
- Play the recording for the students to check their answers. Ask them why Elcano is famous.

> 1 was   2 was   3 completed   4 sent
> 5 was   6 asked   7 sailed   8 died
> 9 continued   10 arrived   11 started
> 12 returned
>
> He completed the first voyage round the world.

Cultural note

Juan Sebastián Elcano (born 1476, died 1526) Juan Sebastián Elcano was a Spanish navigator who commanded a ship that circumnavigated the world in the early sixteenth century.

Listening (SB page 87)

1 🌐 2.68

- Look at the photographs of the three famous people with the class. Elicit any information that they know about them. Encourage use of the past simple. For example, *Leonardo da Vinci was a painter*; *Beethoven wrote music*; *Mother Teresa helped poor people*.
- Play the recording and ask the students to note down the order in which the people are mentioned. Check answers with the class.

> 1 c) Mother Teresa
> 2 b) Beethoven
> 3 a) Leonardo da Vinci

2.68 (I = Interviewer; P = Pat; E = Eva;
C = Carla)

I: *Who's your hero in history?*
P: *Mother Teresa.*
I: *Why?*
A. *Because she lived a very simple life and she gave all her time and her love to poor people.*

2
I: *Who's your hero in history?*
E: *Beethoven.*
I: *Why?*
E: *Because he went deaf, but he wrote wonderful music.*

3
I: *Who's your hero in history?*
C: *Leonardo da Vinci.*
I: *Why?*
C: *Because he was a genius. He did so many different things. He painted the Mona Lisa and he designed the first helicopter. Also, he was a vegetarian and he loved animals.*

Cultural notes

Leonardo da Vinci (born 1452, died 1519)
Leonardo da Vinci was an Italian Renaissance artist, famous for paintings such as the *Mona Lisa* and *The Last Supper*. He also made designs, some hundreds of years ahead of his time, for the helicopter, the armoured tank, the calculator, and many others. He contributed greatly to the study of anatomy, astronomy, and civil engineering too.

Ludwig van Beethoven (born 1770, died 1827)
Ludwig van Beethoven was a German composer and pianist. In his late twenties, he began to lose his hearing and became totally deaf. Nevertheless, throughout his life he continued to produce masterpieces, and he's widely regarded as one of classical music's greatest composers.

Mother Teresa (born 1910, died 1997)
Mother Teresa was an Albanian Catholic nun who founded the Missionaries of Charity in India. In 1952, she opened her first Home for the Dying in Calcutta. Over the years, Mother Teresa created many homes for the dying and the unwanted throughout the world. In 1979, she was awarded the Nobel Peace Prize.

2

Look at the example with the class, then ask them to put all the other verbs in brackets into the past simple. Check answers with the class and explain any difficult vocabulary.

a) went, wrote
b) painted, designed
c) lived, gave

3

Ask the students to discuss in pairs which sentence in Exercise 2 describes which famous person in Exercise 1. Play the recording again and then check answers with the class.

a) Beethoven
b) Leonardo da Vinci
c) Mother Teresa

4

• You could set the preparation for this for homework so that the students have time to look up some information on their heroes. Ask them to choose one person and to tell a partner about their hero. If they do written preparation for this, go round checking that they're using past simple verbs correctly.

• When the students have finished telling each other about their heroes, ask them to report back to the class about their partner's hero, and what they've found out about him or her.

Extra activity

• Do a chain memorisation activity based on the past simple forms the students have seen in this unit.

• Write on the board *Yesterday, I went to London and I …,* and encourage a confident student to finish the sentence, e.g. *bought a car.* Then ask another student to repeat the sentence and add another element using a different verb.

• You'll find a full explanation of this technique in the Practical methodology section of the Introduction.

If your students need further practice, you could use Photocopiable Worksheet *12 Communication* here.

Useful phrases (SB page 88)

1 **2.69**

• Ask the students if they send cards to friends on their birthdays. Ask them on what other occasions they send cards to people.

• Give the students time to look at the pictures of greetings cards. Then ask them to match the special occasions listed in the box with the greeting cards.

• Play the recording for them to check their answers.

1 f   2 c   3 b   4 e   5 d   6 a

2 🔵 2.70

- Focus the students' attention on the pictures and ask them to decide what the situations are. Read out the messages in the box and ask them to match each one to a conversation, and use it to complete the gaps.
- Play the recording for them to listen and check, and explain any difficult vocabulary.

> a) Congratulations!
> b) Good luck!
> c) Happy birthday!

3 🔵 2.71

Play the recording for the students to listen and repeat. Then elicit the kinds of situations in which these would be appropriate messages. (*Congratulations!*: a new baby, a wedding, passing a driving test, passing an exam, etc. *Good luck!*: taking a driving test, taking an exam, starting a new job, etc. *Happy birthday!*: birthdays only.)

4

- Pairwork. Elicit from the class what would be an appropriate message for each of the situations (You're 21 today: *Happy birthday!* or *Congratulations!* as it's a 'special' birthday; You've passed an exam: *Congratulations!*; You're in a race: *Good luck!*).
- Put the students into pairs and ask them to choose one situation and write a conversation. Go round, giving help and encouragement. Then ask them to practise their conversations. Go round and note any particularly good ones that you can ask the students to perform for the class.

5

Ask the students to discuss their last special occasions in pairs, and to report back to the class on what their partners said.

Vocabulary *Extra* (SB page 89)

Verb phrases

1

- Focus the students' attention on the list of words and point out that they're all to do with verb phrases. Remind the students that the underlining indicates the syllable of the word that has the strongest stress. Check that the students can pronounce all of the words correctly.
- Ask the students to look at the pictures and match each one with one of the phrases. Point out that the first one has been done for them.
- You could then ask them to check with a partner before checking with the class.

6	get divorced	4	play basketball
2	get married	13	play football
7	go cycling	8	play golf
3	go sailing	14	play tennis
12	have an operation	5	use a computer
1	listen to music	10	watch TV
11	lose a race	9	win a race

2

Point out that the activities contain a mixture of regular and irregular verbs. Put the students in pairs to decide on the past simple form of each of the verbs phrases from Exercise 1.

6	got divorced	4	played basketball
2	got married	13	played football
7	went cycling	8	played golf
3	went sailing	14	played tennis
12	had an operation	5	used a computer
1	listened to music	10	watched TV
11	lost a race	9	won a race

Writing
Workbook page 51
Building a personal life history from notes

Photocopiable resource materials
Grammar: *Steffi Graf* (Teacher's notes page 136. Worksheet page 180.)
Vocabulary: *Bingo!* (Teacher's notes page 137. Worksheet page 181.)
Communication: *Snakes and Ladders* (Teacher's notes page 137. Worksheet page 182.)

Test CD
See *Test Unit 12* on the CD.

DVD
Programme 6: *Solo sailor*

🔵 CD-ROM
For more activities go to Unit 12: *Hero*.

> For the best activities for beginner students, see pages xvi–xxi
>
> For practical methodology, from *Classroom interaction* to *Writing*, see pages xxii–xxxv
>
> What can your students do now? See self-evaluation checklists on pages xxxvi–xlvi

Review D *Teacher's notes*

These exercises act as a check of the grammar and vocabulary that the students have learnt in Units 10, 11 and 12 of the Student's Book. Use them to find any problems that students are having, or anything that they haven't understood and which will need further work.

Grammar (SB page 90)

Remind the students of the grammar explanations they read and the exercises they did in the *Grammar Extra* on pages 132 and 133 of the Student's Book.

1

Point out to the students that you use the present continuous to describe things that are happening at the moment. Ask them to look at the illustration and complete the sentences. Check answers.

a) is speaking	d) is working
b) is drinking	e) is eating
c) is reading	f) is sleeping

2

Go through the example question with the class and then ask the students to complete the questions. Check that they've formed all the questions correctly before they answer them.

a) Are   b) Is   c) Is   d) Are

a) Yes, they are.
b) No, she isn't.
c) Yes, he is.
d) No, they aren't.

3

Ask the students to underline the correct words and check answers with the class. If anyone makes a mistake, remind them that *I*, *he*, *she* and *it* take *was*, and *you*, *we* and *they* take *were*.

1 Were	2 was	3 Was	4 wasn't
5 Was	6 wasn't	7 Were	8 were

4

Remind the students of the difference between regular verbs and irregular verbs. Regular verbs form the past simple with *d*, *ed* or *ied*. Irregular verbs each have their own past simple form. Ask them to complete the table and check answers with the class.

1 stopped	2 want	3 finished	4 study
5 became	6 buy	7 spoke	8 know

5

- Students complete the sentences. Check answers before moving on to the second stage of the exercise.

a) was born	d) graduated
b) had	e) went
c) started	f) arrived

- Ask the students to make the sentences true for themselves. Go round, monitoring and giving help. Then put them in pairs to compare their sentences.
- Ask several students to read their sentences out to the class.

6

This exercise gives the students an opportunity to identify mistakes, a skill that will be useful when they come to check their own work. They have the advantage here of seeing what the correct sentence should be in each case.

1 a) ~~I reading a really good book.~~
2 b) ~~Paul's working?~~
3 a) ~~What you are doing?~~
4 a) ~~We wasn't happy with the hotel.~~
5 b) ~~The car stop near the school.~~
6 a) ~~I taked the bus to work.~~

Vocabulary (SB page 91)

1

Students complete the crossword. When they've finished, ask several of them to describe what they're wearing today.

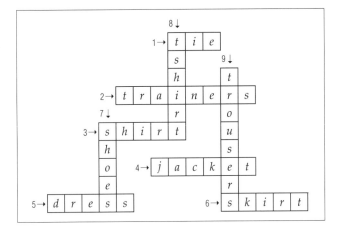

2

- Remind the students that certain nouns join with particular verbs to make verb phrases. Ask them to complete the questions and check their answers before moving on to the next stage of the exercise.

- Then ask the students to work individually to answer the questions for themselves. Finally, put them in pairs to compare their answers.

a) make   b) do   c) play   d) read
e) make   f) do

3

Remind the students that they studied ordinal numbers in Unit 8 and Unit 11. Ask the students to underline the correct words and check answers with the class.

a) first   b) second   c) fourth   d) tenth
e) eleventh   f) twelfth

4

Ask the students to work individually to complete the sentences. They should then read their answers aloud to a partner.

a) January   b) February   c) March
d) July   e) December

Cultural notes

(Saint) Valentine's Day (14th February)
(Saint) Valentine's Day is the traditional day on which lovers send each other cards. These are often anonymous. Approximately 85 percent of these cards are bought by women.

Saint Patrick's Day (17th March)
Saint Patrick's Day celebrates Saint Patrick (386–493), the patron saint of Ireland. It's a national holiday in the Republic of Ireland. It's also celebrated in many countries by people of Irish descent.

US Independence Day (4th July)
In the United States, Independence Day (also called the Fourth of July), is a national holiday celebrating the Declaration of Independence on July 4, 1776. There are many parades, barbecues, picnics, baseball games, and various other events.

5

Remind the students that with some sports you use *go* and with some you use *play*. Look at the example with the class and then point out the different time expressions in the prompts. Ask the students to write sentences for the other pictures, being sure to use *go* or *play* correctly and to use the correct tense.

a) Andy played basketball last week.
b) Britt is playing football now.
c) Carole plays tennis for her country. (Present simple because it is a general statement rather than an indication of what she is doing right now.)
d) Dan went cycling yesterday.
e) Erica goes sailing every week.

If your students need further practice, you could use Photocopiable Worksheet *Review D* here.

Pronunciation (SB page 91)

1

Ask various students to read out the example words. Then ask them to put the words from the box into the correct columns, according to their stress patterns. Encourage them to say them aloud so that they can hear the patterns and get a feeling for what sounds right. Check answers with the class.

1 and 2
A: cheque, helped, jeans
B: <u>foot</u>ball, <u>jac</u>ket, <u>star</u>ted
C: <u>au</u>dience, <u>bas</u>ketball, <u>yes</u>terday
D: a<u>ma</u>zing, fan<u>tas</u>tic, Sep<u>tem</u>ber

2 🌐 2.72

Ask the students to underline the stressed syllables, then play the recording for them to check their answers. Play it a second time for them to repeat the words.

Reading & Listening (SB page 92)

1 🌐 2.73

- Focus the students' attention on the photo. Tell the students that the photo is of Lily Byrne and her granddaughter. Go through the events of Lily's life with the class, then play the recording and ask them to read the text. Allow them to work in pairs to decide the correct order of the events.

- When you have checked answers, go through the text, giving help with any difficult vocabulary.

a) 5	b) 4	c) 6	d) 3	e) 1	f) 2

2 ⊕ 2.74

- Focus the students' attention on the photo at the bottom of the page and explain that this is a photo from Lily's childhood. Tell them they're going to listen to Lily talking about her early years, and that they have to decide if the sentences are true or false. Go through the sentences to make sure they understand them and know what information they're listening for.

- Play the recording as many times as necessary. Ask the students to mark the sentences true or false. Check answers before they correct the false sentences.

> a) False. (She was born in a village near Dublin.)
> b) False. (Her father was a farmer.)
> c) True.
> d) True.
> e) False. (Mr O'Sullivan was her teacher. She married Cyril Murphy.)
> f) False. (He was twenty-five.)

⊕ 2.74

I was born in a little house in a village near Dublin.
It was a very small house – very small – and I had ten brothers and sisters. My father was a farmer, and life was hard. My parents were very poor – they had no money.

When I was seven, I went to school in the village. There was one class and one teacher – Mr O'Sullivan. He was great! I loved school and I loved books. I wanted to go to university and become a doctor. But then, when I graduated from school, I started work on the farm. I was sixteen.

I got married when I was twenty. My husband, Cyril, was twenty-five.

3

- Explain to the students that they'll need to use information from both the reading text and the listening to complete the sentences. If necessary, play the recording again. Check answers with the class.

- Ask the students to use the sentences about Lily as a framework for writing about their own childhoods. Tell them to work individually and to include one false sentence without telling anyone what it is. Go round, monitoring and giving help.

- Finally, put the students in pairs to take turns reading out their sentences. Ask them to try to identify their partner's false sentence.

> a) Lily was born on 6th May 1922 in Ireland.
> b) She lived in a very small house.
> c) She had ten brothers and sisters.
> d) She started school when she was seven.
> e) She loved school and books.

Writing & Speaking (SB page 93)

1

When checking answers, ask the students to read out the full sentences, including the word *when*. Allow them to refer back to the previous page to get the right information.

> a) 5: She started school when she was seven.
> b) 2: She started university when she was forty.
> c) 4: She got married when she was twenty.
> d) 1: She graduated from university when she was forty-five.
> e) 3: She started work on the farm when she was sixteen.

2

Give the students time to think of their answers and write them down. Then ask them to compare sentences in pairs and to report back to the class on their partner's sentences.

3

Give the students time to think of ideas and complete the information about their chosen person. Then put them in pairs to tell their partner about the person.

4

This could be set for homework and the results could be displayed in the classroom for everyone to read. If you do it in class, go round giving help with vocabulary.

Before the next lesson

Collect some holiday photos to show the class. Also encourage the students to bring in some holiday photos of their own, which you can use in the lesson to do more work on questions and talking about travel.

Photocopiable resource materials

Review D: Song – *What a Wonderful World* (Teacher's notes page 137. Worksheet page 183.)

Test CD

See *Test Review D* on the CD.

For the best activities for beginner students, see pages xvi–xxi

For practical methodology, from *Classroom interaction* to *Writing*, see pages xxii–xxxv

What can your students do now? See self-evaluation checklists on pages xxxvi–xlvi

13 Travel *Overview*

Section	Aims	What the students are doing
Vocabulary **SB page 94**	*Vocabulary*: travel phrases	• Listening to and repeating travel phrases. • Identifying sounds associated with travel.
Reading & Writing **SB page 94**	*Reading skills*: reading for detail *Writing skills*: writing short texts	• Completing texts with travel phrases. • Writing a short factual text.
Reading **SB page 95**	*Reading skills*: reading for detail	• Reading a text and identifying places mentioned in it. • Completing a summary.
Grammar **SB page 96**	*Grammar*: past simple negative and question forms; time expressions	• Completing questions and answers. • Completing a table. • Practising using time expressions. • Talking about different ways to travel.
Vocabulary **SB page 96**	*Vocabulary*: holidays	• Listening to and repeating words and phrases to do with holidays. • Categorising words according to holiday preferences.
Pronunciation **SB page 97**	*Pronunciation*: vowel differentiation	• Identifying words in lists that have different vowel sounds.
Grammar **SB page 97**	*Grammar*: *Wh* questions	• Forming *Wh* questions about a conversation. • Completing a conversation. • Talking about holidays.
Listening & Speaking **SB page 97**	*Conversation skills*: fluency practice	• Listening to a man talking about his best holiday and identifying the answers he gives. • Talking about the students' best holiday.
Useful phrases **SB page 98**	*Vocabulary*: phrases which are useful when buying a train ticket	• Listening to a conversation and completing it with numbers. • Listening to and repeating useful phrases for making enquiries at a station. • Writing and practising a new. conversation.
Vocabulary *Extra* **SB page 99**	*Vocabulary*: revision of words from the unit: holidays	• Matching pictures with words.
Writing **WB page 55**	Sequencing: *first, then, after that, finally* Describing a trip	

13 Travel *Teacher's notes*

Quick revision

Play *Irregular verb hangman*. This is like a normal game of Hangman except that instead of writing just one word, you write two, both the infinitive form and the past simple form. So, for example, *go went*.

You will find a full explanation of this technique in the Practical methodology section of the Introduction.

Vocabulary (SB page 94)

Travel phrases

1 🔘 3.01

Focus the students' attention on the travel phrases in the margin. Point out that all the modes of transport given use *by*, with the exception of *on foot*. Play the recording for the students to listen and repeat.

Extra activity

Ask for a show of hands to demonstrate who has used each of these modes of transport within the last week. Elicit any other modes of transport the students can think of (*by balloon, by horse/on horseback, by helicopter, by tram, on skis, by ferry, by ship*).

2 🔘 3.02

- Explain that the students are going to hear some noises which are associated with travel. Ask them before they listen to write the numbers 1 to 8 on a piece of paper. As they hear each noise, they should note down next to the appropriate number what they think the correct travel phrase is.
- Check answers with the class.

1 by motorbike	2 by train	3 by air
4 by bicycle	5 on foot	6 by car
7 by boat	8 by bus	

3 Pairwork

- The pairwork exercise for this unit is on pages 120 and 125. Put the students in pairs and tell them who will be Student A, and who will be Student B.

- While they're doing the exercise, go round monitoring and giving help. Take note of any errors, which may need focusing on later, and also any examples of good language use, which you can praise.

Reading & Writing (SB page 94)

1

Focus the students' attention on the two photos and ask them to read the texts and complete the information. Check they understand by asking questions such as *How long was Robin Knox-Johnston's journey? What was the name of his boat? When did the Choudhurys go around the world by car? How long did it take?* etc.

a) By boat.   b) By car.

Cultural notes

Robin Knox-Johnston (born 1939)
Robin Knox-Johnston was the first man to circumnavigate the globe non-stop and single-handed in April 22nd 1969. In 1994, together with Peter Blake, he won the Jules Verne Trophy for the fastest circumnavigation on their second attempt. Their time was 74 days, 22 hours, 18 minutes and 22 seconds.

Mohammed and Neena Salahuddin Choudhury
Mohammed Salahuddin Choudhury and his wife Neena of Calcutta, India hold the records for the first and fastest circumnavigation of the world by car. Their first journey in 1989 took them 69 days, 19 hours and 5 minutes, and began and finished in Delhi, India. The couple set off again two years later. This time, they took in the six continents in a record 39 days and 20 hours.

2 🔘 3.03

- Ask the students to work individually to complete the text, using the information given in Exercise 1.
- Allow the students to compare their results in pairs before playing the recording for them to check their answers.

1 by boat	2 48,197	3 days	4 hour
5 June	6 April		

3

Point out that the students can use the text in Exercise 2 as a model. As they write, go round giving help and encouragement. Ask several students to read out their texts.

> *Model answer*
>
> Mohammed and Neena Salahuddin Choudhury went round the world by car. They travelled 40,750 kilometres. The journey took 69 days, 19 hours and 5 minutes. They started the journey on 9th September 1989, and finished on 17th November 1989.

Reading (SB page 95)

1 🌐 3.04

- Ask the students if they know who Ewan McGregor and Charlie Boorman are. If they do, ask them to name any films with them in. Go through the countries in the list and make sure that the students can pronounce all of them. Alaska /əˈlæskə/, Australia /ɒsˈtreɪljə/, Britain /ˈbrɪtən/, Canada /ˈkænədə/, Italy /ˈɪtəliː/, Kazahkstan /ˈkæzækstɑːn/, Mongolia /mɒŋˈɡəʊliə/, Russia /ˈrʌʃə/, Siberia /saɪˈbɪəriə/, Ukraine /ˈjukreɪn/.

- Focus the students' attention on the photos and then ask the students to read and listen to the text, ticking the places that Ewan and Charlie visited. Then check answers with the class.

> They visited: Alaska, Britain, Canada, Kazakhstan, Mongolia, Russia, Siberia, Ukraine and the USA.

Cultural notes

Alaska

Note that Alaska is the odd one out in the list as it's not a country, but a state within the United States of America, even though it's separated from most of the other states by a part of Canada. So, anybody who has visited Alaska has visited the USA.

Ewan McGregor (born 1971)

Scottish actor Ewan McGregor acted in the British films *Shallow Grave* and *Trainspotting*. He's since appeared in a number of internationally successful films, including *Star Wars Episodes II* and *III*, in which he played Obi-wan Kenobi. His other films include *Rogue Trader*, *Moulin Rouge* and *Black Hawk Down*.

Charlie Boorman (born 1966)

Son of film director John Boorman, Charlie Boorman started acting at the age of six, and has been acting ever since. He's appeared in films such as *The Bunker*, *On Edge* and *The Emerald Forest*. He's been riding motorcycles since he was seven. He met Ewan McGregor while filming *The Serpent's Kiss*, and their journey around the world on motorbikes was filmed for a television series called *Long Way Round*.

2 🌐 3.05

- Remind the students of the summaries they completed and wrote in the previous section. Then ask them to find the information in the text in Exercise 1 to complete this summary.

- Allow the students to compare their texts in pairs before playing the recording for them to check their answers.

> | | | |
> |---|---|---|
> | 1 Ewan McGregor | 4 three |
> | 2 motorbike | 5 April |
> | 3 30,395 | 6 July |

3

- Pairwork. Put the students in pairs to discuss their last long journey. Go round, giving help and encouragement, and make sure that both students get a chance to talk about their journey.

- Ask the students to report back to the class on what their partner told them.

Grammar (SB page 96)

Past simple

1 🌐 3.06

- Focus the students' attention on the past simple forms in the margin. Read out the example sentences. Then ask the students to complete the questions and answers.

- Play the recording for the students to check their answers. Then play it again for them to listen and repeat.

> a) 'Did they go round the world by motorbike?'
>   'Yes, they did.' 'No, they didn't.'
> b) 'Did they leave London on 14th May 2004?'
>   'Yes, they did.' 'No, they didn't.'
> c) 'Did they travel by car in Siberia?'
>   'Yes, they did.' 'No, they didn't.'
> d) 'Did they arrive in New York on 29th July 2004?'
>   'Yes, they did.' 'No, they didn't.'
> e) 'Did they meet a lot of children?'
>   'Yes, they did.' 'No, they didn't.'
> f) 'Did they sell their motorbikes?'
>   'Yes, they did.' 'No, they didn't.'

Language notes

Grammar: contractions

- Your students have already used the auxiliaries *do/don't* and *does/doesn't* to form questions, short answers and negative sentences in the present simple. In the past simple, the auxiliary *did/didn't* functions in exactly the same way. For example in *yes/no* questions and short answers: *Did you go shopping yesterday? Yes, I did.* And in open questions and negative sentences: *What did you buy? I didn't buy anything.*

- Note that there's only one form *did* for first, second and third persons.

- Note also that you use the infinitive form of the verb after the auxiliary *did/didn't* rather than the past form. For example, *I didn't leave*, not *I didn't left*, and *Did he go?* not *Did he went?*

2

Ask the students to ask and answer the questions in Exercise 1, using the information on page 95 to help them if necessary.

a) Yes, they did.
b) No, they didn't. (They left London on 14th April.)
c) No, they didn't. (They travelled by train.)
d) Yes, they did.
e) Yes, they did.
f) Yes, they did.

3

Go through the columns of the table with the class, and point out that *I went last week* and *I went a week ago* mean the same thing. Ask them to complete the table, making it true for today. Check answers with the class.

4

- Focus the students' attention on the example speech bubbles and read them out. Demonstrate the activity with a confident student, prompting the student to reply with an equivalent expression.

- Put the students in pairs and ask them to take turns to give a prompt with *in* or *last*, and reply with the equivalent expression using *ago*.

5

Go through the example speech bubbles with the class, then ask one or two students to answer the questions truthfully. Then put the students in pairs, and tell them to take turns being the person asking the questions, and the person answering them. Go round, monitoring and giving help. Take note of any interesting answers and get those students to perform their short dialogues for the class.

6 *Grammar Extra* 13

Ask the students to turn to *Grammar Extra* 13 on page 134 of the Student's Book. Here they'll find an explanation of the grammar they've been studying and further exercises to practise it.

1
a) I didn't have coffee for breakfast.
b) I didn't go shopping.
c) I didn't do the housework.
d) I didn't watch a film on television.
e) I didn't walk to work.
f) I didn't buy a newspaper.
g) I didn't write a letter.
h) I didn't make dinner.

3
a) Did you have coffee for breakfast yesterday?
b) Did you go shopping yesterday?
c) Did you do the housework yesterday?
d) Did you watch a film on television yesterday?
e) Did you walk to work yesterday?
f) Did you buy a newspaper yesterday?
g) Did you write a letter yesterday?
h) Did you make dinner yesterday?

If your students need further practice, you could use Photocopiable Worksheet *13 Grammar* here.

Vocabulary (SB page 96)

1 🌐 3.07

- Focus the students' attention on the pictures and ask them what kinds of things they like to do when they're on holiday. Elicit a few ideas and put them on the board. Then ask for a few things that they don't like to do on holiday and write them up too in a different column.

- Focus attention on the box of words and phrases. Explain any that the students don't understand. Play the recording for them to listen and repeat. Then ask for individual repetition of the words and phrases.

2

- Focus the students' attention on the columns and ask them to work individually to put the items from Exercise 1 into the correct columns for them. Emphasise that there are no right or wrong answers here.

- Put the students in pairs to compare and discuss their lists. Find out if there is any consensus in the class about what should go in each list.

If your students need further practice, you could use Photocopiable Worksheet *13 Vocabulary* here.

Pronunciation (SB page 97)

1

Encourage the students to say the words aloud. Explain any words they don't know.

2 🌐 3.08

- Point out that in line 1, *hat* is underlined, and explain that this is because its vowel sound is different from that of the other words in the group. Ask them to read each group of words aloud and to decide which word has a different sound. Warn them that words with similar spellings aren't always pronounced the same (*what, hat*), and that words with different spellings can sometimes be pronounced the same (*wear, hair*).
- Allow them to compare results in pairs, and encourage them to read the words aloud to each other.
- Play the recording for them to check their answers. Then play it a second time for them to repeat the words.

> a) hat   b) here   c) know   d) how
> e) way   f) bean

Grammar (SB page 97)

Wh questions

1 🌐 3.09

- Focus the students' attention on the information about *Wh* questions in the margin. Ask three students to read out the questions given there. Point out the positions of the pronouns *you*, *he* and *they*, and that they come after the auxiliary verb (*did*), but before the main verb in each case.
- Focus the students' attention on the exercise and establish that the six questions are incomplete. Ask them to complete them by putting the subject *you* in the correct position. Play the recording to check answers. Then play it again for them to repeat.

> a) Where did you go?
> b) Why did you go there?
> c) When did you go?
> d) Who did you go with?
> e) How did you travel?
> f) What did you do?

2 🌐 3.10

Go through the example with the class and establish that they have to choose one item from the box to match each question in Exercise 1. Allow them to compare answers in pairs before playing the recording for them to check.

> a) 4   b) 6   c) 3   d) 2   e) 1   f) 5

3

- Take some holiday photos to class. Show them to the students and encourage them to ask questions such as *Where did you go? What did you see? How did you travel? Where did you stay?* etc.
- Demonstrate the activity with a confident student first. Then put the students into pairs to take turns asking about holidays. Encourage them to report back to the class on what their partner said. They can use their holiday photos you asked them to bring in to the lesson here.

Extra activity

Ask the students to mill. Get them to ask each other questions about what they did last weekend. Ask the class to decide who had the best weekend.

If your students need further practice, you could use Photocopiable Worksheet *13 Communication* here.

Listening & Speaking (SB page 97)

1 🌐 3.11

Go through the questions and possible answers with the class. Then play the recording for the students to listen and underline the answers that the speaker gives. Check answers with the class.

> a) the Maldives
> b) last December
> c) five friends
> d) by air
> e) in a house near the beach
> f) swimming with sharks
> g) two weeks

> 🌐 3.11
>
> *My best holiday was in the Maldives. It was last year, in December. I went with five friends. We went by air from London to Colombo in Sri Lanka, and then to the Maldives. We stayed in a house near the beach. We went to the beach every day, and one day we went swimming with sharks. That was amazing. We stayed for two weeks and we had a great time.*

2

- Pairwork. Tell the students that they're going to tell a partner about their best holiday. Give them time to prepare what they're going to say, using the questions and sentences in Exercise 1 for inspiration. Allow them to make notes, but discourage them from writing out a script.
- Put students in pairs and make sure that they take turns to tell each other about their best holiday. Go round, giving help and encouragement.

Useful phrases (SB page 98)

1 🔊 3.12

- Focus the students' attention on the illustration and ask them to say where the conversation is taking place (at a railway station). Go through the numbers in the box, then tell the students to read the conversation at the same time as they listen to it, and to decide where the numbers should go.

- Allow the students to compare results in pairs before playing the recording again for them to check. Explain any unknown vocabulary. You may need to point out that the man is at a station in London, and so when the woman says that the train arrives in Paris at 12.25 *local time*, this is the time in Paris (which is usually one hour ahead of London) and not the time in London. Explain that the man says 'Oh, dear!' at the end because he can't buy a ticket from the woman at the information desk, and he doesn't have a lot of time before the train leaves to get one from the ticket office.

1 9.03	2 12.25	3 12	4 8.51

Language note

Vocabulary: *sir/madam*

The terms *sir* and *madam* are used as a sign of respect, most often heard said nowadays in hotels, restaurants, shops, train stations, airports, etc. by the staff.

2 🔊 3.13

Ask the students to find the useful phrases in the conversation in Exercise 1. Play the recording for them to listen and repeat. Ask for individual repetition of the phrases around the class.

3

- Pairwork. Go through the information with the class, then ask them to write similar conversations to the one in Exercise 1 about the train to Brussels.

- When the students are practising their conversations, encourage them to act them out so that the information clerk is sitting behind a desk, and the passenger approaches carrying a bag. Go round, monitoring and giving help. Choose some pairs to perform their conversations for the class.

Vocabulary *Extra* (SB page 99)

Holidays

- Focus the students' attention on the list of words and point out that they're all to do with holidays: modes of transport and things to do on holiday. Remind the students that the underlining indicates the syllable of the word that has the strongest stress. Check that the students can pronounce all of the words correctly.

- Ask the students to look at the pictures and match each one with one of the expressions. Point out that the first one has been done for them.

6	by air	4	a mountain
3	by boat	11	on foot
8	by bus	13	a road
10	by car	2	sightseeing
12	by motorbike	9	sunbathing
5	by train	7	a swimming pool
1	cold weather	14	a tent

Writing

Workbook page 55

- Sequencing: *first, then, after that, finally*
- Describing a trip

Photocopiable resource materials

Grammar: *My last holiday* (Teacher's notes page 138. Worksheet page 184.)

Vocabulary: *A fantastic holiday* (Teacher's notes page 138. Worksheet page 185.)

Communication: *Marco Polo* (Teacher's notes page 139. Worksheet page 186.)

Test CD

See *Test Unit 13* on the CD.

💿 CD-ROM

For more activities go to Unit 13: *Travel*.

For the best activities for beginner students, see pages xvi–xxi

For practical methodology, from *Classroom interaction* to *Writing*, see pages xxii–xxxv

What can your students do now? See self-evaluation checklists on pages xxxvi–xlvi

14 Circus *Overview*

Section	Aims	What the students are doing
⊕ Reading **SB page 100**	*Reading skills*: reading for detail	• Reading an article and matching names of performers with their photos. • Marking sentences true or false. • Talking about visiting a circus.
⊕ Grammar **SB page 101**	*Grammar*: can/can't	• Completing questions and answers. • Completing factual sentences.
⊕ Pronunciation **SB page 101**	*Pronunciation*: distinguishing between *can* and *can't*.	• Listening and identifying the correct sentence.
Speaking & Writing **SB page 102**	*Conversation skills*: asking questions about ability *Writing skills*: summarising	• Writing questions for a survey, asking them and recording the answers. • Writing a paragraph to report the results of the survey.
⊕ Grammar **SB page 103**	*Grammar*: How many ...?	• Writing and asking questions using *How many?*
⊕ Vocabulary **SB page 103**	*Vocabulary*: parts of the body	• Listening to and repeating the parts of the body. • Performing actions.
⊕ Useful phrases **SB page 104**	*Vocabulary*: phrases which are useful when talking about illness	• Listening to conversations and completing them with words for illnesses. • Listening to and repeating useful phrases for talking about health and making suggestions.
Vocabulary *Extra* **SB page 105**	*Vocabulary*: revision of words from the unit: body; illness	• Matching pictures with words.
Writing **WB page 59**	Online form filling (a simple CD)	

Warm-up

Take some small balls to class. If you can juggle, demonstrate to the class (saying *I can juggle*) and find out if anyone else can do it, and what other tricks they can do. Use this as an introduction to the subject of circuses, and to the use of *can* and *can't*.

Reading (SB page 100)

1 🌐 3.14

- Focus the students' attention on the photos. Teach the word *circus*, but don't pre-empt Exercise 3 by asking too many questions about the students' experiences of circuses. Ask the students to say what they can see in the photos. Then play the recording and ask them to read and listen to the article.

- Allow them time to discuss in pairs and match the performers with their photos. Check answers with the class and explain any difficult vocabulary. (A *palomino* is a kind of horse which is a golden colour with a white mane and tail. The *ring-master* is the person in charge of the circus who introduces the various performers.)

> a) Nell: 1
> b) Gerald: 6
> c) Nancy: 3
> d) Tweedy: 5
> e) the Kenyan Boys: 2
> f) Oleg: 4

Cultural notes

Nell Gifford (born 1976)
Nell Gifford has been interested in circuses since the age of six. After finishing school, she went to the United States for a year and worked in a circus. She then studied at Oxford University, but after meeting her husband Toti, set up Gifford's Circus with him.

Gifford's Circus
Gifford's circus first opened in 2000 and is very popular in southern England, where it tours during the summer months. It's based on a traditional 1930s style circus. It has twelve acts and is also involved in education. Young people are invited to go on tour with the show and experience the life of a touring circus.
For more information, go to www.giffordscircus.com

2

Give the students time to read the article again. Answer any questions they may have and then allow them to discuss the sentences in pairs. Check answers with the class. Encourage students to correct the false sentences.

> a) False. (It started in 2000.)
> b) True.
> c) True.
> d) False. (Gerald is the ring-master.)
> e) True.
> f) False. (The performers are from many different countries.)

3

- Pairwork. Read the example speech bubbles with the class and remind the students of the use of *ago*, which they studied in Unit 13.

- The students then discuss in pairs when they last went to a circus. Go round, giving help and encouragement.

Grammar (SB page 101)

can / can't

1 🌐 3.15

- Go through the information about *can* and *can't* in the margin, and give the students some examples of things you can and can't do (*I can drive, I can't swim*, etc.). Ask them a few *Can you?* questions.

- Then ask the students to complete the questions and answers about the circus.

- Play the recording for the students to check their answers. Then play it again for them to repeat the questions and answers.

> a) 'Can Nell Gifford perform on a horse?'
>   'Yes, she can .' 'No, she can't.'
> b) 'Can Gerald do circus tricks?'
>   'Yes, he can.' 'No, he can't.'
> c) 'Can Nancy dance and sing?'
>   'Yes, she can.' 'No, she can't.'
> d) 'Can the Kenyan Boys do acrobatics?'
>   'Yes, they can.' 'No, they can't.'
> e) 'Can Oleg lift 150 kilogrammes?'
>   'Yes, he can.' 'No, he can't.'

Language notes

Grammar: *can* for ability

- In Unit 1, *can* was introduced for requesting and giving permission. For example, *Can you repeat that?*

- Another major use of *can* is to do with ability, and that is the concept covered in this unit. You use *can* to say that you know how to do something:
  I can swim. I can't dance. Can you play golf?

- Notice that the pronunciation of *can't* is /kɑːnt/.

2

Ask the students to look back at the article on page 100 of the Student's Book and decide what the correct answers are. Check with the class.

> a) Yes, she can.
> b) No, he can't.
> c) Yes, she can.
> d) Yes, they can.
> e) Yes, he can.

3 ⊕ 3.16

- Ask the students to work in pairs and to discuss whether the sentences should be completed with *can* or *can't*. Allow them to compare their results with another pair.

- Play the recording for the students to check their answers. Then play it again for them to repeat the sentences.

> a) Cats can see in the dark.
> b) Lions can't run long distances.
> c) Horses can sleep on their feet.
> d) Lions can swim.
> e) Horses can see colours.
> f) Elephants can't jump.

4 Grammar *Extra* 14

Ask the students to turn to *Grammar Extra* 14 on page 134 of the Student's Book. Here they'll find an explanation of the grammar they've been studying and further exercises to practise it.

> 1
> a) I can speak English, but I can't speak Japanese.
> b) I can ride a bicycle, but I can't ride a horse.
> c) I can drive a car, but I can't drive a bus.
> d) I can play the guitar, but I can't play the piano.
> e) I can read music, but I can't read Chinese.
> f) I can play football, but I can't play tennis.
> 3
> a) Can I help you?
> b) Can you hear me?
> c) Can I use your dictionary?
> d) Can you answer the door?
> e) Can you pass the salt?
> f) Can I have a cappuccino?
> 4
> *Probable answers:*
> a) 1   b) 3   c) 4   d) 6   e) 2   f) 5

Pronunciation (SB page 101)

⊕ 3.17

- Point out the phonetic symbols in the instructions and elicit the pronunciation of *can* and *can't* from the students. Make sure that they're making a distinction between the two sounds.

- Tell the students that as they listen to the recording, all they have to do is to decide whether the speakers say *can* or *can't*, and to tick the correct sentences.

- Check answers with the class.

- Play the recording again for the students to listen and repeat.

> a) Jim can swim.
> b) Lance can't dance.
> c) Clive can drive.
> d) Lee can ski.
> e) Dell can't spell.
> f) Dwight can't write.

If your students need further practice, you could use Photocopiable Worksheet *14 Communication* here.

Speaking & Writing (SB page 102)

1

- Focus the students' attention on the *Class talents* panel and then go through the instructions. Point out that the correct question in each case will be *Can you ....?* (You might also like to point out the use *of How many people can ...?* and say that you'll be looking at *How many?* in the next grammar section.)

- Check that everyone has formulated their question correctly.

- Allow time for the students to mingle and ask everyone in the class their question. Point out that to record the answers, they just need to put a tick every time someone says *yes*, and a cross when someone says *no*.

2

- As a whole class, find out what questions were asked and what the results were. Write the questions on the board (or get the students to do it), and put the number of ticks and crosses after each one in columns headed *yes* and *no*.

- Before the students write their paragraphs, read out the example speech bubble with the class. Ask a selection of students to make similar sentences based on the information on the board.

- Also focus their attention on the Language toolbox which will provide some useful language for making their written paragraphs a little more varied and coherent. Make sure that they understand *everybody* means all of the people and *nobody* means no people, and go through the example paragraph beginning with them before asking the students to write their own paragraph.

- Go round, monitoring and giving help. You could ask some students to read out their paragraphs to the class.

Grammar (SB page 103)

How many ...?

1 🌐 3.18

- Remind the students that they saw the question *How many?* in the survey in the previous section (*How many people can cook an omelette?* etc.). Go through the example question and answer in the margin with the class. Elicit other questions and answers, perhaps based on the survey they did in the last section, particularly if the results are still on the board.

- Focus the students' attention on the example in the exercise. Elicit the answer to b), and then ask the students to complete the rest of the questions. Allow them to compare in pairs.

- Play the recording for the students to check their answers. Then play it again for them to listen and repeat.

> a) How many players are there in a basketball team?
> b) How many letters are there in the English alphabet?
> c) How many strings are there on a violin?
> d) How many days are there in September?
> e) How many states are there in the USA?
> f) How many sports are there in a decathlon?

Language note

Grammar: *How many*

How many can only be used with countable nouns such as *chairs* and *people*. It can't be used with uncountable nouns such as *money* and *water*. You have to use *How much* with these nouns.

2 🌐 3.19

- In pairs, the students can take turns to ask and answer the questions.

- Play the recording for the students to check their answers. Then play it again for them to listen and repeat.

> a) 5   b) 26   c) 4   d) 30   e) 50   f) 10

> 🌐 3.19
> a) *There are five players in a basketball team.*
> b) *There are twenty-six letters in the English alphabet.*
> c) *There are four strings on a violin.*
> d) *There are thirty days in September.*
> e) *There are fifty states in the USA.*
> f) *There are ten sports in a decathlon.*

Extra activity

- The pairwork activity introduces *How many* with *have* and with the simple past. For some students, you'll need to do a 'bridge activity' to prepare them for the writing.

- Ask the students questions such as:
  How many cats do you have?
  How many T-shirts do you have?
  How many computer games do you have?
  How many magazines did you read last month?
  How many TV programmes did you see yesterday?
  How many CDs did you buy last month?

- Get the students to write one *How many* question with *have* and one with the simple past. Check these and then get the students to mill, asking each other their questions.

3 Pairwork

- The pairwork exercise for this unit is on pages 120 and 125 of the Student's Book. Put the students in pairs and tell them who will be Student A, and who will be Student B.

- While they're doing the exercise, go round monitoring and giving help. Take note of any errors which may need focusing on later, and also any examples of good language use which you can praise. Note any pairs whose work is particularly good so you can ask them to perform their conversations to the class.

If your students need further practice, you could use Photocopiable Worksheet *14 Grammar* here.

Vocabulary (SB page 103)

1 🌐 3.20

- Focus the students' attention on the photo. Then give them time to look at the labels.
- Play the recording for the students to listen and repeat. Ask for individual repetition of the various items and check that the students can pronounce all the words correctly. Pay particular attention to *stomach* /'stʌmək/, encourage them to say the *th* /θ/ sound at the end of *mouth* correctly, and make sure that they notice the difference between the pronunciation of the vowels in *tooth* /tuːθ/ and *foot* /fʊt/.

2 🌐 3.21

Explain that the speaker on the recording will tell them to touch certain parts of their body. Explain *touch* as well as *left* and *right*. Then play the recording and ask them to follow the instructions. Teach them *Clap your hands* at the end.

> 🌐 **3.21**
>
> *Touch your head.*
> *Touch your mouth.*
> *Touch your nose.*
> *Touch your back.*
> *Touch your stomach.*
> *Touch a tooth.*
> *Touch your left ear.*
> *Touch your right eye.*
> *Touch your left arm.*
> *Touch your right foot.*
> *Touch your left leg.*
> *Clap your hands!*

3

Pairwork. Put the students in pairs to play a similar game. They take turns to tell each other which body part to touch.

> ### Extra activity
>
> To add a bit more interest, you could teach them *Touch your nose **with** your leg, Touch your head **with** your arm*, etc., and get the other student to respond with *I can't* if such an action is impossible.

If your students need further practice, you could use Photocopiable Worksheet *14 Vocabulary* here.

Useful phrases (SB page 104)

1 🌐 3.22

- Focus the students' attention on the first picture. Teach *What's the matter?* and point out that the woman on the right isn't feeling well. Go through the words in the box and ask the students to decide which applies to this woman. Encourage them to pronounce *ache* /eɪk/ correctly, and point out that the stress in words with *ache* goes on the first part of the word. Then ask them to look at the other pictures, read the conversations and complete them.
- Play the recording for them to check their answers. Go through any difficult words with them

> a) headache   b) toothache   c) backache
> d) stomach ache

2 🌐 3.23

Play the recording for the students to listen and repeat the useful phrases. Ask for individual repetition afterwards to make sure that they're saying them correctly. Pay attention to the pronunciation of *aspirin* /'æsprɪn/.

3

- Pairwork. In pairs, the students practise the conversations, taking turns to be the person with the problem. Go round, giving help and encouragement, and checking that they are pronouncing everything correctly.
- When they've finished, ask what other problems people might have and what advice could be offered by a sympathetic friend.

Vocabulary *Extra* (SB page 105)

Body

- Focus the students' attention on the list of words and point out that they're all to do with parts of the body. Remind the students that the underlining indicates the syllable of the word that has the strongest stress. Check that the students can pronounce all of the words correctly.
- Ask the students to look at the picture and match each part of the body with one of the expressions. Point out that the first one has been done for them.

8	arm	1	head
9	back	11	leg
4	ear	5	mouth
2	eye	3	nose
12	foot	10	stomach
7	hand	6	tooth

Illness

- Focus the students' attention on the list of words and point out that they're all to do with illnesses. Remind the students that the underlining indicates the syllable of the word that has the strongest stress. Check that the students can pronounce all of the words correctly.

- Ask the students to look at the pictures and match each one with one of the words. Point out that the first one has been done for them.

> 2 backache
> 4 headache
> 3 stomach ache
> 1 toothache

Writing

Workbook page 59

Online form filling (a simple CV)

Photocopiable resource materials

Grammar: *How many?* (Teacher's notes page 139. Worksheet page 187.)

Vocabulary: *Pictionary* (Teacher's notes page 139. Worksheet page 188.)

Communication: *Can you drive?* (Teacher's notes page 140. Worksheet page 189.)

Test CD

See *Test Unit 14* on the CD.

DVD

Programme 7: *Let me entertain you*

CD-ROM

For more activities go to Unit 14: *Circus*.

For the best activities for beginner students, see pages xvi–xxi

For practical methodology, from *Classroom interaction* to *Writing*, see pages xxii–xxxv

What can your students do now? See self-evaluation checklists on pages xxxvi–xlvi

15 Future *Overview*

Section	Aims	What the students are doing
🌐 Reading & Speaking **SB page 106**	*Conversation skills*: talking about future ambitions	• Reading a list of ten things to do before you die. • Making their own lists and discussing the items on the list.
🌐 Grammar **SB page 107**	*Grammar*: *would like to*	• Completing questions with *Do you like* and *Would you like to*. • Asking and answering questions. • Choosing the correct form in sentences.
🌐 Vocabulary **SB page 107**	*Vocabulary*: time expressions	• Answering questions about different times. • Asking questions about the future.
🌐 Reading & Speaking **SB page 108**	*Reading skills*: reading for detail	• Completing a questionnaire about the future. • Discussing results with a partner.
🌐 Grammar **SB page 108**	*Grammar*: future (*be going to*)	• Completing questions and answers. • Asking and answering questions about the future.
🌐 Pronunciation **SB page 109**	*Pronunciation*: stress	• Using chants to practise future questions.
🌐 Listening & Speaking **SB page 109**	*Listening skills*: listening for detail *Conversation skills*: fluency practice	• Listening to an interview and deciding whether the people give the same or different answers. • Talking about a lottery win.
🌐 Useful phrases **SB page 110**	*Vocabulary*: phrases which are useful when saying goodbye	• Matching a conversation to a picture. • Reading and completing conversations in which people say goodbye. • Listening to and repeating useful phrases.
🌐 Vocabulary *Extra* **SB page 111**	*Vocabulary*: revision of useful phrases from the all units	• Matching pictures with words.
Writing **WB page 63**	Writing an email to a friend about future plans.	

Quick revision

- Have a 'Spelling Bee' to revise any vocabulary you feel needs reviewing.

- Say a word and ask one of the stronger students to spell it. Write what they say on the board and ask the class to check if the spelling is correct. Continue with other words and other students.

Reading & Speaking (SB page 106)

1 🔘 3.24

- Focus the students' attention on the photos and find out if anyone has actually done, seen or visited any of the things pictured.

- Point out the structure *I'd like to*, explaining that *I'd* is the contracted form of *I would* and that *it* refers to the future. Give the students a couple of minutes to discuss in pairs whether they'd like to do these things listed or not. (You can play the recording if you wish.) They then put ticks and crosses as appropriate.

- Finally, find out from the class who would like to do which things, and which are the most and least popular.

Cultural notes

The Lord of the Rings (photo 3)

The Lord of the Rings is an epic fantasy by the British author J R R Tolkien. Frodo Baggins and his companions attempt to return a powerful magic ring to a mountain to be destroyed, and prevent its power falling into the wrong hands. Three film adaptations have been made of the story, the most recent being the Oscar winning films directed by Peter Jackson, released in three installments in 2001, 2002 and 2003.

The Taj Mahal (photo 4)

The Taj Mahal is a monument in the city of Agra in India. It was built between 1631 and 1654, by a workforce of more than twenty thousand, as a mausoleum for Mughal Emperor Shah Jahan's favourite wife, Mumtaz Mahal, who died in childbirth.

The Pope (photo 5)

The Pope is the head of the Catholic Church. In addition to his service in this spiritual role, the Pope is also head of state of the independent sovereign state of the Vatican City, a city-state and nation entirely enclosed by the city of Rome.

Machu Picchu (photo 6)

Machu Picchu is a pre-Columbian Inca ruin located on a high mountain ridge in Peru. It was built in about 1440, and was inhabited until the Spanish conquest of Peru in 1532. It was then forgotten for centuries until it was rediscoverd in 1911. Today, thousands of tourists visit Machu Picchu each year. In 1983 Machu Picchu was designated a UNESCO World Heritage Site.

Mount Everest (photo 7)

Mount Everest is the tallest mountain in the world. It's 8,848 metres above sea level. It's part of the Himalaya mountain range and lies on the border of Nepal and Tibet. The first people to climb Mount Everest were Edmund Hillary and Tenzing Norgay on 29th May 1953.

The Pyramids (photo 10)

Built by the ancient Egyptians, the Pyramids at Giza, just outside Cairo, are amongst the largest man-made structures every made. The Great Pyramid of Giza is one of the Seven Wonders of the Ancient World, and the only one to survive into modern times.

2

The students should work individually to produce their own lists. They then compare with a partner to see how similar they are.

Grammar (SB page 107)

would like to

1 🔘 3.25

- Remind the students that they asked questions using the structure *Do you like ...?* in Unit 4. Elicit a few questions along the lines of *Do you like fruit? Do you like Chinese food?* Focus the students' attention on the information about *Would you like to ...?* in the margin, and point out that this structure isn't used for asking about general likes and dislikes, but for asking about future wishes. Explain that *wouldn't* is the contracted form of *would not*.

- Students add the correct question to the columns in the table.

- Play the recording to confirm the answers. Then play it a second time for the students to listen and repeat the questions.

> Question 1: Do you like …?
> Question 2: Would you like to …?

Language note

Grammar: *Would like*

It may be useful to explain to the students that *Would you like to …?* is a softer and more polite way of saying *Do you want to …?*

2

Put the students in pairs to take turns asking and answering the questions. Go round, giving help where needed and checking that the students are forming the questions and answers correctly.

3 🌐 3.26

- This exercise provides a further check that the students have grasped the difference between *like* and *would like*, this time using statements rather than questions. Do the first one with the class as an example, and then ask them to work individually to choose the correct forms in the remainder of the sentences.
- Play the recording for the students to check their answers. Then play it a second time for them to listen and repeat.
- Ask the students to decide which sentences are true for them and to discuss this with a partner.

a) 'd like to	d) doesn't like
b) likes	e) 'd like to
c) wouldn't like to	f) 'd like to

Extra activity

Get the students to work in small groups to prepare a questionnaire containing questions starting *Would you like to …* Go round and check the questions, giving help with vocabulary.

Form new groups with one person from each of the old groups. Tell the students to ask and answer each other's questionnaire.

Vocabulary (SB page 107)

1

Ask the students to answer the questions individually, or in pairs. Check the answers with the class.

2 🌐 3.27

Go through the questions with the class and explain any difficult vocabulary. Then play the recording for students to listen and repeat.

3

Put the students in pairs to ask and answer the questions.

Reading & Speaking (SB page 108)

1 🌐 3.28

- Go through the questionnaire with the class. (You can play the recording if you wish.) Focus the students' attention on the use of *(be) going to* in the questions. Explain that it's used to talk about future plans. Play the recording and ask the students to complete the questionnaire for themselves with ticks and crosses.
- Go through the key, explaining that someone who is *spontaneous* doesn't plan ahead, but will make a sudden decision to do something.

Language notes

Grammar: *(be) going to*

- There's no future tense in English, but there are various ways of talking about the future including *(be) going to*, the present continuous and *will*.
- *(be) going to* is the most common way to talk about future plans and intentions, and is the future form that is presented in this unit. It's usually used when you've already decided about a future action – you 'know' what you're going to do.
- When *(be) going to* is used with *go*, it's often shortened. For example: *I'm going to go shopping* becomes *I'm going shopping.*
- *Going to* is often written in an abbreviated form as *'gonna'* in pop songs. Encourage students to use the full form when doing their own writing. (Unless they're writing pop songs!)

2

Ask the students to compare their results in pairs, and to discuss whether they think the questionnaire's assessment of their personality is accurate.

Grammar (SB page 108)

Future: *(be) going to*

1 🌐 3.29

- Go through the information in the margin about the future *(be) going to*, and elicit some more questions and answers using *(be) going to* from the students. Then ask them to complete the exercise. Allow them to compare results in pairs, but don't check answers at this stage.
- Play the recording for the students to check their answers. Then play it again for them to listen and repeat.

2

Put students in pairs to take turns asking and answering the questions. Remind them that *I don't know* is an appropriate response if the answer is neither *yes* nor *no*.

3 Pairwork

• The pairwork exercise for this unit is on pages 120 and 125 of the Student's Book. Put the students in pairs and tell them who will be Student A, and who will be Student B.

• While they're doing the exercise, go round monitoring and giving help. Take note of any errors which may need focusing on later, and also any examples of good language use which you can praise. Note any pairs whose mimes are particularly good, so you can ask them to perform them to the class for the other students to guess.

4 *Grammar Extra* 15

Ask the students to turn to *Grammar Extra* 15 on page 134 of the Student's Book. Here they'll find an explanation of the grammar they've been studying and further exercises to practise it.

1
a) I'm going to sell my house tomorrow. /
   I'm not going to sell my house tomorrow.
b) I'm going to get up before 8.00 a.m. tomorrow. /
   I'm not going to get up before 8.00 a.m. tomorrow.
c) I'm going to drive a car tomorrow. /
   I'm not going to drive a car tomorrow.
d) I'm going to play tennis tomorrow. /
   I'm not going to play tennis tomorrow.
e) I'm going to buy a new mobile phone
   tomorrow. / I'm not going to buy a new mobile
   phone tomorrow.
f) I'm going to walk to work tomorrow. /
   I'm not going to walk to work tomorrow.
2
a) Are you going to sell your house tomorrow?
b) Are you going to get up before 8.00 a.m. tomorrow?
c) Are you going to drive a car tomorrow?
d) Are you going to play tennis tomorrow?
e) Are you going to buy a new mobile phone
   tomorrow?
f) Are you going to walk to work tomorrow?

3
a) She's going to watch television.
b) He's going to listen to music.
c) They're going to play football.
d) They're going to learn to dance/go dancing.

Extra activity

• Refer the students back to the questionnaire in the Reading and Speaking section on page 108.

• This time ask them to work in pairs, and ask and fully answer the questions, e.g. *What are you going to do this evening? I'm going to watch TV.*

Pronunciation (SB page 109)

1 🌐 3.30

Play the recording once for the students to listen and read the chant. Then play it again for them to repeat. For further practice, divide the class in half and get them to chant alternate lines. Encourage them to put the emphasis on the question words and the main verbs. You could point out that in normal speech *(be) going to* isn't usually stressed.

2 🌐 3.31

• Give the students a couple of minutes to complete the chants. Allow them to compare answers in pairs before playing the recording for them to check. Then play the recording a second time for them to repeat the chants.

• As before, you can practise them again by dividing the class into teams, and giving different lines or different chants to each one.

B
WHO are you going to SEE?
WHEN are you going to SEE them?
WHY are you going to SEE them?
WHAT are they going to SAY?
C
WHO are you going to MEET?
WHEN are you going to MEET her?
WHY are you going to MEET her?
WHAT's she going to SAY?

If your students need further practice, you could use Photocopiable Worksheet *15 Communication* here.

Listening & Speaking (SB page 109)

1 🌐 3.32

• Focus the students' attention on the photo of Justin and Kelly. Tell them that they've won the lottery. Find out how many of your students play the lottery and whether they've ever won anything, or if they know anyone who has.

- Tell the students they're going to listen to an interview with Justin and Kelly. Ask them what they think they'll talk about (what they'll do with the money). Go through the questions with the class and ask them to listen as you play the recording, and put a tick or a cross according to whether both Justin and Kelly give the same answer to the questions, or whether their answers are different.

---

a) ✗ b) ✗ c) ✗ d) ✗ e) ✗

🌐 3.32 (I = Interviewer; J = Justin; K = Kelly)

I: *Congratulations! You won €10 million. How are you going to celebrate?*

J: *Oh, <u>we're going to have a big party with all our friends</u>.*

K: *No, no, we're not going to have a big party. <u>We're going to have a quiet party</u> with our family. And then we're going to go on holiday.*

I: *Where are you going to go?*

K: <u>*To India.*</u>

J: <u>*To America.*</u>

K: *I want to see the Taj Mahal.*

J: *And I want to see the Grand Canyon.*

I: *Um, are you going to buy a new house?*

K: *Yes, <u>we're going to buy a house in Spain</u>.*

J: *France. <u>We're going to buy a house in France.</u>*

K: *Spain.*

I: *And are you going to give some money to your family?*

K: *Yes. <u>We're going to buy a new car for my mother.</u>*

J: *A new car for your mother? <u>I want a new car.</u>*

I: *Do you think you're going to be happy?*

K: <u>*Oh yes! Of course.*</u>

J: *Hmm!*

2

- Go through the instructions with the class and then ask them to work individually to make their plans for the future. Go round, giving help and encouragement. If they're slow to respond, tell them how you'd answer the questions, giving full answers to explain your choices, and give reasons rather than just one-word responses.

- Pairwork. Students tell each other about their plans for the future and what they'll buy with the money they've won.

- Ask them to report back to the class on what their partners said, and find out how many of the students think they're going to be happy, and how many don't.

Useful phrases (SB page 110)

1 🌐 3.33

- Focus the students' attention on the illustrations and point out that each shows a situation in which someone is saying goodbye.

- Go through the conversation with the class and play the recording. Then ask the students to decide which picture they think best illustrates the conversation.

- Check answers with the class. If you want to do some more practise of *going to*, ask questions about the conversation, such as *When is Tim going to come back? What's Tim going to do when he arrives? Is he going to write to his parents? What's he going to send them?*

Picture c.

---

2 🌐 3.34

- The two conversations here match the remaining pictures in Exercise 1.

- Go through the words in the box and ask the students to listen to the recording, and use them to complete the conversations. Check answers with the class. Point out the different forms of goodbye which are used in informal (*Bye*) and formal (*Goodbye*) situations.

---

1 week   2 holiday   3 See   4 Monday
5 good

Language note

Vocabulary: *Ms*

Traditionally, all men were addressed as *Mr* (pronounced /mɪstə/), but single women were called *Miss*, and married women *Mrs* (pronounced /mɪsɪz/). The modern form *Ms* (pronounced /məz/ or /mɪz/ is a direct equivalent of *Mr*, and can be used for both single and married women.

3 🌐 3.35

Go through the useful phrases and ask the students to find them in the conversations in Exercises 1 and 2. Then play the recording for them to listen and repeat. Ask for individual repetition of the items, checking that the students are pronouncing them correctly and using appropriate intonation.

4

Pairwork. The students practise the conversations in Exercises 1 and 2. Encourage them to act them out, using any suitable props. This will help them in getting the correct intonation.

If your students need further practice, you could use Photocopiable Worksheet *15 Grammar* here.

Vocabulary *Extra* (SB page 111)

Useful phrases: revision

1

- Point out that this is revision of phrases from the Useful phrases section throughout the coursebook.
- Focus the students' attention on the phrases and check that the students can pronounce them correctly.
- Ask them to match each of the phrases with one of the pictures. Point out that the first one has been done for them.
- Allow the students to compare answers in pairs before checking with the class.

---

a) 6   How much are these?
b) 9   This is John.
c) 8   Can I speak to Mr Brown, please?
d) 3   What time is it in London?
e) 1   Excuse me. Is there a bank near here?
f) 5   Would you like a cup of tea?
g) 4   Can I have a cappuccino, please?
h) 2   Can I help you?
i) 10 It's my English exam today.
j) 7   What's the matter?

---

2   3.36

- Go through the responses with the class and encourage them to pronounce them correctly. Then ask them to match each one of the phrases in Exercise 1 with each of the responses. Point out that the first one has been done for them.
- Play the recording for them to check their answers. Then play it again for them to listen and repeat the conversations.

---

f) 1 No, thanks.
e) 2 Er, yes – over there.
j) 3 I have a toothache.
b) 4 Nice to meet you.
d) 5 It's 9.30 in the morning.
i) 6 Oh, good luck!
g) 7 Small, medium or large?
a) 8 Twenty euros.
h) 9 Yes, I'm looking for a tie.
c) 10 I'm sorry. He's out.

  3.36 (W = Woman; M = Man)

a) W: *How much are these?*
   M: *Twenty euros.*

b) W: *This is John.*
   M: *Nice to meet you.*

c) M: *Can I speak to Mr Brown, please?*
   W: *I'm sorry. He's out.*

d) W: *What time is it in London?*
   M: *It's 9.30 in the morning.*

---

e) M: *Excuse me. Is there a bank near here?*
   W: *Er, yes – over there.*

f) M: *Would you like a cup of tea?*
   W: *No, thanks.*

g) M: *Can I have a cappuccino, please?*
   W: *Small, medium or large?*

h) W: *Can I help you?*
   M: *Yes, I'm looking for a tie.*

i) W: *It's my English exam today.*
   M: *Oh, good luck!*

j) M: *What's the matter?*
   W: *I have toothache.*

3

Pairwork. Students choose three of the dialogues to practise. Go round, giving help and encouragement. Ask several confident pairs to perform their dialogues for the class.

If your students need further practice, you could use Photocopiable Worksheet *15 Vocabulary* here.

Writing

Workbook page 63

Writing an email to a friend about future plans

Photocopiable resource materials

Grammar: *What do you know?* (Teacher's notes page 140. Worksheet page 190.)

Vocabulary: *Blockbusters* (Teacher's notes page 141. Worksheet page 191.)

Communication: *What's she going to do?* (Teacher's notes page 143. Worksheet page 192.)

Test CD

See *Test Unit 15* on the CD.

CD-ROM

For more activities go to Unit 15: *Future*.

For the best activities for beginner students, see pages xvi–xxi

For practical methodology, from *Classroom interaction* to *Writing*, see pages xxii–xxxv

What can your students do now? See self-evaluation checklists on pages xxxvi–xlvi

Review E *Teacher's notes*

These exercises act as a check of the grammar and vocabulary that the students have learnt in the final three units of the Student's Book. Use them to find any problems that students are having, or anything that they haven't understood and which will need further work.

Grammar (SB page 112)

Remind the students of the grammar explanations they read and the exercises they did in the *Grammar Extra* on pages 134 and 135 of the Student's Book.

1

The first three exercises practise the past simple. Ask the students to look at the pictures and complete the sentences about Tina and Bob's trip to Scotland. Check answers with the class.

a) went, travelled	d) visited, didn't see
b) stayed	e) went
c) didn't like	f) made, didn't want

2

Instead of getting the students to write these questions down, you could elicit them orally around the class and get other students to answer each one in turn.

> a) Did they travel by plane?
> b) Did they stay in a tent?
> c) Did they like the food?
> d) Did they see the monster?
> e) Did they go to a disco?
> f) Did they make some new friends?
> g) Did they want leave?
>
> a) No, they didn't. They travelled by train.
> b) No, they didn't. They stayed in a hotel.
> c) No, they didn't.
> d) No, they didn't.
> e) No, they didn't. They went to a pub.
> f) Yes, they did.
> g) No, they didn't.

3

Check that the students have completed the questions correctly before putting them in pairs to ask and answer them.

> a) Where b) What c) Who d) How many
> e) How

4

Remind the students of the work they did on *can* and *can't* in Unit 14. As the students write their questions, go round checking that they're forming them correctly. Then put them in pairs to take turns asking and answering the questions.

> a) Can you cook spaghetti?
>   (Yes, I can. / No, I can't.)
> b) Can you do circus tricks?
>   (Yes, I can. / No, I can't.)
> c) Can you lift thirty kilogrammes?
>   (Yes, I can. / No, I can't.)
> d) Can you play basketball?
>   (Yes, I can. / No, I can't.)
> e) Can you read *The Lord of the Rings* in one day?
>   (Yes, I can. / No, I can't.)
> f) Can you touch your nose with your foot?
>   (Yes, I can. / No, I can't.)

5

This exercise practises some of the forms from Unit 15. Check answers with the class before asking the students to tick the sentences that are true for them. Then ask them to compare their results in pairs.

> a) I'd like to meet
> b) I'd like to read
> c) I'm going to buy
> d) I'd like to visit
> e) I'm going to see
> f) I'm going to have

6

- This exercise gives the students an opportunity to identify mistakes, a skill that will be useful when they come to check their own work. They have the advantage here of seeing what the correct sentence should be in each case.

- If the students get any of these wrong, refer them back to the relevant sections of the units.

1 a) ~~When you start this book?~~
2 b) ~~Jan went to Santander by boat?~~
3 b) ~~I can to swim.~~
4 a) ~~You like a drink?~~
5 b) ~~How many days there are in February?~~
6 b) ~~I am going watch TV tonight.~~

If your students need further practice, you could use Photocopiable Worksheet *Revision E* here.

Vocabulary (SB page 113)

1

Point out that the illustrations are clues for the words that fit in the crossword. Allow the students to work in pairs to complete the crossword if they wish.

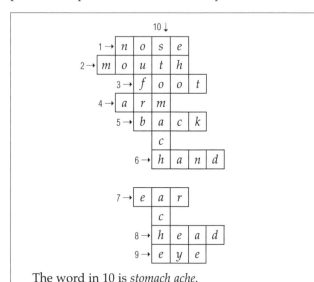

The word in 10 is *stomach ache*.

2

Remind the students that Unit 13 was all about travel. The illustrations should help them to complete the words. Point out that all the modes of transport here (with the exception of *on foot*) use *by*.

> a) plane   b) motorbike   c) car   d) boat
> e) bicycle   f) train   g) bus   h) on foot

3

- Point out that *friend* is the odd word out in a) because both the other items are places rather than people. When checking answers, ask the students to say why each one is the odd word out.

> a) friend (friend is a person; the others are places)
> b) shark (shark is a fish; the others are places)
> c) weather (weather is the only one not a place)
> d) family (family is the only one not a place)
> e) tent (the others are things to do; tent is a place to stay)
>   or: sport (the others are words to do with holidays)
> f) road (the others are words for travel)

4

- Remind the students that they studied time expressions with *ago*, *in* and *last* in Unit 13, and time expressions with *in* and *last* in Unit 15. Then ask students to complete the time expressions. Check answers with the class.

- Students then rewrite the sentences so that they're true for them. They then compare their sentences with a partner.

> a) in   b) Last   c) ago   d) next   e) in
> f) ago   g) last   h) next

Pronunciation (SB page 113)

1

Remind the students of the use of the large and small stress boxes and the underlining. Ask three students to read out the words in the table, and encourage them to use the correct intonation. Then ask the students to put the other words in the box in the correct columns. Encourage them to say the words aloud as they do this to give them a feel for what sounds right. Check answers with the class.

> 1 and 2
> A: <u>birth</u>day, <u>jour</u>ney, <u>moun</u>tain, <u>wea</u>ther
> B: <u>bi</u>cycle, <u>dan</u>gerous, <u>holi</u>day, <u>no</u>body
> C: a<u>go</u>, ar<u>rive</u>, ho<u>tel</u>, per<u>form</u>

2 🌐 3.37

Point out the underlining in the examples in the table in Exercise 1, then ask the students to underline the stressed syllables in the other words. Play the recording for them to check their answers. Then play it a second time for them to listen and repeat.

Reading & Listening (SB page 114)

1 🌐 3.38

Focus the students' attention on the photos and tell them that they show the members of a rock band. Go through the question with the class so that they know the information they are looking for. Then play the recording and ask them to read the article as they listen. Check the answer to the question.

> Amy sings. Tom plays the piano. Baz plays the guitar. Olly plays the drums.

2

Give the students time to read the article again. Then ask them to find the answers to the questions. Go round, giving help and encouragement. Check answers with the class, perhaps by getting one student to call out a question and choosing another student to answer it.

a) Two.
b) Four months.
c) April.
d) Tom.
e) He would like to visit the Te Papa Museum.
f) Because it's summer in New Zealand (in January).

3

Give the students time to think about where they should put the missing words and allow them to compare in pairs before checking with the class.

a) How long are you going to stay in New Zealand?
b) Where are you going to go after New Zealand?
c) When did you start the tour?
d) How do you usually travel?
e) What do you all like doing when you're not working?

4 🌐 3.39

Play the recording so that the students can check their answers to Exercise 3 again.

🌐 3.39 (D = Darren; A = Amy)

D: *I have Amy from White Nights here in the studio. Amy, welcome.*
A: *Thanks. It's good to be here.*
D: *How long are you going to stay in New Zealand?*
A: *We're going to stay for six days.*
D: *Great! Where are you going to go after New Zealand?*
A: *We're going to go to Australia. We have two concerts in Sydney.*
D: *Ah. When did you start the tour?*
A: *We started four weeks ago – on 22ⁿᵈ of December.*
D: *Four weeks ago? I see. How do you usually travel?*
A: *Usually by plane. We sometimes travel by car on very short journeys, but we usually go by plane.*
D: *What do you all like doing when you're not working?*
A: *Well, Baz likes sightseeing – and he loves museums. Olly likes all sports, so he usually tries to find somewhere to swim or play football. Tom and I like shopping, and that's where we spend all of our time and money.*
D: *Thank you very much for coming in, Amy. I hope you have a good time here in New Zealand, and please come back soon.*
A: *Thank you very much.*

5

Play the recording again and ask the students to make notes on Amy's answers to the questions in Exercise 3. You may need to play the recording more than once, and pause it at appropriate places, so that they can do this. Check answers with the class.

a) Six days.
b) Sydney, Australia.
c) Four weeks ago.
d) Usually by plane (sometimes by car).
e) Baz likes sightseeing (he loves museums). Olly likes sports. Tom and I like shopping.

Writing & Speaking (SB page 115)

1

Read the announcement with the class, explaining any difficult vocabulary, and ask what they've won. Ask if any of the photos show places that they'd like to go to.

A round-the-world ticket for two people to visit four countries.

2

Give the students a couple of minutes to rewrite the questions, then check answers.

a) Where are you going to go?
b) Why do you want to go there?
c) How are you going to travel?
d) What are you going to do there?

3

• Pairwork. Put the students into pairs and explain that as the prize is for two people, they have to decide which four countries they'd both like to visit.

• When the students have chosen four countries, they should answer the questions in Exercise 2 for each country they'd like to visit, and write the answers in the form of a short paragraph. Go through the example with them and explain that they can use this as a model.

• The students then read their ideas to another pair and listen to their round-the-world trip. They then decide whose is the best round-the-world trip.

4

The first question here is designed to focus the students' attention on the fact that separate paragraphs contain separate ideas. Olly's email has four paragraphs and each has a different subject. Ask the students to read the email and decide which paragraph contains which information. Then go through the email and explain any difficult words.

a) Paragraph 2
b) Paragraph 1
c) Paragraph 3
d) Paragraph 4

5

- Encourage the students to use Olly's email as a model, but to add any ideas of their own that they would like. Emphasise that they should put different topics in separate paragraphs. Go round giving help and encouragement, and supplying any vocabulary the students need.

- The emails could be displayed in the classroom for everyone to read. Alternatively, you could 'send' each email to a different pair, and ask them to write a short reply.

Photocopiable resource materials

Review E: *The Revision Game* (Teacher's notes page 143. Worksheet page 193.)

Test CD

See *Test Review E* on the CD.

For the best activities for beginner students, see pages xvi–xxi

For practical methodology, from *Classroom interaction* to *Writing*, see pages xxii–xxxv

What can your students do now? See self-evaluation checklists on pages xxxvi–xlvi

Resource materials

Worksheet	Activity and focus	What students are doing
Unit 1		
1 Grammar *It's her pen*	Groupwork: card game Possessive determiners *this* and *these*	Asking about common objects
1 Vocabulary *What's his name?*	Pairwork: famous people game Alphabet and spelling	Connecting first names and surnames Spelling aloud
1 Communication *What's your number?*	Personal information and numbers Spelling aloud	Asking questions to complete ID cards
Unit 2		
2 Grammar *Where is it?*	Groupwork: writing Places in the UK Prepositions *in* / *near*	Looking at a map and writing sentences
2 Vocabulary *Bingo!*	Pairwork: *Bingo* game Countries / nationalities	Playing *Bingo* Listening to countries and identifying nationalities
2 Communication *How much is it?*	Pairwork: information exchange Prices / technology	Asking prices in euros and completing advertisements
Unit 3		
3 Grammar *Who is he?*	Pairwork: finding connections Possessive *'s*	Asking questions to match celebrities and their children
3 Vocabulary *Who's his wife?*	Reading and problem-solving Possessive *'s* Family	Interpreting a text to complete a simple family tree Comprehension questions
3 Communication *My family*	Groupwork: information exchange Possessive *'s* *How old ...?* Family	Asking about names and ages of family members
Review A *The Revision Game*	Groupwork: board game Revision of structures from Units 1–3	Choosing the correct sentences

Worksheet	Activity and focus	What students are doing
Unit 4		
4 Grammar *Do you like it?*	Groupwork: game *like* + adjective / noun *Do you like ...?*	Putting nouns and nationality adjectives together Asking questions about likes
4 Vocabulary *Categories*	Team vocabulary game Vocabulary revision: classroom objects, colours, countries, family	Working together to think of words as quickly as possible beginning with a given letter
4 Communication *My favourite ...*	Groupwork: board game *My favourite ... / Do you like ...?*	Asking and talking about favourite things
Unit 5		
5 Grammar *Have, live, speak, work*	Pairwork: Pelmanism game 1st and 3rd person present simple Pronoun / verb / noun combinations	Making logical and correctly formed sentences
5 Vocabulary *What's the job?*	Groupwork: card game Present simple Jobs	Miming or drawing a job for other students to guess
5 Communication *Knowing you*	Groupwork: board game Personal information Interests and hobbies	Asking questions and finding out about other students in the group
Unit 6		
6 Grammar *The same time*	Whole class: mingle activity Routines and clock times	Asking questions and finding students in the class with the same routines
6 Vocabulary *Time of day*	Pairwork: Pelmanism game Routines and clock times Present simple	Making logical sentences about someone's personal routine
6 Communication *A day in a job*	Groupwork: information exchange Daily routines and clock times Jobs	Asking about times and routines and guessing jobs
Review B *Friday, I'm In Love*	Listening and reading Revision of vocabulary from Units 4–6	Listening to and reading a song Identifying words and sounds
Unit 7		
7 Grammar *Old Town, New Town*	Pairwork: information exchange *Is there a ...?* Features of a city	Asking about and finding locations of places on a map
7 Vocabulary *Famous places*	Groupwork: Pelmanism game Places in a city Famous landmarks	Identifying types of landmark
7 Communication *My town*	Pairwork: information exchange Choice of amenities	Inventing a perfect town and finding out about a partner's town

RESOURCES   Teacher's notes

Worksheet	Activity and focus	What students are doing
Unit 8		
8 Grammar *Our flat*	Pairwork: information exchange Furniture *Is there a ...? / Are there any ...?*	Asking and finding out about items of furniture
8 Vocabulary *Password!*	Team game: word association Furniture and equipment	Quickly identifying items of furniture through mime and word association
8 Communication *Do you like him?*	Groupwork: card game *Do you like ...?* Object pronouns	Categorising people and things into likes/dislikes
Unit 9		
9 Grammar *Are you healthy?*	Pairwork: questionnaire Adverbs of frequency Personal routines	Asking questions and completing a form in pairs Deciding how healthy your partner is
9 Vocabulary *Do you eat it?*	Groupwork: card game Present simple Vocabulary revision	Putting the correct verb with an item of vocabulary and asking a partner about it
9 Communication *Small or large?*	Groupwork: role play *Can I have ...? / Would you like ...?* Restaurant choices	Choosing options from a menu in a restaurant situation
Review C *The Revision Game*	Groupwork: board game Revision of structures from Units 7–9	Choosing the correct sentences
Unit 10		
10 Grammar *I'm wearing blue jeans*	Groupwork: card game Colours and clothes Present continuous	Using card combinations to make sentences about what other students are wearing
10 Vocabulary *Crossword*	Pairwork: crossword completion Clothes	Working in pairs to complete the crossword, each student having half the picture clues
10 Communication *What am I doing?*	Team miming game Present continuous Vocabulary revision	Miming actions for other members of the team to guess
Unit 11		
11 Grammar *It's a lie!*	True/False game *was/were*	Using prompt cards to tell the truth or lie about a given time in the past
11 Vocabulary *What are the numbers?*	Pairwork: writing game race *There are ...* Time	Writing sentences to categorise numbers, for example: *There are seven days in a week*
11 Communication *Going out*	Whole class: mingle activity *Would you like ...?* Times and days Entertainment	Inviting a partner to go to an event Giving and receiving tickets

Worksheet	Activity and focus	What students are doing
Unit 12		
12 Grammar *Steffi Graf*	Groupwork: jigsaw reading Past simple regular and irregular affirmative	Sequencing and pairing sentence halves to make short biography
12 Vocabulary *Bingo!*	Pairwork: *Bingo* game Irregular past simple verbs	Playing *Bingo* Listening to infinitives and identifying past tenses
12 Communication *Snakes and Ladders*	Groupwork: board game Past simple Personal information	Playing *Snakes and Ladders* Making sentences using the verb in the square
Review D *What a Wonderful World*	Listening and reading Revision of vocabulary from Units 10–12	Listening to and reading a song Identifying words and pictures
Unit 13		
13 Grammar *My last holiday*	Whole class: mingle activity Past simple Holidays	Asking *Yes/No* questions about other students' most recent holidays
13 Vocabulary *A fantastic holiday*	Pairwork: information exchange *was/were* Adjectives	Asking about and describing aspects of a holiday using prompts
13 Communication *Marco Polo*	Pairwork: information gap *Wh* questions: past simple	Asking questions to complete a short biography about Marco Polo
Unit 14		
14 Grammar *How Many?*	Team quiz *How Many ...?* *Have/has* Vocabulary revision from Units 1-14	Reading and discussing multiple choice quiz answers
14 Vocabulary *Pictionary* Animals Possessive *'s*	Groupwork: *Pictionary* game Parts of the body Describing a picture correctly	Drawing an animal or human body part
14 Communication *Can you drive?*	Whole class: mingle activity *can* for ability	Asking questions to get information about students' abilities
Unit 15		
15 Grammar *What do you know?*	Team race Structures and vocabulary revision	Reading aloud and answering questions in teams
15 Vocabulary *Blockbusters*	Team race Vocabulary revision	Identifying words correctly to move across a playing board
15 Communication *What's she going to do?*	Pairwork: questionnaire *going to* for prediction	Predicting a partner's activities for the following weekend
Review E *The Revision Game*	Groupwork: board game Revision of structures from Units 13–15	Choosing the correct sentences

Teacher's notes

1 Grammar It's her pen

Page 144

Activity

Groupwork: card game.

Focus

Possessive determiners. *this/these*.
Asking about common objects.

Preparation

Make one copy of the worksheet for every three
students in the class. Cut up the cards on each
worksheet.

Procedure

- Put the class into groups of three. If the class does
  not divide into threes, include a group of four or join
  one of the groups yourself. Give one set of cards to
  each group.
- Ask each student to turn three cards face up in front
  of them. Everyone in the group should look at all the
  cards for one minute and try to memorise them.
- Ask one student in each group to collect the cards
  together and mix them up. Then they should put
  them in a pile face down in the middle of their group.
- Demonstrate by taking a card from the pile in one
  group, e.g. a picture of a pen. Ask one of the
  students: *What's this?* or *What are these?* and
  encourage them to answer – *It's (They're) his / her / my
  / your pen (pens).*
- If the answer is correct, he or she can keep the card.
  If not, it goes to the bottom of the pack.
- Write up the word *Pen*. Ask the students for the
  question and possible replies and write these up.
  Write up the word *Pens* and do the same for
  plurals:

  A: *What's this?*   *What are these?*

B: *It's*	*his*	*pen.*	*They're*	*his*	*pens.*
	her			*her*	
	my			*my*	
	your			*your*	

- Ask one student from each group to demonstrate
  with the student sitting on their left.
- Tell the students to continue in the same way in their
  groups, taking turns to turn over a card and ask the
  student sitting on their left.

- Monitor the groups. When the students gain in
  confidence, erase the model from the board.
- At the end of the activity the student with the most
  cards is the winner.

1 Vocabulary What's his name?

Page 145

Activity

Pairwork: famous people game.

Focus

First names. The alphabet and spelling.

Preparation

Make one copy of the worksheet for each student in the
class.

Procedure

- Write up your first name with the vowels missing,
  but including the capital letter at the beginning.
  Ask the students for the missing letters.
- Write up a few first names of students in class with
  the vowels missing. After each one ask the class what
  the letters are and what the name is.
- Hand out the worksheet and point out the number
  six example. Ask students to complete the name
  Tiger.
- Ask students to work together in pairs to connect
  and complete the other names.
- When the students have finished, read out the
  numbers of the names in random order and choose a
  student to say and spell the name of the person. If
  time permits, go through the names twice, or until
  everyone in class has had a few goes.

Variation

To start the activity, find some photos of celebrities,
celebrity couples and children from a magazine such as
Hello. Show these quickly to the class for students to
shout out the names.

```
 1  John (Lennon)
 2  Venus (Williams)
 3  George (Clooney)
 4  William (Shakespeare)
 5  Albert (Einstein)
 6  Tiger (Woods)
 7  Marilyn (Monroe)
 8  Quentin (Tarantino)
 9  Nelson (Mandela)
10  Elizabeth (Windsor)
```

1 Communication What's your number?

Page 146

Activity

Mingle activity. Finding out personal details.

Focus

First names and surnames. Letters and numbers.

Preparation

Make one copy of the worksheet for every four students in the class and cut them up so that there is one card per student.

Procedure

- Hand out one ID card to each student. As you hand it out tell the students: *This is you.*

- Demonstrate how to fill in the table using the board: ask a student his or her first name – as written on their ID card. Ask the spelling and write the name in the table on the board.

First name	Elizabeth
Surname	
Passport number	
Mobile number	

- Ask students what the questions are for each row and write them up on the board:

  What's your first name? – Can you spell that, please?
  What's your surname?
  What's your passport number?
  What's your mobile number?

- Tell the students that they have to find three new people's information as quickly as possible. The first one to finish is the winner.

- Ask everyone to stand in the middle of the room. Ask them to mingle and speak to three other students to complete their tables.

- Check students have the correct information for all four cards by asking the questions to the whole class.

Extension

Students ask each other the questions in pairs and write down their partner's real information. They can make up passport or mobile numbers if they want to.

2 Grammar Where is it?

Page 147

Activity

Groupwork: writing. Finding out about the UK.

Focus

Prepositions *in/near*.

Preparation

Make one copy of the worksheet for each student in the class.

Procedure

- Write up the name of a small town near the city where your students are learning English, e.g. Guadalajara. Then write these sentences with gaps:

  Guadalajara is _____ Spain.
  Guadalajara is _____ Madrid.

- Ask students which words could fill the gaps – *in*, *near*.

- Hand out the worksheet and teach the pronunciation of places on the map:

  London – /ˈlʌndən/
  Edinburgh – /ˈedɪnbrə/
  Birmingham – /ˈbɜːmɪŋəm/
  Loch Lomond – /lɒk ˈləʊmənd/
  Windsor Castle – /ˌwɪnzə ˈkɑːsl/
  Thorpe park – /ˌθɔːp ˈpɑːk/
  Giant's Causeway – /ˌdʒaɪənts ˈkɔːzweɪ/
  Glasgow – /ˈglɑːzgəʊ/
  Stratford-upon-Avon – /ˈstrætfəd əpɒn ˈeɪvən/
  Ballycastle – /ˈbælikɑːsl/
  Manchester – /ˈmæntʃɪstə/

- Demonstrate to the students by writing an example on the board:

  London is in England. Windsor Castle is near London.

- Encourage the class to continue in the same way in their groups, starting with the place name, and write sentences with *in* and *near*. Monitor and make sure that they work together, writing about one place / city at a time.

- When everyone has finished, go through the sentences in random order around the classroom.

Extension

If your students have access to the internet, ask them to find photos of the places in the worksheet. In the next lesson use the photos to revise today's sentences.

Hold up a photo and follow this dialogue:

T: What is this?
St: It's Windsor Castle.

T: Is Windsor Castle near London?
St: Yes, it is. / No, it isn't.
Ask individual students to stand and hold up their
photo for the class to see. They then ask and answer the
same questions with another student.

2 Vocabulary *Bingo!*

Page 148

Activity
Pairwork: *Bingo!* game.

Focus
Countries and nationalities.

Preparation
Make one copy of the worksheet for every twelve
students in the class. Cut each worksheet into six cards.

Procedure
- Write up *Bingo!* in large letters. Find out how many
  students know the game. For some classes you may
  need to explain the rules: show a *Bingo* card to the
  class. Explain the game by saying: *I say a country. You
  put an X on the nationality* and demonstrate with
  Italy, crossing off **Italian** on the card. Point out that
  they need to get a line in any direction. When they
  get a line they shout *Line!* When they get all the
  nationalities on their card they shout *Bingo!*
- Hand out a *Bingo* card to each pair of students.
- Read out the countries in the order given below.
- Go round checking that everyone is crossing off the
  nationalities. Give a point to the first five pairs to get
  a line. Give another point to the first pair to shout
  out *Bingo!*

America – Brazil – Britain – France – Germany – Italy –
Japan – Poland – Spain

2 Communication How much is it?

Page 149

Activity
Pairwork: information exchange.

Focus
Asking the prices of things. Technology vocabulary.

Preparation
Make one copy of the worksheet for each pair of
students in the class, and a copy for yourself. Cut each
worksheet into two.

Procedure
- Hold up a copy of worksheet A and ask students
  what things are in the advertisement: **computer,
  camera, mobile phone**. Hold up both worksheets, A
  and B, and show that they are different.
- Put the students in pairs and hand out different
  worksheets to Students A and B in each pair.
- Demonstrate an example, e.g. *How much is the
  Kompak KP190?*. Write the answer in the empty price
  tag and show the class.
- Ask the class to continue in their pairs, taking turns
  to ask and answer questions. Ask students not to
  show each other their worksheets.
- When everyone has finished, ask the whole class the
  prices of different items and allow students to shout
  out the answers. If any pairs finish early ask them to
  compare worksheets and check prices.

Variation
Use a real advertisement section from a newspaper,
make two copies and blank out different prices for
Students A and B. Then make copies for each pair of
students in the class.

3 Grammar Who is he?

Page 150

Activity
Pairwork: matching celebrities and their children.

Focus
Possessive *'s*.

Preparation
Make one copy of the worksheet for each student.

Procedure
- Hand out a worksheet to each student. Check they
  know the symbols for male (♂), indicating *son*, and
  female (♀), indicating *daughter*.
- Ask students to work in pairs and find the
  connections between the celebrities and their
  children. Note that not all the celebrities' children are
  included on the worksheet.
- Write up an example on the board:
  Brooklyn is David Beckham__ son.
- Ask the students what goes in the gap: the
  apostrophe *'s*.
- Ask students what the question is. Write it above the
  corresponding answer on the board: *Who is Brooklyn?*
- Choose another child on the worksheet and ask a
  pair of students to ask and answer the question for
  the class.
- Ask the class to continue in the same way in pairs.
  When they seem confident, erase the model from the
  board.

3 Vocabulary Who's his wife?

Page 151

Activity

Reading and problem solving.

Focus

Possessive 's. Family vocabulary.

Preparation

Make one copy of the worksheet for each student in the class, plus one for yourself.

Procedure

- Teach the words **uncle, aunt** and **cousin** by drawing a simple family tree for your own family on the board. Below this write gapped sentences for the words *uncle, aunt* and *cousin*, e.g.

  Chris is my _____ .
  Debby is my _____ .

- Ask one student to read out the instructions for Exercise 1 on the worksheet. Repeat this to the class, showing where they write names on the picture.

- Allow students to work in their own time to read the text and write in the missing names of the family members. When they finish, get them to compare answers with the student sitting next to them.

- Check the answers. If you can project the picture on the board, get students to come up to the board and write the names there.

- Ask students to work in pairs to write the answers to Exercise 2.

- Check the answers to Exercise 2.

- Ask students to write three more questions for their partner to answer.

Extension

Ask students to bring in their own family photographs to the next lesson. They then work in groups with a photo belonging to someone in another group and guess the family relationships, e.g. *This is Henri's brother. That's his grandfather….* The owner of the photo then joins the group to tell them who is who.

---

1 Clockwise from the top left:
   Maria, Jenny, Brad, Linda, Derek, Anna, Kevin, Sandra, Colin, Cathy.

2 a) Maria
   b) Sandra
   c) Derek
   d) Maria and Brad
   e) Kevin

3 Students' own answers.

---

3 Communication My family

Page 152

Activity

Groupwork: other students' families.

Focus

Family vocabulary. Possessive 's. *How old is…?*

has (extension)

Preparation

Make one copy of the worksheet for every four or five students in the class. You'll need two dice for each group.

Procedure

- Teach the words **uncle, aunt** and **cousin** by drawing a simple family tree for your own family on the board. Below this write a gapped sentence for the words *uncle, aunt* and *cousin*, e.g.
  Paul is my _____ .

- Write up this dialogue:
  A: _____ _____ your brother's name?
  B: My brother's name is Martin.
  A: _____ _____ is he?
  B: He's 25.

- Encourage students to help you complete the gaps: *What is, How old.*

- Put the students in groups of four or five.

- Hand out a worksheet and two dice to each group.

- Demonstrate how to play: roll the dice and ask a student the questions in the dialogue, e.g. roll a 2 and ask a student: *Do you have a son?* If he or she doesn't have a son, ask another student. Follow this question with: *What's your son's name?*

- Tell the groups to continue in the same way, taking it in turns to throw the dice, and ask another student in the group the questions.

Variation

Some students may have lost a family member and this could be a difficult topic in a group situation, especially for younger students. You may wish to begin the activity by seeing how happy students are to draw their own family trees.

Extension

Ask students to make notes about others in the group and then report back, e.g.

Kira has a son. Her son's | name is Pavel.
                   His |

Review A The Revision Game

Page 153

Activity
Groupwork: board game.

Focus
Revising main structures from *New Inside Out* Beginner Student's Book Units 1–3.

Preparation
Make one copy of the worksheet for every three or four students in the class, and one for yourself. You will need one counter for each student, and one coin and a copy of *New Inside Out* Beginner Student's Book for each group.

Procedure
Ask the students to work in groups of three or four. Hand out the worksheets, one to each group. One person is the 'Checker'. The Checker doesn't play the game.

1 Players place their counters on different squares marked START.

2 The first player throws the coin and moves the counter as follows:
'Heads' = two squares
'Tails' = one square

3 When a player lands on a square, they must choose the correct sentence, a) or b).

4 The Checker then turns to the Grammar *Extra* section on pages 126 and 127 and checks the answer. If the player is right, they can wait for their next turn. If the player is wrong, they miss a turn.

5 The first player to reach FINISH is the winner.

```
Player 1: 1 b  2 b  3 b  4 a  5 b  6 a  7 a  8 a
Player 2: 1 b  2 b  3 b  4 a  5 a  6 a  7 b  8 a
Player 3: 1 b  2 a  3 b  4 a  5 a  6 b  7 a  8 b
```

4 Grammar Do you like it?

Page 154

Activity
Groupwork: finding connections between words.

Focus
I like + adjective / noun order. *Do you like …?*

Preparation
Make one copy of the worksheet for every three or four students in the class. Cut it into separate words. Make a copy of the worksheet for yourself.

Procedure
- Put the class into small groups and spread out one set of cards face up in the middle of each group. Ask students to match the nationalities with the nouns. Students need to agree on the best way to put the words together.

- While the students are putting the words together write this dialogue on the board:
  A: _____ you like French wine?
  B: Yes, I _____ .
  A: Do you _____ English coffee?
  B: No, I _____ .

- When they have finished putting the words together, ask the students which words go in the gaps on the board – *Do, do, like, don't*.

- Tell students to ask other students in their group questions, following the dialogue on the board.

> The order of the words on the worksheet shows a possible way of putting them together.

4 Vocabulary Categories

Page 155

Activity
Teamwork: vocabulary game.

Focus
Vocabulary and spelling revision – colours, classroom objects, family, countries.

Preparation
Make one copy of the worksheet for every two teams of three or four students. Make a copy of the worksheet key for yourself. Cut each worksheet into two.

Procedure
- Divide the class into teams of three or four students.

- Give each team a copy of the worksheet.

- Ask students: *What begins with the letter C?* They then have to write a word beginning with *C* in as many columns as possible, e.g. *computer, cousin, China.* Write these on your worksheet as an example to show students.

- Make sure that someone from each team is chosen to do the writing on their worksheet.

- Tell the class this is a race; they must write their words very quickly.

1 Ask the same question: *What begins with the letter A?* and wait for a short time before moving on to the next letter. Use the letters in this order:

A – B – D – F – G – J – M – O – P – R – S – T – W – Y

2 After the last letter read out the answers from the list below and ask one student to check the teams' worksheets. They should give one point for every correctly spelled word that is written in the correct column.

colours	things in class	family	countries
black	bag	aunt	America
blue	book	brother	Brazil
brown	computer	cousin	Britain
green	dictionary	daughter	China
grey	mobile phone	father	France
orange	pen	grandmother	Japan
pink	picture	grandfather	Poland
red	student	mother	Russia
white	teacher	sister	Spain
yellow		son	

3 The team with the most points is the winner.

4 Communication My favourite …

Page 156

Activity

Groupwork: board game.

Focus

Vocabulary practice. *My favourite … Do you like …?*

Preparation

Make one copy of the worksheet for every four students in the class. You will need one dice for each group and one counter for each student (or get them to use a small personal item such as a pencil sharpener).

Procedure

- Write up this dialogue:

    A: *My favourite drink is coffee.*
    B: *Do you like white coffee?*
    A: *Yes, I do. | No, I don't.*

- Put the students into groups of four.
- Explain that they are going to play a game and show them the dice and the title of the worksheet.
- Place a copy of the game in the middle of each group and hand out counters and a dice.
- Demonstrate for each group in turn how the game works: students take it in turns to throw the dice. When they land on a square they tell the group their favourite thing in that category. The student on their right then asks them a *'Do you like …?'* question about the topic in the square.
- The first student to finish ends the game.

5 Grammar *Have, live, speak, work*

Page 157

Activity

Pairwork: Pelmanism game.

Focus

1st and 3rd person present simple.

Pronoun / verb / noun combinations.

Preparation

Make one copy of the worksheet for every three students in the class. Cut this into separate cards.

Procedure

- Put the class in groups of three.
- Spread out a set of cards face down in the middle of one of the groups and demonstrate how to play the game:

    1 Turn over one small rectangular card, one square card and one large rectangular card.

    2 If the cards go together, keep them and have another go, for example:

    If they do not go together, turn them face down again. (The cards go together in two ways: the pronoun and verb must match, e.g. *He live*<u>s</u> …, and the sentence must make sense, e.g. *I like in London* does not match.)

    3 The student sitting on the right then turns over three cards.

    4 The student with the most sentences at the end is the winner.

- Ask the class to play the game in their groups.
- Monitor the groups as they play, making sure that the cards they keep are correct sentences.

5 Vocabulary What's the job?

Page 158

Activity

Groupwork: card game using mime and pictures.

Focus

Present simple.
Jobs vocabulary.

Preparation

Make one copy of the worksheet for every four students in the class. Cut this into cards. You will need one large piece of paper per group – flipchart size or larger.

Procedure

- Write up the word *Jobs* in large letters and ask students to give you a few examples.
- Show the class a pack of cards. Tell them the cards have jobs written on them.
- Take one card and without showing it to the class, say *This is my job* ... Ask the class to guess what it is using drawings on the board and / or mime. e.g.

  Actor – Drawing of a stage
  Artist – Mime someone adding brushstrokes and looking away from picture to something he is painting
  – Drawing of a painter's palette and brush

- The student who guesses the job keeps the card. Do another two or three examples if necessary.
- Put the class in groups of four or five students. Put a large sheet of paper in the middle of each group and a pack of cards in the middle of each sheet of paper.
- Students take a card in turn and describe the job with pictures and mime. They should draw their pictures on the large sheet of paper. Whoever guesses the job first gets the card.
- The student with the most cards at the end is the winner.

Variation

If you think your students may need help remembering the jobs they learned in the Student's Book, you could write the list of sixteen jobs on the board for them to refer to while they are playing the game.

Extension

If the groups have an interesting selection of drawings, ask the students to get up and look at the other groups' pictures. Can they guess the jobs?

5 Communication Knowing you

Page 159

Activity

Groupwork: board game.

Focus

Personal information and interests vocabulary.

Preparation

Make one copy of the worksheet for every four students in the class. You'll need one dice for each group of four.

Procedure

- Put the students in groups of four and place a worksheet and a dice in the middle of each group. Write up two questions for the first category and ask students to think of possible questions for the other categories and write them on the board, e.g.

  1 *Where do you live?*
     Do you live in a house or an apartment?

  2 *What's your _____'s name?*
     How old is your _____?
     Do your parents have a _____?
     Do your friends like _____?

  3 *What's your favourite food / drink?*
     Do you like _____?
     Do you eat _____?

  4 *What music do you like?*
     What's your favourite TV programme / film?
     Who's your favourite actor?

  5 *What's your favourite sport?*
     Do you like _____?
     Who's your favourite _____ player?

  6 *What do you do?*
     Where do you work / study?
     What languages do you speak?
     What's your dream job?

- Roll a dice. The number you roll indicates the category, numbered 1 to 6, e.g. if you roll a 3, ask a student a question about food and drink. The student answers.
- Instruct the class to continue in the same way in their groups, with students taking it in turns to roll the dice and ask another student in the group a question.

6 Grammar The same time

Page 160

Activity

Whole class mingle activity: form filling.

Focus

Routines and clock times.

Preparation

Make one copy of the worksheet for each student in the class and one for yourself. Fill in the second column of the worksheet for yourself.

Procedure

- Hand out one worksheet to each student.
- Ask everyone to work on their own to fill in the second column on the worksheet. Show them yours as an example.
- When they have finished, demonstrate the next stage of the activity: walk around asking students the first few questions. When you find someone who does a thing at the same time as yourself, say: *And me! Look – same time.* Show him or her the time you wrote on your worksheet and write his or her name in the column on the right. Show the class.
- Ask everyone to stand in the middle of the room. Ask them to mingle and find other students who have the same routine in different things – getting up, breakfast time, etc.

- When most of the class have finished ask everyone to sit down again.
- Find out from the class which students have found someone who has the same, or almost the same daily routine.

6 Vocabulary Time of day

Page 161

Activity

Pairwork: Pelmanism game.

Focus

Routines and clock time.

in the evening / in the afternoon / in the morning

Present simple.

Preparation

Make one copy of the worksheet for every three or four students in the class. Cut this into cards.

Procedure

- Put the class in small groups of three or four.
- Spread out a set of cards face down in the middle of one of the groups and demonstrate how to play the game:

  1 Turn over a rectangular card and a square card, e.g.

  2 Say a complete sentence in the first person:

     I get up at half past seven in the morning. If the group agrees that the cards go together and make a logical sentence, keep them and have another go. If the group does not think they go together, turn them face down again.

  3 It is then the next student's go to turn over two cards.

  4 The student with the most cards at the end is the winner.

- Ask the class to play the game in their groups. Monitor and make sure that students say a sentence every time they turn over a pair of cards.

Extension

At the end, ask everyone to put their cards back in the middle of the table face up. They then match the times and actions, and put them in order from morning to night.

6 Communication A day in a job

Page 162

Activity

Groupwork: information exchange and guessing game.

Focus

Daily routines and clock times.

Jobs.

Preparation

Make one copy of the worksheet for every four students in the class. Cut this into cards.

Procedure

- Write up this dialogue. Ask students if they can complete the gaps – *time, at.*

  A: What _____ do you get up?

  B: I get up _____ 7.30.

- Under the dialogue write the following tables:

have	breakfast
	lunch
	dinner
	coffee

  go to work
  get to work
  finish work
  get home
  go to bed

- Divide the class into groups of four. If the class does not divide into fours include a group of three.
- Ask the groups to work together and practise the expressions on the board. They each take turns to ask the student opposite them a *What time do you ...?* question.
- Tell the class you have a job card for each student in the group – they must keep their card secret (show this by holding a card close to your chest).
- Give a different job card to every student in each group. Check they know what the job is.
- Put a set of word cards in the middle of each group.
- Demonstrate with one of the groups: turn over a card from the middle and ask a question to every student in the group, which they answer *as the person on their card.*
- Ask all the groups to continue in the same way, taking turns to ask a question to the other students in their group.
- When all the question cards have been used up, ask the students to guess the other jobs in their group.

Review B *Friday, I'm In Love*

Page 163

Activity

Pairwork: song.

Focus

Revising vocabulary from *New Inside Out* Beginner Student's Book Units 4–6; rhyming words at the ends of song lines.

Preparation

Make one copy of the worksheet for each pair of students in the class. Get the recording ready (1.89).

Procedure

- Explain to students that they are going to listen to a song in English by The Cure. Ask the class if anyone knows the group or the names of any of their songs.

- Remind students of the correct order of the days of the week by asking them to call them out quickly when you point to different students around the class.

- Remind students which days are the weekend (*Saturday* and *Sunday*).

  1 Give out the worksheets, one to each pair of students. Ask them to look at the list of days in Exercise 1 and tick once for each time that they hear a day in the song. Note that after the first run through there is a repeat of the first two verses. Monday and Friday are each sung twice more. (For example, *Monday* is heard six times). Play the song and ask each pair to complete the first exercise together. Check the answers as a class.

  2 Ask the students to read the song again, working on their own to underline three colour words.

  3 Tell the students that songs often contain words which have the same sound. Ask them which rhyming words in the first verse go with *blue* (*too* and *you*). Now ask students to look at Exercise 3 and complete each group of words with a word from the box, like *you* in the example. They should check their answers in pairs. Play the recording for them to check their answers.

  4 Now ask the students to complete Exercise 4 individually. They decide which days of the week they like and write a tick in the box, and which days they don't like (cross). They then compare their choices with a partner's.

  5 Then each student should choose a day to complete each sentence in Exercise 5. Ask various students in the class to read out their sentences and compare which are the popular days and which the unpopular. Encourage them to stress the adjectives *great* and *terrible*.

> 1: Monday 6
> Tuesday 6
> Wednesday 6
> Thursday 6
> Friday 8
> Saturday 2
> Sunday: 2
>
> 2: blue, grey, black
>
> 3: a) you   b) apart   c) late   d) back   e) instead

7 **Grammar** Old Town, New Town

Page 164

Activity

Pairwork: identifying city features.

Focus

Is there a …? Are there any …?

Finding out about local amenities.

Prepostitions *in* and *near*.

Preparation

Make one copy of the worksheet for each pair of students in the class. Cut the worksheet into two.

Procedure

- Put the students in pairs. Tell the class that Student A lives in New Town and Student B lives in Old Town.

- Hand out one worksheet to each student, saying *You're Student A, you're Student B* as you go round.

- Write up this model dialogue on the board and ask the students to decide which words go in the gaps – *there, in, isn't*:

  A: Is _____ a bank in New Town?
  B: Yes, there is. It's _____ Archway Road.
      OR
      No, there _____.

- Ask the students to help you write the same model for plurals: *Are there any cafés in New Town?* and write this up next to the first model.

- Ask the class to continue in their pairs, asking each other questions to find out the identity of the buildings in their maps. They use the question prompts on the right of their worksheets.

- When they have finished, ask the pairs to compare their maps and see if they have got things in the same places.

- Write up this model on the board and ask the students which words go in the gaps – *in, near*:

  A: Is there a restaurant _____ Old Town?
  B: Yes, there is. It's _____ the hotel.

- Ask the whole class a few more questions with *Is there a …?* and accept answers with *It's near… .*

- Ask the students to work together in different pairs and continue asking and answering questions in the same way.
- At the end ask individual students where they would like to live – in Old Town or New Town.

Extension

If you have access to an interactive whiteboard, use Google Earth to look at New York City, asking students to make *there is/are* sentences.

7 Vocabulary Famous places

Page 165

Activity

Groupwork: Pelmanism game.

Focus

Vocabulary of places in a town or city.

Preparation

Make one copy of the worksheet for every four or five students in the class, cut into cards. Make one copy of the worksheet for yourself.

Procedure

- Put the class in groups of four or five students.
- Show the class a picture card (large) and matching word card (small). Tell them they have to find the cards that go together.
- Spread out a set of cards face down in the middle of each group.
- Demonstrate how to play for each group:
  1 Take turns to turn over a large and small card.
  2 If they go together, keep them and have another go. If they do not go together, turn them face down again.
  3 It is then the next student's turn.
  4 When all the cards have gone from the table the student with the most cards is the winner.
- At the end of the game ask the groups to return their picture cards to the middle of the table face upwards.
- Each group now works together as a team to identify the famous landmark in each picture. The team that gets the most places correct is the winner.

Extension

If you can find photos of the landmarks in the worksheet, revise them in the next lesson: Divide the class into two teams, left and right. Show the class the photos very quickly. The team that shouts out the name of the landmark each time gets a point.

---

1 The Sydney Opera House (theatre)
2 The Louvre (museum)
3 Central Park (park)
4 Red Square (square)
5 Trafalgar Square (square)
6 Charles Bridge (bridge)
7 Venus de Milo (statue)
8 The River Thames (river)
9 The Statue of Liberty (statue)
10 Burj-Al-Arab Hotel (hotel)
11 Ipanema Beach (beach)
12 The Golden Gate Bridge (bridge)

7 Communication My town

Page 166

Activity

Pairwork: information exchange.

Focus

Near my house, there's a …
Inventing a perfect town with amenities.

Preparation

Make one copy of the worksheet for each student in the class plus one for yourself. Fill your own copy in before the lesson by drawing in ten buildings and giving them names from the list down the side of the worksheet.

Procedure

- Write up the title of the activity:

  perfect
  My/town

- Tell the class they can invent their perfect town. Show them a blank copy of the worksheet and point to the house in the middle. Say: *This is where you live – number 1 Park Road. There aren't any shops.* Show the class the copy that you filled in for yourself and describe it, e.g.

  This is my perfect town. Near my house there's a cinema. There isn't a football stadium! Near my house there's a beautiful park.

- Hand out the worksheet. Explain that there are twenty-two places in the list, but that they can only choose ten of them.
- Ask everyone to work on their own. They draw the places near their house and write the names on them.
- When everyone has finished ask the class to sit in pairs. If there is an odd number of students, make a group of three. Ask the students to compare their maps by taking turns to tell their partner about their town, for example:

  Near my house there's a …

Extension

If the students in class know the area where the school is located, ask them two questions about local amenities – one singular and one plural, e.g

Is there a bank near here? Are there any good bars near here?

Write the two questions you asked next to each other on the board. Ask the class for the answers and write them under the questions.

Yes, there is.   *Yes, there are.*
No, there isn't.   *No, there aren't.*

Ask the class to work in small groups and ask questions about the local area using the words on the worksheet.

8 Grammar Our flat

Page 167

Activity

Pairwork: information exchange.

Focus

Is there a …? Are there any …?
Furniture vocabulary.

Preparation

Make one copy of the worksheet for each student in the class plus one for yourself. Write in seven items of furniture on your flat plan before the lesson.

Procedure

- Ask the students to work individually. Hand out the worksheet. Tell the students that they can choose seven items of furniture they would like in their flat from the sheet, and write the names of the items in the rooms. They should keep their flat plans secret.

- Show the class your flat plan. Use your items to ask one of the students about their flat:

  Teacher: Is there a TV in your flat?
  Student: Yes, there is.
  Teacher: Are there any books in your flat?
  Student: No, there aren't.

- Show the class that you have ticked the TV picture on your worksheet, to show that you have the same as the student.

- Tell the students they have to find out how many items are the same as their partner. Ask the students to work in pairs to find out about each other's flats.

- Monitor and check that students are using both plural and singular forms.

- At the end of the activity check which pairs have most items the same. Maybe they can share a flat!

Extension

If you feel the students are confident, ask them to write sentences about their real accommodation. Write up these sentence frames on the board:

There is a_____ in my _____. (kitchen / bedroom / living room)
There are _____ in my _____.
There aren't any _____ in my _____ .

8 Vocabulary Password!

Page 168

Activity

Team game: word association.

Focus

Furniture vocabulary and related words.

Preparation

Make one copy of the worksheet for each team of five students plus one copy for yourself. Cut the words up into separate cards – one pile for each team.

Procedure

- Put the class in three or more teams of four or five students. Tell each team they going to help each other guess some furniture words using a different word or mime.

- Demonstrate for the students by picking up the first card from the pile e.g. *piano*. Say *music*, then *play*, then *big*, and wait until a student calls out *piano*. Give them the card. Pick up another card e.g. *bed* and mime pulling back the covers and going to sleep.

- Give each team a pile of cards and ask them to sit together to begin the game. Remind students that they must not say the word on the card.

- The winning team is the first to get rid of their pile of cards.

8 Communication Do you like him?

Page 169

Activity

Groupwork: talking about likes and dislikes.

Focus

Do you like …? Object pronouns.

Preparation

Make one copy of the worksheet for each group of students in the class. Cut this up into cards.

Procedure

Write these pronouns on the board:

Subject	Object
He	him
She	_____
It	_____
They	_____

- Ask the students to complete the list of object pronouns.
- Write up the title of the activity: *Things we like and things we don't like.*
- Put the students in groups of three or five or seven.
- Demonstrate the activity with one of the groups: show them a card, e.g. A bottle of cola, and ask the individual students in the group: *Do you like it?* If most of them like cola, put it to one side on the table and say: *These are things we like.* Do another example, e.g. with *snow.* If most of the group dislikes it, put it to the other side and say: *These are things we don't like.*
- Ask the class to continue in their groups: students take it in turns to turn a card face up. They all say if they like it/them/her/him, and then ask the others and put the card to one side or the other.
- You can help the students with any words they want to know.

9 Grammar Are you healthy?

Page 170

Activity

Pairwork: questionnaire.

Focus

Adverbs of frequency. Personal routines.

Preparation

Make one copy of the worksheet for each student in the class, plus one for yourself.

Procedure

- Hand out the worksheet.
- Demonstrate how to fill in the worksheet: write the first name of one of the students at the top. Ask him or her the first three questions and tick one of the boxes next to each question – *always, usually, sometimes* or *never.*
- Now show how healthy you think he or she is by putting a cross on the line at the bottom of the worksheet. Show the class what you have done.
- Ask everyone to work in pairs. If there is an odd number of students, work with one student yourself.

- Ask the class to take turns to go through the questions in their pairs. Each student fills in the worksheet for their partner and then puts a cross on the line at the bottom to show how healthy they think he or she is.
- When everyone has finished, find out which students have a cross at or near the 'healthy' or 'unhealthy' ends of the line.

9 Vocabulary Do you eat it?

Page 171

Activity

Groupwork: card game.

Focus

Present simple: *Do you …?*
Vocabulary revision.

Preparation

Make one copy of the worksheet for every four students in the class. Cut this into separate cards. You will need one piece of paper for each group divided into four boxes with the headings *eat, go to, play* and *speak.*

Procedure

- Write these words on the board:

  fruit   discos   basketball   French

- Ask students to call out the verbs that people use with these words, but not *like* – (*eat, go to, play, speak*) and write these above the words.
- Explain to students that they are going to play a card game. They have to decide quickly which verb the words on the cards go with.
- Put the class in groups of four and give one pile of cards (face down) and one piece of paper to each group.
- Demonstrate with one of the groups by turning over the top card and asking the students to decide which verb box it goes in.
- Tell the groups to play the game by turning over the cards and putting them in the correct box. Shout *Go!* to begin the game.
- When the first group has finished shout *Stop!*
- Ask students to work in pairs with the person opposite. They should ask a question using each card. Demonstrate with a student and write the example on the board:

Teacher:	Do you go to discos?
Student A:	Yes, I do. / No, I don't.
Teacher:	Do you eat eggs?
Student B:	Yes, I do. / No, I don't.

- Ask students to take turns choosing a card and asking the questions. Go round and monitor. Make sure they are using the correct verb.

9 Communication Small or large?

Page 172

Activity

Groupwork: role play.

Focus

Can I have …? Would you like …?
Restaurant food and drink vocabulary.

Preparation

Make one copy of the worksheet for each student in the class, plus one for yourself.

Procedure

- Ask students to work in pairs to match the food and drink items in the column on the left with the most suitable options in the column on the right.

- Check the connections they have made by going through the list with the whole class.

- Tell students that they are in a restaurant. Check that they know *waiter* and *customer*. Ask them to use their lists to help you write a short dialogue on the board:

  Waiter: Good evening, Sir / Madam.
  Customer: Good evening. Can I have a sandwich, please?
  Waiter: Yes. Would you like white or brown bread?
  Customer: Brown, please.

- Put the class into groups of three or four and choose a waiter for each group.

- Pretend to be the waiter and demonstrate the roleplay with one group. Each customer should order two things and the waiter gives them the options and then writes down the order.

- Encourage students to sound friendly and polite during the roleplay.

Review C The Revision Game

Page 173

Activity

Groupwork: board game.

Focus

Revising main structures from *New Inside Out* Beginner Student's Book Units 7–9.

Preparation

Make one copy of the worksheet for every three or four students in the class, and one for yourself. You will need one counter for each student, and one coin and a copy of *New Inside Out* Beginner Student's Book for each group.

Procedure

Ask the students to work in groups of three or four. Hand out the worksheets, one to each group. One person is the 'Checker'. The Checker doesn't play the game.

1 Players place their counters on different squares marked START.

2 The first player throws the coin and moves the counter as follows:
  'Heads' = two squares
  'Tails' = one square

3 When a player lands on a square, they must choose the correct sentence, a) or b).

4 The Checker then turns to the Grammar *Extra* section on pages 130–131 and checks the answer. If the player is right, they can wait for their next turn. If the player is wrong, they miss a turn.

5 The first player to reach FINISH is the winner.

Player 1: 1 b 2 b 3 a 4 b 5 b 6 a 7 a 8 a	
Player 2: 1 b 2 a 3 b 4 a 5 a 6 b 7 b 8 a	
Player 3: 1 a 2 b 3 b 4 a 5 b 6 b 7 a 8 b	

10 Grammar I'm wearing blue jeans

Page 174

Activity

Groupwork: card game.

Focus

Present continuous.

Colours and clothes.

Preparation

Make one copy of the worksheet for every three students in the class. Cut this into separate cards.

Procedure

- Put students in groups of three with a pile of cards face up in the middle of each group. If there is an extra student make one group of four.

- Demonstrate the game. Say three sentences about the clothes you're wearing, using the colours and items on the cards, but don't use the first person. Write the colour and clothes item on the board first, e.g.

  black trousers
  white top
  black shoes

  Then say and write sentences on the board as a model:

  Teacher: This person is wearing black trousers. This person is wearing a white top. This person is wearing black shoes. Who is it?

  Students should be able to guess.

- Tell the class that they need to test their memory. Two students in each group should close their eyes. The other student picks out three different colour and clothes cards which describe someone in the classroom. They then make sentences for the other students using the present continuous.
- When someone has guessed who it is, they open their eyes again. The first student in the group to guess correctly asks the others to close their eyes, and continues to choose cards which describe another person in the class.
- Make sure everyone has at least one turn each.

Extension

Ask students to walk around the room, mingling with each other for about 15 seconds. Shout *Stop!*, and ask each student to stand back to back with the nearest person and describe what they're wearing.

Demonstrate by standing next to someone and making sentences about the student they are back to back with: *You're wearing …* , making as many sentences as possible. Then students turn round to check if they're right.

10 **Vocabulary** Crossword

Page 175

Activity

Pairwork: complete a crossword.

Focus

Clothes vocabulary.

Preparation

Make one copy of the worksheet for each pair of students in the class. Cut it in half. Make another copy for yourself.

Procedure

- Ask the students to work in pairs. If there is an odd number of students, two can work together as Student A or B.
- Show the class the worksheet. Point out that one is for Student A and one is for Student B.
- Explain that the class is going to complete the crossword. A and B help each other. Student A has a picture with half the words for the crossword. Student B has a picture with the other half of the words.
- Hand out the worksheet. Demonstrate with one of the Student A's worksheets by saying the answer to clue number 1:

  Number 1 – Jeans : J – E – A – N – S

- Make sure that everyone writes the word *jeans* in number 1 down.

- Students continue in the same way, taking it in turns to look at their picture and say the numbers, items of clothing and spellings. Note that 12 has an 'across' (trainers) and 'down' (tie) which you may want to point out to students as you go round listening.
- At the end ask the whole class if anyone can guess the word for number 5.

```
                      1J
        2S  3H  O   E   S          4J
    5K      A       A              A
6S  H   I   R   T       N          C
        M               S   O  C  K  S
    7B  O   O  8T   S               E
        N       S              9T  O  P
C   L   O   T   H   E 10S    11D
        I       K           R
        12T R   A   I   N   E   R   S
13S U   I   T       R           S
        E       T               S
```

10 **Communication** What am I doing?

Page 176

Activity

Team game: miming.

Focus

Present continuous. Vocabulary revision.

Preparation

Make one copy of the worksheet and cut it up.

Procedure

- Divide the class into two teams. Ask them to think of a name for their team, e.g. a local football team. Write the two team names on the board.
- Put the pile of mime cards on the table in front of you. Take the top one and look at it. Then put it to one side. Stand in front of the class and ask the class *'What am I doing?'* – mime eating a fish (dividing the meat from the bone, pulling a bone from your mouth etc.) The class must work out exactly what you are doing, so if a student says *You are eating*, ask *What am I eating?* The first team to guess correctly gets a point. Put this on the board under their team name.

- Ask one student from each team to come to the front of the class. Show them a card from the pack. They mime the action for their team, who have thirty seconds to guess what it is. If they guess correctly, they score a point. If time runs out, the other team can have a guess. If they guess correctly, they get the point and then continue with their own turn.

- The team with the most points at the end is the winner.

11 Grammar It's a lie!

Page 177

Activity

Groupwork: True/False game.

Focus

was/were

Preparation

Make one copy of the worksheet for every three students in the class. Cut this into cards.

Procedure

- Place a pack of cards on the table in front of you. Take the top card and use the prompt written on it to make a sentence, e.g.

  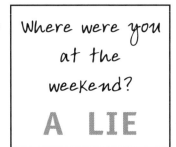

  Where were you at the weekend?

  A LIE

  I was in New York at the weekend.

- Ask the class if the statement is true or a lie.

- Show the class the prompt written on the card.

- Write up the prompt and the sentence.

- Do another example with a truth card.

- Divide the class into groups of three. If the class does not divide into threes, allow a group of four or allow two students to work together as one.

- Place a pack of cards in the middle of each group.

- Tell the class the rules of the game:

  1 Take it in turns to take a card. Keep it hidden from the other students in the group.

  2 Answer the question on the card with a true sentence or a lie.

  3 The student on your left decides if your sentence is true or a lie. If he or she is correct give him or her the card. If he or she is wrong, give the card to the other student.

  4 The student with the most cards at the end of the game is the winner.

Variation

Give a choice of adjectives to add to the sentences:

amazing	brilliant	expensive	nice
awful	excellent	fantastic	terrible
boring	exciting	great	wonderful

Include one of the adjectives in your example:
I was in New York at the weekend. It was amazing!

11 Vocabulary What are the numbers?

Page 178

Activity

Pairwork: writing game.

Focus

There are …
Time vocabulary: clock time, months, etc.

Preparation

Make one copy of the worksheet for each student in the class, plus one for yourself.

Procedure

- Put the class in pairs. If there is an odd number of students allow a group of three, or divide the whole class into groups of three.

- Tell the class this is a race. They have to write ten sentences and the first pair to finish is the winner.

- Hand out the worksheet. Ask the whole class: *What are these numbers?* If no-one can guess, write the word *Time* on the board. Elicit an example for one of the *60s* on the worksheet. Write the sentence for the class:

  There are sixty seconds in a minute.

- Ask the class to continue in pairs. They should write ten more sentences for the rest of the numbers on their worksheet. Monitor and make sure they write their answers in words, not numbers.

Variation

Instead of handing out the worksheet, make a transparency of it and project it onto the board.

  60   There are sixty seconds in a minute.
  60   There are sixty minutes in an hour.

24	There are twenty-four hours in a day.
7	There are seven days in a week.
4	There are four weeks in a month.
28	There are twenty-eight days in February.
30	There are thirty days in April, June, September and November.
31	There are thirty-one days in January, March, May, July, August and October.
365	There are three hundred and sixty-five days in a year.
52	There are fifty-two weeks in a year.
12	There are twelve months in a year.

11 Communication Going out

Page 179

Activity

Whole class: mingle activity.

Focus

Would you like …? Times and days.

Entertainment vocabulary.

Preparation

Make two copies of the worksheet for every twelve students in the class. If there are more than twelve in the lesson, divide the class into two groups. Cut the worksheet up into separate tickets and put them together so that each student gets two copies of the same ticket. Keep the pair of tickets for yourself.

Procedure

- Show the class your tickets and say *I have two tickets to a fantastic disco.* Write up the information on the ticket:

- Write up the following mini dialogue and elicit the words for the gaps – *like, with, OK:*

  – Would you _____ to go to a disco _____ me?

  – Yes, _____.

- Under the reply write the questions on the board:

  When is it?

  Where is it?

  How much is it? / How much does it cost?

- Walk around and ask students if they'd like to go to the disco with you. When a student agrees practice the questions and answers with him or her.

- Give him or her one of your tickets and tell the class what tickets you have, e.g.

  Yukio and I have two tickets for a disco on Saturday evening.

- Tell them that the tickets are all on Friday evening, Saturday afternoon or Saturday evening. Tell them they must <u>give</u> a ticket to one student and <u>take</u> a ticket from another student.

- Hand out the tickets.

- Ask everyone to stand in the middle of the room and mingle until they have found someone to go out with.

- When everyone has finished, ask the class to sit down again. Ask individual students at random around the class to tell everyone what tickets they have, e.g.

  Lien and I have two tickets for a disco on Friday evening. Carla and I have two tickets for a festival on Saturday afternoon.

12 Grammar Steffi Graf

Page 180

Activity

Groupwork: jigsaw reading.

Focus

Past simple regular and irregular affirmative forms.

Preparation

Make one copy of the worksheet for every three students in the class and cut it into separate phrases.

Procedure

- Write on the board: *Steffi Graf – Tennis Champion.*

- Tell the class this is the story of the tennis player Steffi Graf. Briefly show the pictures on the worksheet to the class.

- Tell the class this is a race. Steffi Graf's story is on some pieces of paper and every sentence is in two pieces. Hold up the halves of the first sentence to demonstrate. Write the sentence on the board:

Steffi Graf was	born in 1969.

- Underline and remind students about the capital letter at the beginning of the sentence and the full stop at the end.

- Put the class in small groups of about three.

- Spread out the sentence halves in the middle of each group.

- Ask the groups to put the sentences together and to put the completed sentences in order.

- The first group to finish is the winner.

Extension

Ask the students to write out the completed story. Before you begin this task take away the following parts of the jigsaw so that the students are writing some of it from memory.

*Steffi Graf was
Her father taught
She practised tennis
In 1987 she became
Steffi Graf retired
In 2001 she married*

12 **Vocabulary** *Bingo!*

Page 181

Activity

Pairwork: *Bingo!* game.

Focus

Irregular past simple verbs.

Preparation

Make one copy of the worksheet for every twelve students in the class. Cut each worksheet into six cards.

Procedure

- Write up *Bingo!* in large letters. Find out how many students know the game and pair off any who do not know with those who do.
- For some classes you may need to explain the rules: show a *Bingo!* card to the class. Explain the game by saying: *I say a verb. You put an X on the past tense.* Demonstrate with the verb *become*. Say the word and cross off *became* on your card. Show the class what you have done. Point out that they need to get a line in any direction. When they get a line they shout: *Line!* When they get all the words on their card they shout: *Bingo!*
- Hand out a *Bingo* card to each pair of students.
- Read out the infinitive of the verbs in the order given below. Go round checking that everyone is crossing off the past tenses.
- Give a point to the first three pairs to get a line. Give another point to the first three pairs to get *Bingo*.

become – have – get – write – sell – give – speak – do – run – eat – sit – buy – go – tell – lose – win – see – think

12 **Communication** *Snakes and Ladders*

Page 182

Activity

Groupwork: *Snakes and Ladders* game.

Focus

Past simple regular and irregular verbs – affirmative form. Exchanging personal information.

Preparation

Make one copy of the worksheet for every three or four students in the class. You will need one dice for each group and a counter for each student (or get them to use a small personal item such as a pencil sharpener).

Procedure

- Write the name of this game on the board: *Snakes and Ladders*.
- Show the class the worksheet to teach the words **snake** and **ladder**. Tell the class that in this game you go **up** the ladders and **down** the snakes.
- Put the students in groups of three or four.
- Place a copy of the game and a dice in the middle of each group. Make sure each student has a counter.
- Explain the rules of the game:
  1 Students take turns to roll the dice and move their counters, beginning at the start. If they roll a 3, for example, they move three squares.
  2 When they land on a square they say something about themselves using the verb written in the square. All sentences must be in the past.
  3 When they land at the bottom of a ladder they move up to the top and then say something. When they land on the head of a snake they move to the bottom and then say something.
  4 The first student to get to the finish is the winner.
- Demonstrate a turn for the class, e.g. (throwing a 5) *I had a coffee this morning.*

Review D What a Wonderful World

Page 183

Activity

Pairwork: song.

Focus

Revising vocabulary from *New Inside Out* Beginner Student's Book Units 7–9.

Preparation

Make one copy of the worksheet for each pair of students in the class. Get the recording ready (2.75).

Procedure

- Explain to students that they are going to listen to a song in English by Louis Armstrong. Ask the class if anyone knows why he is famous.

- Ask students what they see outside their window. Encourage them to give you a few examples open class and then ask the students to tell a partner what they can see from their own room at home.

  1 Give out the worksheets, one to each pair of students. Ask them to look at the picture and write the words in the box in the correct place on the picture. Check the answers as a class.

  2 Play the song and ask each student to underline the colours they hear. Check the answers as a class.

  3 Ask students in pairs to write a colour beside each word on the picture.

  4 Now ask students to complete Exercise 4 individually. They may need you to give them a few examples. Ask students to read out their sentences or alternatively compare them with a partner.

---

1 a) sky
   b) trees
   c) clouds
   d) rainbow
   e) babies
   f) friends
   g) roses

2 green, red, blue, white

3 green trees, red roses, blue skies, white clouds

---

13 Grammar My last holiday

Page 184

Activity

Whole class: mingle activity.

Focus

Past simple: negative and question forms.

Holiday vocabulary.

Preparation

Make one copy of the worksheet for each student in the class, plus one for yourself.

Procedure

- Hand out the worksheet.

- Show the class how to complete the worksheet by asking one of the students the question for the first statement:

  Did you go to a hot place?

- Keep asking students until you find someone who went somewhere hot on their last holiday. Write his or her name in the column on the right. Show the class what you have written.

- Ask all the students to stand in the middle of the room. Ask the second question to different students until one says *Yes, I did*. Write their name, and tell all the students to follow your example.

- When about half the class have completed their worksheet ask everyone to sit down again.

- For feedback ask a few questions to students at random using *Did …?* e.g.

  Teacher: Did you go to a hot place?
  Student: Yes, I did. / No, I didn't.

Extension

Use the first five topics in the worksheet to practise this dialogue:

A: When was the last time you went to a hot place?
B: Two years ago / In August. / Last year.

Begin by demonstrating an example with one of the stronger students. Write the example on the board. Put the class in pairs and ask them to use numbers 1 to 5 on the worksheet.

13 Vocabulary A fantastic holiday

Page 185

Activity

Pairwork: information exchange.

Focus

was/were.

Adjectives.

Preparation

Make one copy of the worksheet for each pair of students in the class. Cut these in half.

Procedure

- Write the title of the activity on the board:

  An awful
  A fantastic holiday!!!

- Ask the students to work in pairs. If there is an odd number, one of them can work with you.

- Tell the class that Student A's holiday was fantastic. Student B's holiday was awful.

- Hand out the role cards. Tell students to use the adjectives and nouns to ask and answer questions about their holiday. Demonstrate a few examples and write them on the board:

  Teacher: Margarita, did you have a nice holiday?
  Margarita: Yes. It was fantastic!
  Teacher: Did you like the hotel?
  Margarita: Yes, the room was great.
  Teacher: Did you have a nice holiday, Roberto?
  Roberto: No. My holiday was terrible!
  Teacher: Did you like the hotel?
  Roberto: No, the hotel was noisy.

- Encourage students to sound happy or unhappy when they are responding to the questions.

13 Communication Marco Polo

Page 186

Activity

Pairwork: information gap.

Focus

Wh questions: past simple.

Preparation

Make one copy of the worksheet for each pair of students in the class, and one for yourself. Cut it in half.

Procedure

- Write up the title of the activity on the board:

  Marco Polo – Explorer.

- Ask the students to sit in pairs. If there is an odd number, include a group of three with two students working together.

- Show the class both halves of the worksheet so that they can see that Student A's half is different from Student B's. They both have gaps, but these are in different places. They ask each other questions to get the information to fill in the gaps. Student A has the answers to B's questions and B has the answers to A's questions.

- Hand out the worksheet.

- Ask one of the A students to tell you the first question and write it on the board:

  Where did he live?

- Encourage Student B to say the answer. Ask *How do you spell that?* and write it on the board. Make sure that all the As write the answer on their worksheet.

- Do the same for the second question with one of the B students and write it on the board:

  What languages did he speak?

- Ask for the answer from the A partner and make sure all the Bs write the answer.

- Ask the class to continue in their pairs. Keep monitoring as they ask their questions and fill in their worksheets. Point out that all the questions have the question word *did*.

- When everyone has finished, check the questions, eliciting question and answer from different pairs.

14 Grammar How many?

Page 187

Activity

Teamwork: multiple choice quiz.

Focus

How many ...?

have/has.

Vocabulary revision from Units 1–14.

Preparation

Make one copy of the worksheet for each student in the class, plus one for yourself.

Procedure

- Divide the class into teams of four or five.

- Hand out one worksheet to each team.

- Demonstrate the quiz with the example question. Read the question out loud. Write on the board:

  *I think it's **a**. What do you think?*

- Tell the class to use this way of talking about the questions. They take turns to read out the questions. They need to agree on the correct answer and circle *a*, *b* or *c*. Put a circle on answer *a* on your worksheet to demonstrate.

- Monitor the groups as they work together. Make sure that all the students take turns to read out questions.

- When everyone has finished hand out the rest of the copies of the quiz so that everyone has got one.

- Check the answers by asking students at random to read out the questions and give their team's answer.

- At the end ask each team how many they got correct.

Extension

Ask the teams to write two more questions with *How many ...?* and pass them on to the next team. They answer the questions they receive from another team.

> *Example* a 1c 2a 3a 4c 5b 6c 7a 8a 9b 10a

14 Vocabulary *Pictionary*

Page 188

Activity

Team game: *Pictionary*.

Focus

Parts of the body and animals vocabulary.

Possessive *'s*.

Preparation

Make one copy of the worksheet and cut it up into cards. For the variation prepare one set of cards for each group of four or five students. You will need a clock or watch with a second hand.

Procedure

- Place the set of cards face down on the table in front of you.
- Take one card and look at it. Do a large drawing on the board of what is written on the card, e.g. a dog's head.
- Ask the class: *What is it?* When someone guesses correctly show the class that it is written on the card. Write a model sentence on the board:

  It's a dog's head.

- Divide the class into two teams, A and B, and explain how to play the game:

  1 One student from Team A comes to the front of the class and takes a card. He or she draws a picture of it on the board.

  2 Team A have twenty seconds to guess what it is, for a point. They must get the grammar of the sentence correct. (Point to the apostrophe *'s*.)

  3 If Team A do not guess correctly in twenty seconds, Team B can have a guess. If Team B guess correctly, they score a point.

  4 Then it is Team B's turn.

  5 Continue until all the cards have been guessed.

  6 The team with the most points at the end is the winner.

Variation

Ask students to work in groups of four or five. Place a set of cards in the middle of each group. Each student in the group takes turns to pick up a card and do a drawing. The first student in the group to guess what the drawing is keeps the card. The student with the most cards at the end is the winner.

14 **Communication** Can you drive?
Page 189
Activity
Whole class: mingle activity.

Focus
can for ability.

Preparation
Make one copy of the worksheet for each student in the class.

Procedure

- Hand out the worksheet.
- Show the class how to complete the worksheet. Ask one of the students the question for the first statement:

  Can you drive?

- Continue to ask students until you find someone who can drive. Write his or her name in the column on the right. Show the class what you have written.
- Ask all the students to stand in the middle of the room. Continue asking questions and writing different students' names in the column on the right. Ask the students to join in, asking *Can you …?* questions to other students. They should fill in their worksheets with a different name for each question.
- When about half the class have completed their worksheets, ask everyone to sit down again.
- You may want to ask any confident students who can do the things on the worksheet to demonstrate, e.g. to mime driving a car, to dance salsa, etc.
- To end the activity, ask students to work in pairs asking *Can you …?* questions to their partner which are not in the worksheet.

15 **Grammar** What do you know?
Page 190
Activity
Team race: information exchange.

Focus
Structures and vocabulary revision.

Preparation

Make two copies of the worksheet. Cut these into cards. Shuffle both sets of cards. Make a copy of the worksheet for yourself.

Procedure

- Tell the class they are going to have a race.
- Divide the class into two teams. If necessary, swap some of the team members so that there is a good balance of stronger students in both teams.
- Place the two packs of cards on the desk in front of you, one for Team A and one for Team B.
- Demonstrate how to play the game: take a card from the top of Team A's pack and ask Team A the question on it, for example:

  Teacher: Team A, what language do Austrians speak?
  Student from team A: Austrians speak German.

- Pretend to write the answer on the back of the card.
- Do the same with a different question for Team B, e.g. *How many days are there in September?*

- Tell the class the rules:
  1 One student from each team runs to the teacher's table, takes a card and runs back to their team.
  2 They ask the team the question on the card. The team must listen carefully, and anyone can answer.
  3 The student who asks the question writes the short answer on the back of the card and gives the card to another student in the team.
  4 He or she brings the card back to the teacher's table and takes another card back to the team.
  5 They continue like this until all the cards are finished.
  6 The first team to use up all the cards in their pack is the winner.
- Listen to what each team is saying. If you hear any question forms that cause problems, circle them on your copy of the worksheet. At the end of the activity you can practise these.
- Discuss any answers that the two teams disagree on.

15 Vocabulary *Blockbusters*

Page 191

Activity
Team race: *Blockbusters* game.

Focus
Revision of vocabulary from the Student's Book.

Preparation
Make a transparency of the worksheet. If you do not have an overhead projector, make an A3 sized photocopy.

Procedure
- Divide the class into two teams.
- Project the game onto the whiteboard, or attach your A3 copy to the board.
- Tell the class they are going to play a game. Explain the rules:

Team A's aim is to connect the top and the bottom of the board. Team B needs to connect the left and the right of the board.

As well as trying to connect one side to the other each team should try to block the other's progress. The first team that connects two sides of the board is the winner.

All the letters are the initial letters of words from the Student's Book.

1 Team A chooses a letter. To choose a letter *s*, for example, a student on Team A says: *Give us an s*.
2 The teacher then asks a question which requires an answer beginning with *s*, e.g. *What s is something in tea or coffee?*
3 If Team A guess correctly – *sugar* – they keep the hexagon with the letter *s* for their team.
4 Then Team B chooses a letter.
5 When one team has a hexagon the other team cannot use it.
6 The winning team gets to the other side of the board first.

There is a list of some of the vocabulary on the next page with types of clue you can use.

Opposite – e.g. **What b is the opposite of white?**

beautiful	buy	cold	expensive	love	night	stand
big	cheap	come	happy	negative	sit	stop
black		early	hot	new	small	

Can – e.g. **What b can you drink in a bar?**

beer	cigarette	coffee	football	moon	pasta	pilot
bread	cinema	dress	French	motorbike	park	pizza

Example – e.g. **What b is, for example, a dictionary, *Inside Out*, *Don Quixote* …?**

book	colour	family	meal	musician	number	sport
car	drink	housework	month	name	relation	weekday

Category – e.g. **What b is a person in your family?**

artist	daughter	farmer	green	November	sandwich	sugar
afternoon	December	February	horse	piano	Saturday	Thursday
August	dentist	Friday	lion	pink	secretary	Tuesday
Australia	dog	Germany	March	red	September	water
brother	elephant	grandfather	milk	restaurant	sofa	Wednesday
	evening	great	morning	Russia		

Draw, point or **mime** – e.g. **What b is this?** (draw a bridge)

arm	eat	half	mouth	ride	skirt	tennis
boat	egg	hand	nose	river	sleep	tie
carpet	eye	head	paper	road	square	train
chair	foot	hour	pen	run	stomach	trousers
dictionary	fish	leg	plane	shirt	swim	walk
ear	golf	listen	potato	shoes	television	wine
		look	read	shower		

Past – e.g. **What b is the past of break?**

ate	did	had	ran	sent	thought	went
bought	gave	knew	sat	sold	told	won
broke	got	lost	saw	spoke	took	wrote

15 Communication What's she going to do?

Page 192

Activity

Pairwork: guessing game.

Focus

going to.

Preparation

Make one copy of the worksheet for each student, and one for yourself.

Procedure

- Write on the board: *Do you know the other students?*

- Hand out the worksheet. Ask each student to write the name of another student sitting on the other side of the room. Make sure that everyone is included. If there is an odd number of students, ask one of the students to write about you. You will then need to fill in a worksheet for someone else.

- Demonstrate how to fill in the worksheet: using your own copy, write the name of a student in the space provided and put a tick or a cross in the first few rows: put a tick if you think the statements in the column on the left are true and a cross if you think they are not true. Show the class what you have done and tell everyone about it, e.g.

  I think Marie is going to cook dinner on Friday evening. I don't think she's going to have a beer on Friday night.

- Ask the students to fill in their worksheets in the same way. Remind the class that this is about next weekend.

- When the students have finished, ask everyone to stand in the middle of the room.

- Ask the class to find the students they wrote about and check their guesses. Demonstrate with your copy of the worksheet, e.g.

  Teacher: *I think you're going to cook dinner on Friday evening.*
  Marie: *Yes. It's true.*
  Teacher: *I don't think you're going to have a beer on Friday night.*
  Marie: *It's not true. I'm going to have a beer with my friends.*

Review E The Revision Game

Page 193

Activity

Groupwork: board game.

Focus

Revising main structures from *New Inside Out* Beginner Student's Book Units 13–15.

Preparation

Make one copy of the worksheet for every three or four students in the class, and one for yourself. You will need one counter for each student, and one coin and a copy of *New Inside Out* Beginner Student's Book for each group.

Procedure

Ask the students to work in groups of three or four. Hand out the worksheets, one to each group. One person is the 'Checker'. The Checker doesn't play the game.

1 Players place their counters on different squares marked START.

2 The first player throws the coin and moves the counter as follows:
  'Heads' = two squares
  'Tails' = one square

3 When a player lands on a square, they must choose the correct sentence, a) or b).

4 The Checker then turns to the Grammar *Extra* section on pages 134–135 and checks the answer. If the player is right, they can wait for their next turn. If the player is wrong, they miss a turn.

5 The first player to reach FINISH is the winner.

Player 1: 1 b	2 a	3 b	4 a	5 b	6 a	7 a	8 b
Player 2: 1 b	2 b	3 b	4 a	5 a	6 b	7 a	8 a
Player 3: 1 a	2 b	3 b	4 b	5 a	6 a	7 a	8 b

It's her pen

1 Vocabulary

What's his name?

1 J_hn	Monroe
2 V_n_s	Tarantino
3 G_ _rg_	Shakespeare
4 W_ll_ _m	Woods
5 Alb_rt	Mandela
6 T_g_r	Einstein
7 M_r_lyn	Williams
8 Q_ _nt_n	Windsor
9 N_ls_n	Lennon
10 El_z_b_th	Clooney

1 Communication

What's your number?

First name	Elizabeth			
Surname	Jackson			
Passport number	PZ291813			
Mobile number	07906649992			

First name	**Patrick**			
Surname	**Stevens**			
Passport number	**US450603**			
Mobile number	**07947793552**			

First name	Nevita			
Surname	Preston			
Passport number	NZ483662			
Mobile number	070773662509			

First name	Alexander			
Surname	Townsend			
Passport number	UK634327			
Mobile number	07905557857			

 New Inside Out **Beginner Teacher's Book** © Macmillan Publishers Limited 2007

2 Grammar

Where is it?

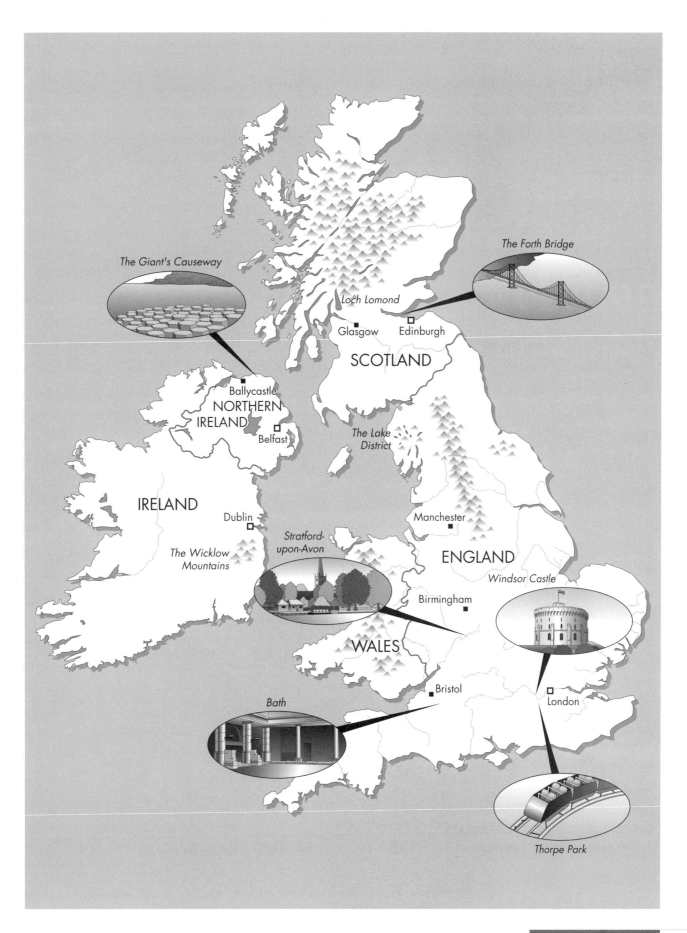

2 Vocabulary

Bingo!

Polish	German	Brazilian	Polish	German	Spanish
French	American	Spanish	Brazilian	Japanese	British
Japanese	Italian	British	Italian	French	American
Polish	Brazilian	French	British	French	Japanese
Italian	Spanish	British	Italian	Polish	Brazilian
American	German	Japanese	Spanish	American	German
Brazilian	Japanese	German	Japanese	American	German
Spanish	British	American	Italian	British	Polish
Polish	French	Italian	Brazilian	Spanish	French

 New Inside Out Beginner Teacher's Book   © Macmillan Publishers Limited 2007

2 Communication

How much is it?

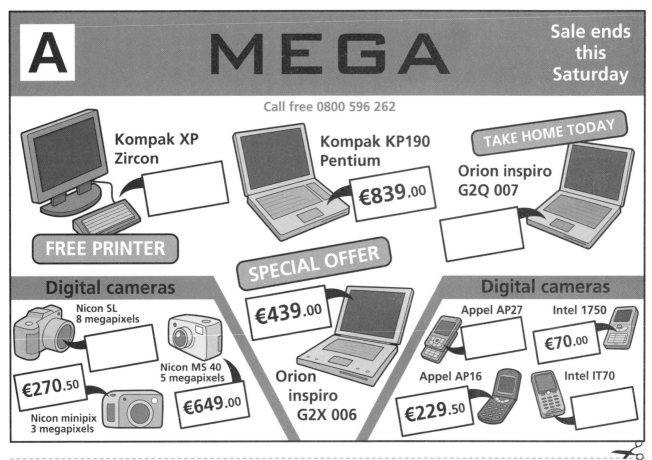

A MEGA — Sale ends this Saturday

Call free 0800 596 262

Kompak XP Zircon — FREE PRINTER

Kompak KP190 Pentium — €839.00

TAKE HOME TODAY — Orion inspiro G2Q 007

SPECIAL OFFER — €439.00 — Orion inspiro G2X 006

Digital cameras
- Nicon SL 8 megapixels
- Nicon MS 40 5 megapixels — €649.00
- €270.50 — Nicon minipix 3 megapixels

Digital cameras
- Appel AP27
- Intel 1750 — €70.00
- Appel AP16 — €229.50
- Intel IT70

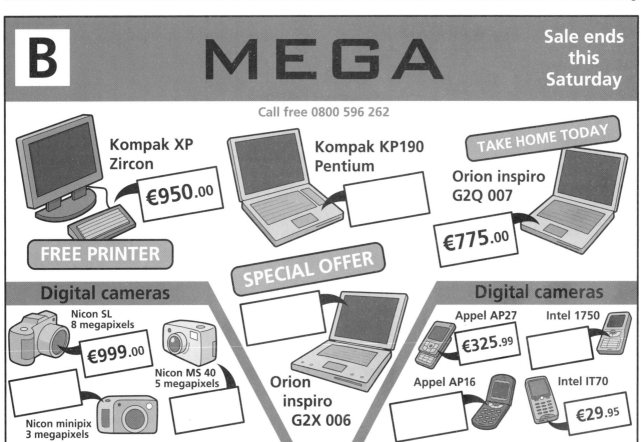

B MEGA — Sale ends this Saturday

Call free 0800 596 262

Kompak XP Zircon — €950.00 — FREE PRINTER

Kompak KP190 Pentium

TAKE HOME TODAY — Orion inspiro G2Q 007 — €775.00

SPECIAL OFFER — Orion inspiro G2X 006

Digital cameras
- Nicon SL 8 megapixels — €999.00
- Nicon MS 40 5 megapixels
- Nicon minipix 3 megapixels

Digital cameras
- Appel AP27 — €325.99
- Intel 1750
- Appel AP16
- Intel IT70 — €29.95

3 Grammar

Who is he?

New Inside Out Beginner Teacher's Book   © Macmillan Publishers Limited 2007

3 Vocabulary

Who's his wife?

1 Read this paragraph and look at the picture of the Johnson family.
Write their names in the boxes.

Colin and Sandra Johnson are grandparents. They have two children; their son's name is Derek and their daughter's name is Maria. Maria has three children. Cathy is seven years old and her sister Anna is five. Their cousin's name is Kevin. Kevin's parents are Derek and Linda. His uncle's name is Brad and his aunt's name is Maria. Brad has a baby. The baby's name is Jenny.

2 Answer these questions:

a) Who's Brad's wife?

....

b) Who's Anna's grandmother?

....

c) What is Linda's husband's name?

....

d) Who are Jenny's parents?

....

e) What is Jenny's cousin's name?

....

3 Write three more questions for your partner.

....

....

....

2 son
3 grandfather
4 father
5 brother
6 uncle
7 cousin
8 aunt
9 sister
10 mother
11 grandmother
12 daughter

Review A

The Revision Game

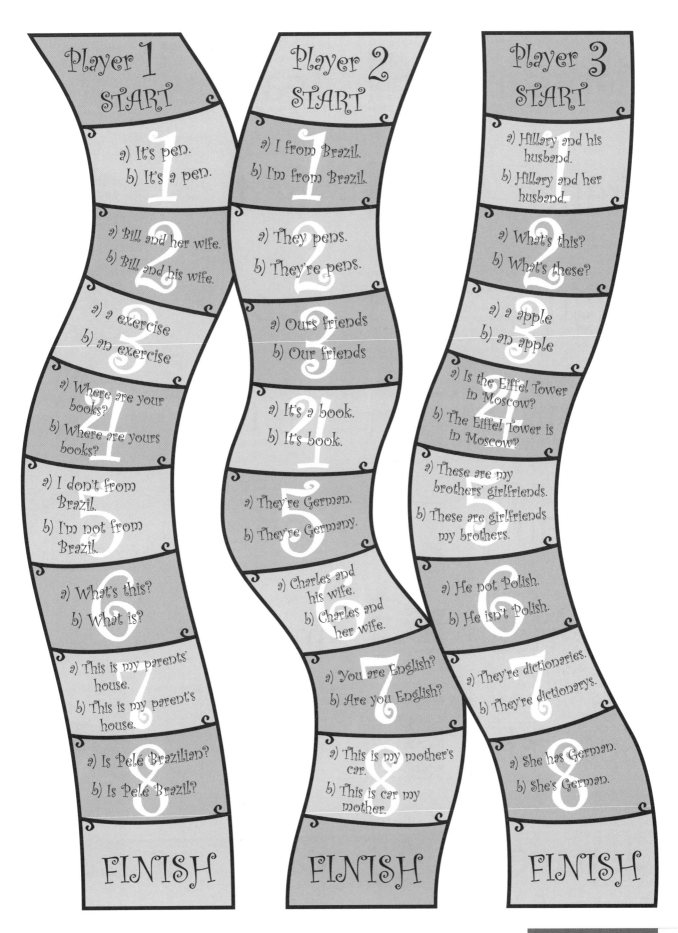

Player 1
START

1.
a) It's pen.
b) It's a pen.

2.
a) Bill and her wife.
b) Bill and his wife.

3.
a) a exercise
b) an exercise

4.
a) Where are your books?
b) Where are yours books?

5.
a) I don't from Brazil.
b) I'm not from Brazil.

6.
a) What's this?
b) What is?

7.
a) This is my parents' house.
b) This is my parent's house.

8.
a) Is Pelé Brazilian?
b) Is Pelé Brazil?

FINISH

Player 2
START

1.
a) I from Brazil.
b) I'm from Brazil.

2.
a) They pens.
b) They're pens.

3.
a) Ours friends
b) Our friends

4.
a) It's a book.
b) It's book.

5.
a) They're German.
b) They're Germany.

6.
a) Charles and his wife.
b) Charles and her wife.

7.
a) You are English?
b) Are you English?

8.
a) This is my mother's car.
b) This is car my mother.

FINISH

Player 3
START

1.
a) Hillary and his husband.
b) Hillary and her husband.

2.
a) What's this?
b) What's these?

3.
a) a apple
b) an apple

4.
a) Is the Eiffel Tower in Moscow?
b) The Eiffel Tower is in Moscow?

5.
a) These are my brothers' girlfriends.
b) These are girlfriends my brothers.

6.
a) He not Polish.
b) He isn't Polish.

7.
a) They're dictionaries.
b) They're dictionarys.

8.
a) She has German.
b) She's German.

FINISH

4 Grammar

Do you like it?

German		tea	
French		food	
English		books	
Brazilian		football	
Italian		coffee	
American		music	
Spanish		wine	
Japanese		cars	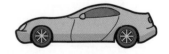

 New Inside Out Beginner Teacher's Book © Macmillan Publishers Limited 2007

4 Vocabulary

Categories

colours	things in class	family	countries

✂

colours	things in class	family	countries

5 Grammar

Have, live, speak, work

I	live	in a house.	We	like	Spanish food.
We	live	with my parents.	She	likes	football.
She	lives	in London.	I	have	an expensive car.
I	work	in an office.	We	have	seven children.
We	work	for Microsoft.	He	has	a Brazilian wife.
He	works	in a hospital.	I	speak	French and German.
I	like	English music.	She	speaks	English.

actor	artist	bus driver	dancer
taxi driver	doctor	farmer	flight attendant
football player	shop assistant	teacher	model
musician	waiter	pilot	secretary

5 Communication

Knowing you

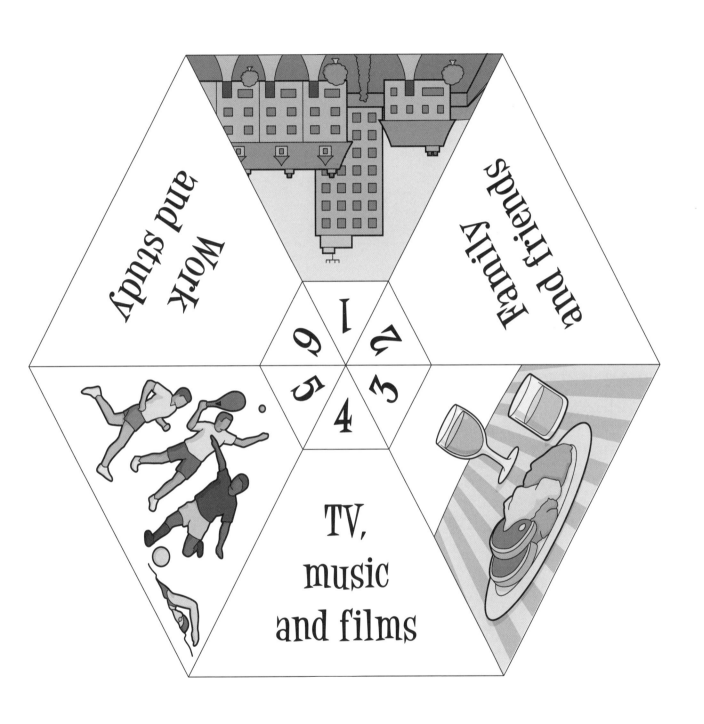

6 Grammar

The same time

What time do you ...	You	Names
get up on weekdays?		
have breakfast on Sundays?		
go to work or school?		
have lunch on Wednesdays?		
finish work or school?		
get home on Fridays?		
have dinner on Saturdays?		
go to bed on weekdays?		

 New Inside Out **Beginner Teacher's Book** © Macmillan Publishers Limited 2007

get up	7.30 a.m.	finish work	5.00 p.m.
have a shower	7.40 a.m.	go to the gym	5.30 p.m.
have breakfast	8.00 a.m.	get home	6.40 p.m.
go to work	8.45 a.m.	have dinner	7.00 p.m.
start work	9.15 a.m.	watch a film on TV	8.00 p.m.
have lunch	1.00 p.m.	read a book	11.00 p.m.
have a coffee	3.30 p.m.	go to bed	11.45 p.m.

6 Communication

A day in a job

	have lunch	go to bed
	get to work	get home
	have breakfast	finish work
	get up	have coffee

Review B

Song: *Friday, I'm In Love*

1 🔊 1.89 **Read and listen to the song. How many times do you hear each day of the week?**

Monday	Tuesday	Wednesday	Thursday	Friday	Saturday	Sunday
✓✓✓✓✓✓						
6						

Friday, I'm In Love

I don't care if Monday's blue,
Tuesday's grey and Wednesday too.
Thursday I don't care about you.
It's Friday, I'm in love.

Monday you can fall apart.
Tuesday, Wednesday break my heart.
Thursday doesn't even start.
It's Friday, I'm in love.

Saturday, wait,
And Sunday always comes too late,
But Friday, never hesitate …

I don't care if Monday's black,
Tuesday, Wednesday – heart attack,
Thursday, never looking back.
It's Friday, I'm in love.

Monday, you can hold your head.
Tuesday, Wednesday stay in bed.
Or Thursday – watch the walls instead.
It's Friday, I'm in love.

Saturday, wait,
And Sunday always comes too late,
But Friday, never hesitate …

2 **Read the song again. <u>Underline</u> three colour words.**

3 **Look at the five pairs of words from the song with the same sound.**
Add another word from the box to each pair.

| a<u>part</u>   late   back   ~~you~~   in<u>stead</u> |

a) blue   too   *you*
b) heart   start   _____
c) wait   hesi<u>tate</u>   _____
d) black   at<u>tack</u>   _____
e) head   bed   _____

Listen again to the song and check.

4 **Tick (✓) the days of the week that you like. Cross (✗) the days of the week that you don't like.**

Monday	Tuesday	Wednesday	Thursday	Friday	Saturday	Sunday
		✗			✓	

Now compare with a partner.

5 **Complete each sentence with a day of the week.**

a) _____ is great!
b) _____ is terrible!

7 Grammar

Old Town, New Town

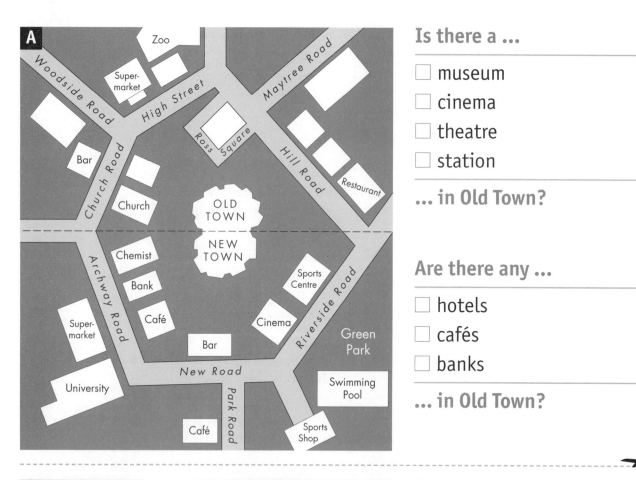

Is there a ...

- ☐ museum
- ☐ cinema
- ☐ theatre
- ☐ station

... in Old Town?

Are there any ...

- ☐ hotels
- ☐ cafés
- ☐ banks

... in Old Town?

✂

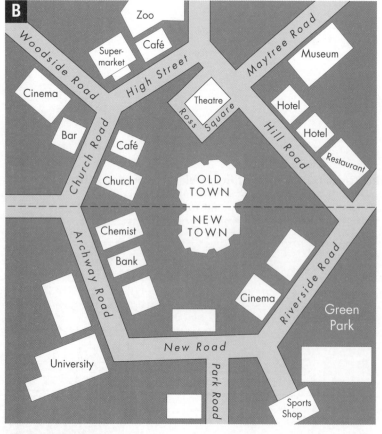

Is there a ...

- ☐ swimming pool
- ☐ bar
- ☐ sports centre
- ☐ theatre
- ☐ supermarket

... in New Town?

Are there any ...

- ☐ cafés
- ☐ hotels
- ☐ restaurants

... in New Town?

7 Vocabulary

Famous places

theatre	museum	park	square	square	bridge
statue	river	statue	hotel	beach	bridge

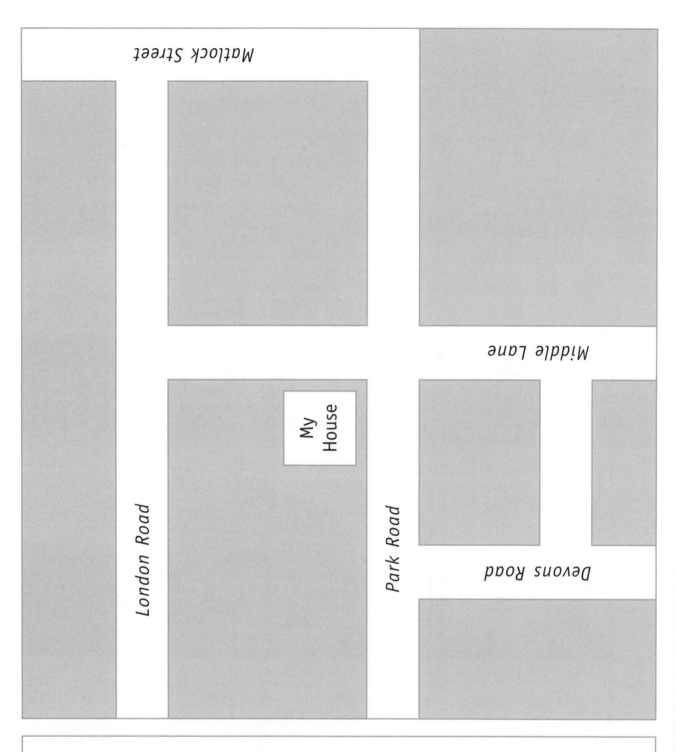

bookshop
bus stop
café
cashpoint
chemist
Chinese restaurant
cinema
disco
fish and chip shop
football stadium
gym
Indian restaurant
museum
park
river
square
supermarket
swimming pool
theatre
train station
underground station
zoo

8 Grammar

Our flat

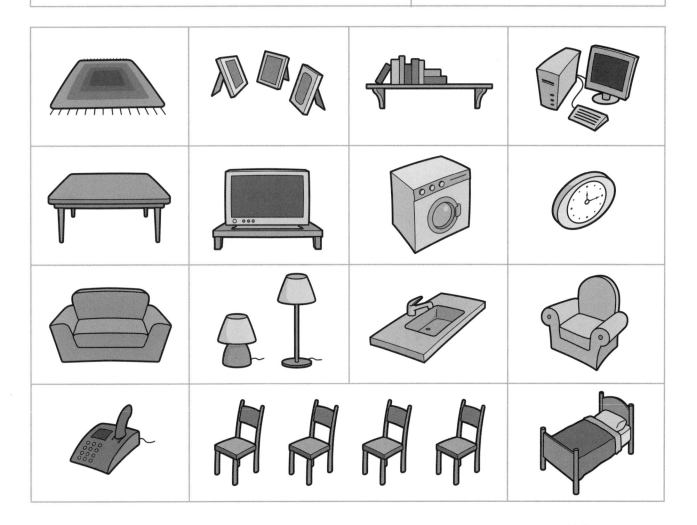

8 Vocabulary

Password!

phone	chairs
computer	*bed*
table	*lamp*
sofa	**cooker**
armchair	*sink*
books	**piano**
washing machine	**clock**
photos	TV

   New Inside Out Beginner Teacher's Book   © Macmillan Publishers Limited 2007

8 Communication

Do you like him?

9 Grammar

Are you healthy?

Name

	Always	Usually	Sometimes	Never
Do you go for a run in the morning?	☐	☐	☐	☐
Do you drink water with meals?	☐	☐	☐	☐
Do you smoke in the evening?	☐	☐	☐	☐
Do you work late at night?	☐	☐	☐	☐
Do you drink beer on Friday evenings?	☐	☐	☐	☐
Do you eat fruit with your lunch?	☐	☐	☐	☐
Do you go to bed early?	☐	☐	☐	☐
Do you go to the gym at the weekend?	☐	☐	☐	☐
Do you drink coffee in the evening?	☐	☐	☐	☐
Do you have sugar in tea or coffee?	☐	☐	☐	☐

Healthy   *Unhealthy*

PHOTOCOPIABLE   *New Inside Out* **Beginner Teacher's Book**   © **Macmillan Publishers Limited 2007**

Do you eat it?

cake	*restaurants*	pasta	noodles
soup	clothes shops	*Chinese food*	**tennis**
basketball	**Italian**	football	fish
Spanish	*cereal*	**oranges**	the piano
eggs	sandwiches	the guitar	*golf*
museums	discos	*Polish*	**French**
biscuits	**theatres**	German	football matches

9 Communication

Small or large?

  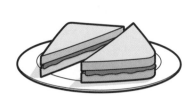 

a beer	white or brown bread
a glass of wine	English or German
a sandwich	black or white
an ice-cream	chocolate or banana
some chips	an orange or an apple
a coffee	red or white
some soup	large or medium
some fruit	potato or tomato

 New Inside Out Beginner Teacher's Book © Macmillan Publishers Limited 2007

Review C

The Revision Game

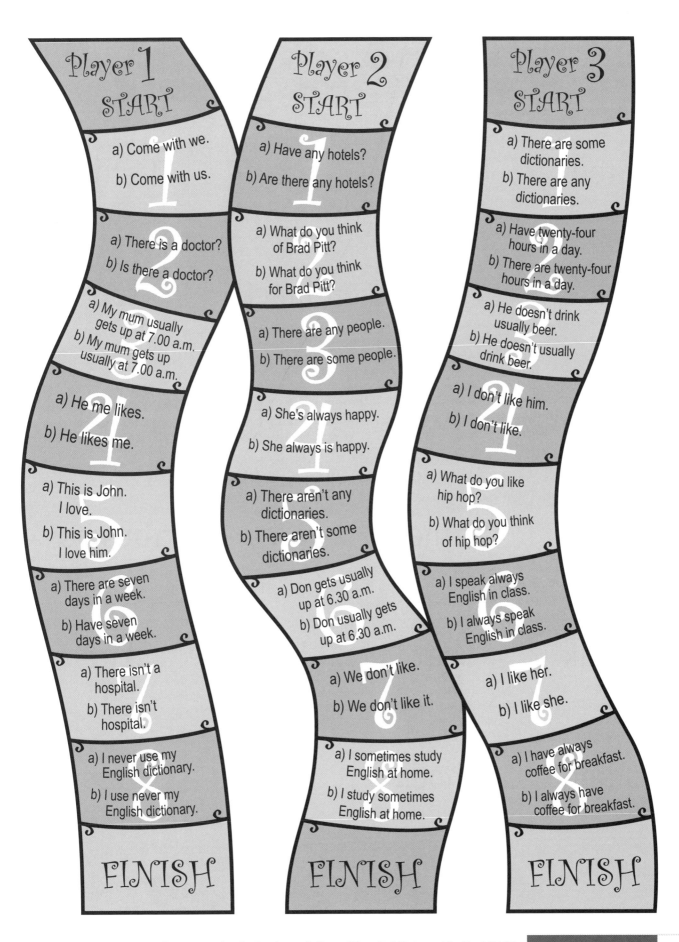

Player 1
START

1. a) Come with we.
   b) Come with us.

2. a) There is a doctor?
   b) Is there a doctor?

3. a) My mum usually gets up at 7.00 a.m.
   b) My mum gets up usually at 7.00 a.m.

4. a) He me likes.
   b) He likes me.

5. a) This is John. I love.
   b) This is John. I love him.

6. a) There are seven days in a week.
   b) Have seven days in a week.

7. a) There isn't a hospital.
   b) There isn't hospital.

8. a) I never use my English dictionary.
   b) I use never my English dictionary.

FINISH

Player 2
START

1. a) Have any hotels?
   b) Are there any hotels?

2. a) What do you think of Brad Pitt?
   b) What do you think for Brad Pitt?

3. a) There are any people.
   b) There are some people.

4. a) She's always happy.
   b) She always is happy.

5. a) There aren't any dictionaries.
   b) There aren't some dictionaries.

6. a) Don gets usually up at 6.30 a.m.
   b) Don usually gets up at 6.30 a.m.

7. a) We don't like.
   b) We don't like it.

8. a) I sometimes study English at home.
   b) I study sometimes English at home.

FINISH

Player 3
START

1. a) There are some dictionaries.
   b) There are any dictionaries.

2. a) Have twenty-four hours in a day.
   b) There are twenty-four hours in a day.

3. a) He doesn't drink usually beer.
   b) He doesn't usually drink beer.

4. a) I don't like him.
   b) I don't like.

5. a) What do you like hip hop?
   b) What do you think of hip hop?

6. a) I speak always English in class.
   b) I always speak English in class.

7. a) I like her.
   b) I like she.

8. a) I have always coffee for breakfast.
   b) I always have coffee for breakfast.

FINISH

10 Grammar

I'm wearing blue jeans

red	jeans	green	T-shirt
blue	shirt	black	top
yellow	suit	white	jacket
green	trainers	grey	trousers
pink	hat	blue	skirt
orange	shoes	red	dress

New Inside Out Beginner Teacher's Book   © Macmillan Publishers Limited 2007

10 Vocabulary

Crossword

Student A

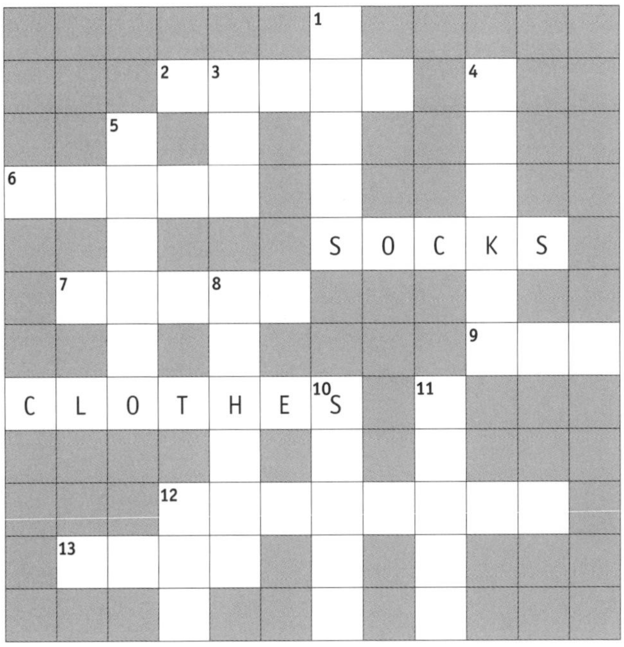

1
2
3
4
5
6
S O C K S
7
8
9
C L O T H E S
10
11
12
13

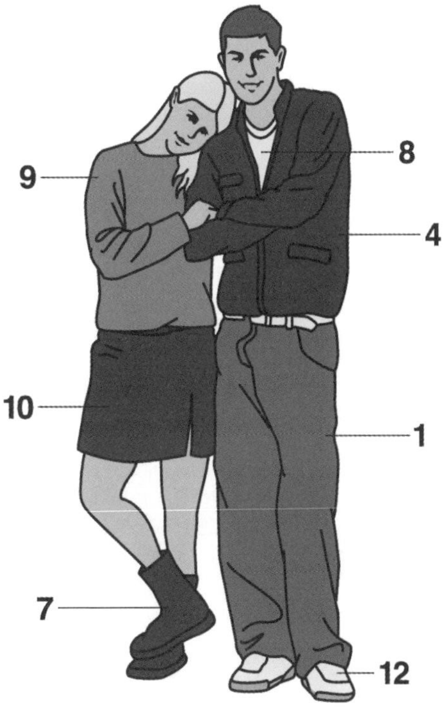

9
8
4
10
1
7
12

Student B

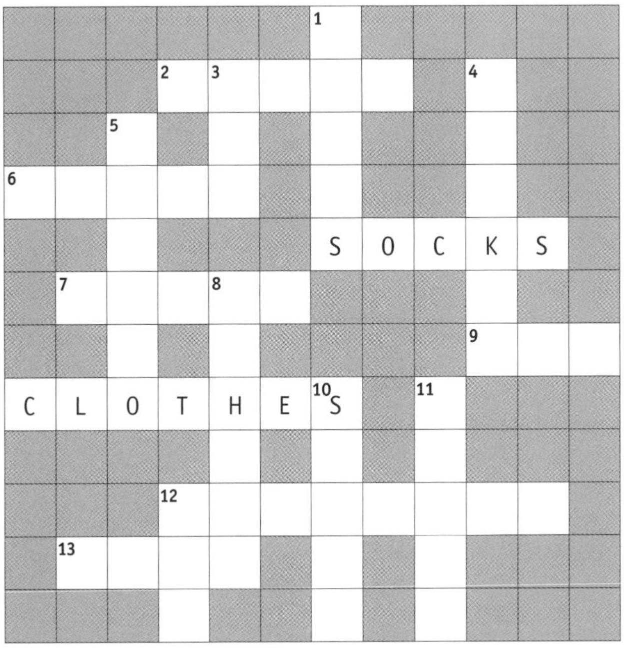

1
2
3
4
5
6
S O C K S
7
8
9
C L O T H E S
10
11
12
13

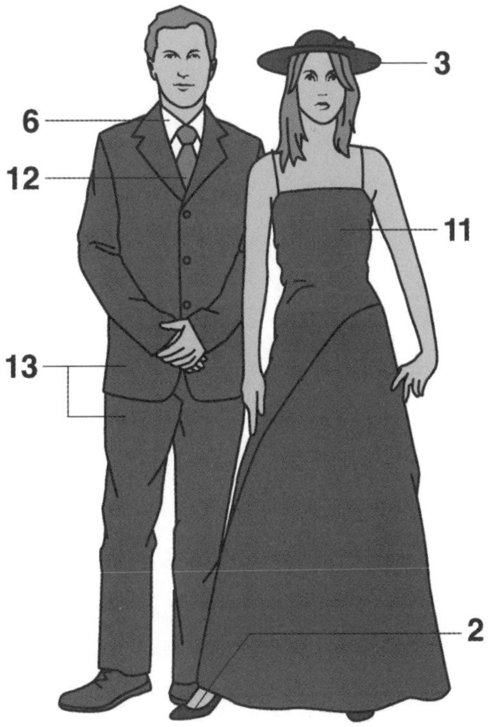

3
6
12
11
13
2

10 Communication

What am I doing?

playing the piano	watching tennis	trying on a jacket	reading a newspaper
drinking wine	watching football on TV	washing clothes	travelling in a plane
eating soup	visiting a museum	listening to music	eating a pizza
making breakfast	having a shower	standing on an underground train	eating spaghetti

PHOTOCOPIABLE *New Inside Out* Beginner Teacher's Book © Macmillan Publishers Limited 2007

11 Grammar

It's a lie!

Where were you last year? **A LIE**	Where were you in 1997? **A LIE**	Where were you at the weekend? **A LIE**	Where were you on Friday night? **A LIE**
Where were you on Saturday morning? **A LIE**	Where were you on Sunday afternoon? **A LIE**	Where were you yesterday afternoon? **A LIE**	Where were you yesterday at midday? **A LIE**
Where were you last night? **A LIE**	Where were you at 11 p.m.? **A LIE**	Where were you at 4 a.m.? **A LIE**	Where were you at 7.30 a.m.? **A LIE**
Where were you in 2004? **TRUE**	Where were you last Monday? **TRUE**	Where were you at the weekend? **TRUE**	Where were you on Friday? **TRUE**
Where were you on Saturday afternoon? **TRUE**	Where were you on Sunday evening? **TRUE**	Where were you yesterday morning? **TRUE**	Where were you yesterday evening? **TRUE**
Where were you at 10.45 p.m.? **TRUE**	Where were you at midnight? **TRUE**	Where were you at 3 a.m.? **TRUE**	Where were you at 8.30 a.m.? **TRUE**

11 Vocabulary

What are the numbers?

 New Inside Out Beginner Teacher's Book © Macmillan Publishers Limited 2007

MANCHESTER UNITED

CHAMPIONS LEAGUE

MANCHESTER UNITED
V
BARCELONA

SATURDAY 19th June
2:00 p.m.

E15
WEST STAND   £42

BARBICAN THEATRE

The Three Sisters
by
Anton Chekov

Friday 18th June
8.00 p.m.

PRICE £27

WIMBLEDON
LAWN TENNIS ASSOCIATION

CENTRE COURT
TICKET
Saturday 19th June

Gates open 1.30 p.m.

£65 incl. V.A.T.

| Day 4 | Level 2 | Gangway 3 | Row F | Seat 035 |

WEMBLEY
ENTERTAINMENTS
presents
the **ROLLING**
STONES
'Still Rolling Tour'
Friday June 18th at 7.00 p.m.
£70

VORTEX DISCO
R&B HOUSE Hip-Hop

DJ DAVE
Saturday 19th June
9.00 p.m. – 2.00 a.m.

£27.50   Admit 1

ODEON
C I N E M A

OXFORD STREET

The UK premiere of

STAR WARS VII

SATURDAY
19TH JUNE
8.00 p.m.
(doors open 7.00 p.m.)

£120 including champagne

RSC

ROYAL
SHAKESPEARE
COMPANY

HAMLET
Royal Theatre

SATURDAY 19th JUNE

Doors open 7.30 p.m.   £35

Summer Party

At John and Mary's house,
3 Ellingfort Road

Music
Beer
Volleyball

Saturday 19th June
11.00 p.m.

£2.50 for food

BRITISH
FORMULA 1
GRAND PRIX

SILVERSTONE
Saturday
19th June

Doors Open 11.00 a.m.
Race begins 1.00 p.m.

Price: £65

The Spitz
Disco & Bar
SALSA
AND SAMBA
NIGHT

Saturday 19th June

8.00 p.m. –3.00 a.m.

£15

JAZZ
IN THE PARK

JAZZ FOR AFRICA
presents

Manu Dibango
Super Etoile de Dakar
Dollar Brand

Victoria Park
Saturday 19th June
2.00 p.m. - 6.00 p.m.

£30 admission

LONDON
Film
FESTIVAL

Friday June 18th
at the

SOUTH BANK
ARTS CENTRE

5.00 p.m. –10.00 p.m.

£24

A NIGHT WITH

Frank Sinatra

EARLS COURT
Saturday 19th June

£49   8.00 p.m.

12 Grammar

Steffi Graf

✂

| Steffi Graf was | born in 1969. |

| Her father taught | her to play tennis. |

| She won her first competition | when she was five. |

| Steffi played her first professional | match in 1982. |

| She practised tennis | four hours a day. |

| In 1987 she became | the number 1 player in the world. |

| She won Wimbledon | in 1988. |

| Steffi Graf retired | from tennis in 1999. |

| In 2001 she married | Andre Agassi. |

| Their daughter Jaz Elle | was born in 2003. |

 New Inside Out Beginner Teacher's Book

12 Vocabulary

Bingo!

had	bought	did	wrote	wrote	sat	bought	spoke
went	became	gave	ate	told	sold	had	ran
ran	told	sat	spoke	gave	went	did	got
sold	won	got	thought	ate	became	lost	won
thought	won	told	got	spoke	lost	got	won
wrote	bought	gave	did	had	did	saw	gave
ran	had	went	sold	told	sold	ran	became
ate	spoke	became	lost	ate	wrote	sat	went
told	sat	gave	spoke	told	got	gave	sold
saw	sold	wrote	ate	spoke	won	had	bought
had	bought	won	did	became	did	ran	went
ran	got	went	became	lost	sold	sat	wrote

12 Communication

Snakes and Ladders

run	give	win		Finish
get home		walk	go	meet
lose	get up	go	play	
watch	visit	break	help	
talk	eat	finish	be	speak
	buy	arrive	wait	ask
Start	sit	cook		have

 New Inside Out **Beginner Teacher's Book** © **Macmillan Publishers Limited 2007**

Review D

Song: *What A Wonderful World*

1 Label the picture with these words from the song.

trees   roses   sky   clouds   rainbow   friends   babies

a)

b)

c)

d)

e)

f)

g)

2 🔘 1.75 **Read and listen to the song.** <u>Underline</u> all the colours you hear.

What A Wonderful World

I see trees of green, red roses too.
I see them bloom for me and you.
And I think to myself, what a wonderful world.

I see skies of blue, and clouds of white,
The bright blessed day, the dark sacred night.
And I think to myself, what a wonderful world.

The colours of the rainbow, so pretty in the sky,
Are also on the faces of people going by.
I see friends shaking hands, saying 'How do you do?'
They're really saying, 'I love you.'

I hear babies crying, I watch them grow.
They'll learn much more than I'll ever know.
And I think to myself, what a wonderful world.
Yes, I think to myself, what a wonderful world.

3 Match the colours with words on the picture.

4 Write three reasons why it's a wonderful world and one reason why it's a horrible world.

It's a wonderful world because _____

_____

_____

It's a horrible world because _____

On his/her last holiday this person...	
1 went to a hot place.	
2 stayed in a tent.	
3 travelled by boat.	
4 went swimming in the sea.	
5 ate in a restaurant.	
6 spoke English.	
7 had a fantastic time.	
8 stayed in this country.	
9 went with his/her mother.	
10 played a sport.	

13 Vocabulary

A fantastic holiday

Student A

Ask Student B about his / her holiday.
Talk about your holiday.

The hotel / room
The restaurant / food / waiters
The buses / trains / cars
The town / houses
The weather
The people
The beach

Use these adjectives: ▼

hot
new fantastic
amazing
quiet delicious
cheap
big happy
great brilliant
beautiful

--✂-

Student B

Ask Student A about his / her holiday.
Talk about your holiday.

The hotel / room
The restaurant / food / waiters
The buses / trains / cars
The town / houses
The weather
The people
The beach

Use these adjectives: ▼

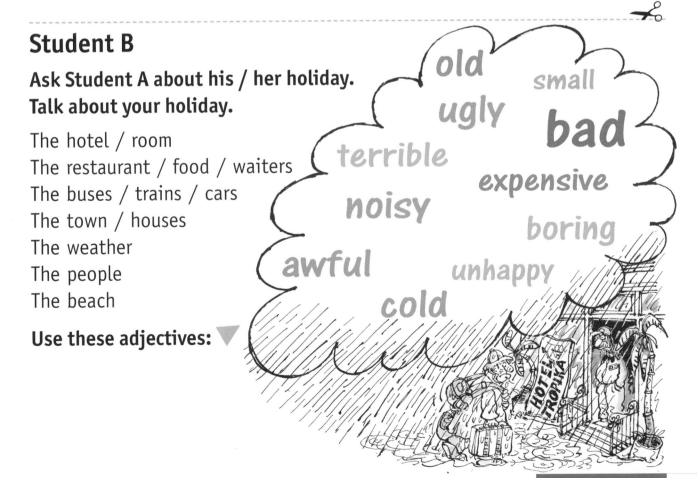

old
small
ugly
bad
terrible
expensive
noisy
boring
awful unhappy
cold

13 Communication
Marco Polo

Student A

Marco Polo was born in 1254 in Dalmatia, Italy. He lived in (1) _____ .
He spoke two languages: Italian and French.

In 1271 Marco Polo traveled to China. He arrived in Bejing in (3) _____ .
He met Kublai Khan and they became friends. Kublai Khan had 10,000 white horses.
Marco Polo stayed in China for (5) _____ years. He also went to
India and he visited Siberia.

In 1292 he left China for the last time. He
travelled home by (7) _____ and he
arrived in Venice in 1295. The journey home took
two years.

He married (9) _____ and they
had three daughters.

Marco Polo died in Venice in 1324. He was
sixty-nine years old.

Student B

Marco Polo was born in 1254 in Dalmatia, Italy. He lived in Venice. He spoke two languages:
(2) _____ and _____ .

In 1271 Marco Polo travelled to China. He arrived in Beijing in May 1275. He met
(4) _____ and they became friends. Kublai Khan had 10,000 white horses.
Marco Polo stayed in China for seventeen years. He also went to India and he
visited (6) _____ .

In 1292 he left China for the last time.
He travelled home by boat and he arrived in
Venice in 1295. The journey home took
(8) _____ years.

He married Donata Badoer and they had three
daughters.

Marco Polo died in Venice in
(10)_____ .
He was sixty-nine years old.

 New Inside Out Beginner Teacher's Book   © Macmillan Publishers Limited 2007

14 Grammar

How many?

Example How many eyes does a person have?
- a 2
- b 4
- c 6

1 How many eyes does a tarantula have?
- a 2
- b 4
- c 8

2 How many sports are there in the Olympic Games?
- a 28
- b 35
- c 43

3 How many yellow taxis are there in New York City?
- a 12,000
- b 20,000
- c 28,000

4 How many stomachs does a cow have?
- a 1
- b 2
- c 4

5 How many days are there in a fortnight?
- a 15
- b 14
- c 12

6 How many countries are there in Europe?
- a 36
- b 40
- c 44

7 How many rooms are there in Buckingham Palace?
- a 429
- b 532
- c 631

8 How many bones does a person have?
- a 206
- b 154
- c 109

9 How many months begin with J?
- a 2
- b 3
- c 4

10 How many bridges are there in London?
- a 30
- b 36
- c 42

a person's arm	a fish's back	an elephant's ears	a cat's eyes
a penguin's foot	a person's hand	a dog's head	a kangaroo's leg
a shark's mouth	an elephant's nose	a cow's foot	a lion's tooth
a cat's ear	a person's foot	a kangaroo's head	a tarantula's leg
a dog's nose	a person's leg	a person's ear	a lion's head

14 Communication

Can you drive?

Can you ...	
drive?	
count from 10 to 1?	
ride a horse?	
say the 23rd letter of the English alphabet?	
stand on your hands?	
dance salsa?	
play golf?	
say the past of *understand*?	
cook Indian food?	
spell your teacher's name?	

15 Grammar

What do you know?

ASK YOUR TEAM

Can you spell the first month of the year?

M	T	W	T	F	S	S
		1	2	3	4	5
6	7	8	9	10	11	12
13	14	15	16	17	18	19
20	21	22	23	24	25	26
27	28	29	30	31		

ASK YOUR TEAM

What was the date three weeks ago?

20 MONDAY	23 THURSDAY
21 TUESDAY	24 FRIDAY
	25 SATURDAY
22 WEDNESDAY	26 SUNDAY

ASK YOUR TEAM

What language do Brazilians speak?

ASK YOUR TEAM

What is your teacher wearing?

ASK YOUR TEAM

When is the next World Cup going to be?

ASK YOUR TEAM

How long does it take to fly to Australia?

ASK YOUR TEAM

What can birds do?

ASK YOUR TEAM

What's the national sport in India?

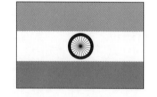

ASK YOUR TEAM

Who's the president of Russia?

ASK YOUR TEAM

What time is it in New York?

ASK YOUR TEAM

What does a shop assistant do?

ASK YOUR TEAM

How did Columbus travel to America?

 New Inside Out Beginner Teacher's Book © Macmillan Publishers Limited 2007

15 Vocabulary

Blockbusters

15 Communication

What's she going to do?

This weekend   NAME

		TRUE	NOT TRUE
	cook dinner on Friday evening	☐	☐
	watch TV on Friday night	☐	☐
	have a beer on Friday night	☐	☐
	go to bed late on Friday night	☐	☐
	get up early on Saturday morning	☐	☐
	read a newspaper on Saturday morning	☐	☐
	talk to friends on the phone on Saturday morning	☐	☐
	play a sport on Saturday afternoon	☐	☐
	buy clothes on Saturday afternoon	☐	☐
	go to the park on Saturday afternoon	☐	☐

 New Inside Out **Beginner Teacher's Book**

Review E

The Revision Game

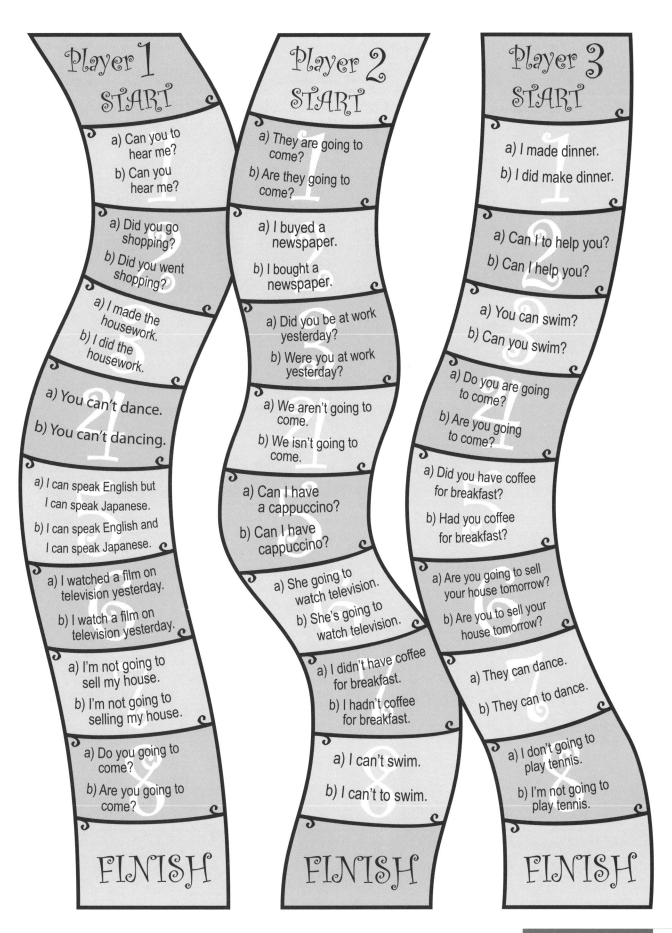